Pool & Billiards

FOR

DUMMIES®

by Nicholas Leider

WILEY

Wiley Publishing, Inc.

Pool & Billiards For Dummies®

Published by
Wiley Publishing, Inc.
111 River St.
Hoboken, NJ 07030-5774
www.wiley.com

Copyright © 2010 by Wiley Publishing, Inc., Indianapolis, Indiana

Published by Wiley Publishing, Inc., Indianapolis, Indiana

Published simultaneously in Canada

For general information on our other products and services, please contact our Customer Care Department within the U.S. at 877-762-2974, outside the U.S. at 317-572-3993, or fax 317-572-4002.

For technical support, please visit www.wiley.com/techsupport.

Wiley also publishes its books in a variety of electronic formats. Some content that appears in print may not be available in electronic books.

Library of Congress Control Number: 2010920660

ISBN: 978-0-470-56553-7

Manufactured in the United States of America

SKY10037787_110122

About the Author

Nicholas Leider has been playing pool since he bought his father a pool table (with his mom's money) for Father's Day when he was 15 years old. But only since joining *Billiards Digest* as an editor in 2007 has he realized how much there is to learn about pool. With 7,000-plus hours spent reading, talking, and writing about the sport, Nicholas is prepared to answer the two Trivial Pursuit questions about pool. You can contact him at nleider12@hotmail.com.

Dedication

This book is dedicated to my parents. To my dad, who provided me with first-hand proof that hard work pays off (even if I'm just making boxes). And to my mom, who has no idea what her strength and determination has meant to our entire family. (Well, I hope she has *some* idea now.)

Author's Acknowledgments

I'd like to thank those people who learned that I'm only on deadline when it's the third deadline I've been given — acquisitions editor Michael Lewis; project editor Kelly Ewing; art director Alicia South; photographer Brien Richmond; and last but not least, technical editor, "Dr. Dave" Alciatore. Thanks also to John Novi, Jr. for allowing us into his home for the photo shoot. And finally, many thanks go to my agent, Marilyn Allen, who has been nothing but supportive.

And a special thanks to those who have taught me so much about this game, especially Larry Schwartz, George Fels, Mike Panozzo, and the rest of the crew at *Billiards Digest*.

Also, I'd like to thank my brother and sister for the constant support (and comic relief), my special ladyfriend, Jenny, for putting up with plenty of nights where I was a little less than sunny, and my friends for allowing me to drop out of society for a few months.

Publisher's Acknowledgments

We're proud of this book; please send us your comments at http://dummies.custhelp.com. For other comments, please contact our Customer Care Department within the U.S. at 877-762-2974, outside the U.S. at 317-572-3993, or fax 317-572-4002.

Some of the people who helped bring this book to market include the following:

Acquisitions, Editorial, and Media Development

Project Editor: Kelly Ewing

Acquisitions Editor: Michael Lewis

Assistant Editor: Erin Calligan Mooney

Editorial Program Coordinator: Joe Niesen

General Reviewer: Dave Alciatore

Senior Editorial Manager: Jennifer Ehrlich

Editorial Supervisor and Reprint Editor: Carmen Krikorian

Editorial Assistant: Jennette ElNaggar

Art Coordinator: Alicia B. South

Photographer: Brien Richmond

Cover Photos: © iStock

Cartoons: Rich Tennant (www.the5thwave.com)

Composition Services

Project Coordinator: Patrick Redmond

Layout and Graphics: Ashley Chamberlain, Carl Byers, Ronald G. Terry, Christine Williams

Proofreaders: Laura L. Bowman, John Greenough

Indexer: Glassman Indexing Services

Publishing and Editorial for Consumer Dummies

    Diane Graves Steele, Vice President and Publisher, Consumer Dummies

    Kristin Ferguson-Wagstaffe, Product Development Director, Consumer Dummies

    Ensley Eikenburg, Associate Publisher, Travel

    Kelly Regan, Editorial Director, Travel

Publishing for Technology Dummies

    Andy Cummings, Vice President and Publisher, Dummies Technology/General User

Composition Services

    Debbie Stailey, Director of Composition Services

Contents at a Glance

Table of Contents

Introduction

. . . . .

Welcome to *Pool & Billiards For Dummies*, where you've got an in to the
sometimes intimidating world of pool. I've written this book to help
you develop in all areas of the entertaining and challenging aspects of pool.
So whether you aren't sure which end is which on a cue stick or you're looking to pick up some tips after hours spent at a pool table, the skill-building
and strategic principles in this book will help you become a better pool player.

You may have picked up this book because you're thinking about taking up
pool as a hobby. The game of pocket billiards is a fantastic, low-impact physical activity that incorporates walking and stretching with a boatload of hand-
eye coordination. Aside from the physical benefits, pool is a social game. You
can play against some friends in a home game room or you can join a league to
make new friends. No matter how you see pool fitting into your life, you'll be
playing with other people, which makes the game that much more enjoyable.

No matter your goals with pool, the game isn't always easy. But it's nothing
near impossible. Some books cover the subject as if you've grown up with a
cue in your hand. But break down all the cool pool lingo and boil down some
of the complex systems, and pool is a sport that anyone can play proficiently.

About This Book

I know that you have plenty of options when it comes to books on pool and
billiards. But I have a few reasons why this book is better than all the rest.

✔ **It's in plain English.** This book isn't a complex treatise on the geometry
and physics involved in pool. Instead, this book is a straightforward look
at a game that anyone with a little determination and time can master.
In *Pool & Billiards For Dummies*, I have one simple goal: If someone
who doesn't know a cue ball from an 8 ball can understand the subject
matter, I've done my job.

To that end, I try to keep the developing player — someone who is just
starting to play pool or someone who has played for awhile but is just
starting to study the game — in mind. When I used to tool around on
the pool table in my house as a teenager, I didn't have much direction,
though that didn't stop me from practicing. But lately, since joining the
staff at *Billiards Digest*, I spend my days reading and talking to the best
minds in the game. These two experiences allow me to cover the technical aspects of pool in an everyday way.

✔ **It's a reference.** You can read this book cover to cover if you want. But I'm guessing you're not going to quit your job to take up pool for hours on end. And because it may take awhile before you're winning world championships, you can use this book as a reference guide. No matter what topic you want to explore on a given night, you can pick up this book and flip to any chapter at any point. If you want to jump to Chapter 20, you don't need to skim the first 19 chapters. Instead, feel free to explore the subjects that interest you.

✔ **It's comprehensive.** Just because this book is written in a way that anyone can understand the subject doesn't mean that it's an incomplete look at the absolute basics of pool. Instead, this book drops a lot of the pool jargon while still covering all the information you need on all the different aspects of the fascinating game of pool.

✔ **It's objective.** I'm not trying to convince you that you absolutely must get a pool table or spend $100 on a pool cue. This book is about increasing your knowledge of the game. I want you to learn how to become the pool player you want to be. That's it!

Conventions Used in This Book

Every book has its own conventions, and this one is no different. To make the most of the information I provide, keep your eye out for these conventions:

✔ Terms I use for the first time are in *italics*. To be sure I keep you up to speed, plain-English explanations or descriptions of these terms are nearby.

✔ When I go through a process in a particular order, I number the steps and put the action part of each step in bold.

✔ Web addresses are in monofont. *Note:* When this book was printed, some Web addresses may have needed to break across two lines of text. If that happened, rest assured that we haven't put in any extra characters (such as hyphens) to indicate the break. So, when using one of these Web addresses, just type exactly what you see in this book, as though the line break doesn't exist.

What You're Not to Read

When you bring this book home, you're not signing up to read every single page. You can jump around to find the information you need. You can also skip the *sidebars* (text in gray boxes) — sidebars are interesting, but they aren't essential to your understanding of the topic at hand. Finally, you can skip anything marked by a Technical Stuff icon. (For more on icons, see "Icons Used in This Book," later in this Introduction.)

Making Assumptions

I'm not saying I know everything about you, but here are a few assumptions I've made about you:

✔ You like to play pool or are thinking about taking up pool as a hobby.

✔ You either own a pool table or have easy access to one, whether it's at a pool hall, bar, or friend's house.

✔ You have little or no experience in learning the proper techniques of a pool stroke.

✔ You may be an experienced pool player who is looking for some additional tips on stroke fundamentals and the mental side of the game.

How This Book Is Organized

As the table of contents shows, this book is divided into six parts. Here's what you can find in each of them.

Part 1: Fundamentals of Pool

Part I is where you discover the fundamentals of a sound stance and stroke. From finding out where your feet go to the proper way of swinging your cue stick from backswing and on through the cue ball, you'll find all this information in this part. In this part, I also cover some of the social etiquette of pool. All in all, Part I gets you set for some of the more in-depth aspects of pool.

Part 11: Controlling the Cue Ball

This part of the book covers one of the most underrated aspects of the game — controlling the cue ball. As any experienced pool player can tell you, the secret of the game isn't so much making the shot at hand. It's about leaving the cue ball in position for your next shot. I've broken up the different ways of controlling the cue ball, so you can read about each process by itself — all on the way to getting a handle on controlling the cue ball.

Part III: Taking Your Shots

If you like the sound of a ball hitting the back of a pocket — and who doesn't? — this is the part of the book for you. In Part III, I dissect some of the many shots you'll face on a pool table. From the opening shot (the break) to some tricky shots like banks, kicks, and caroms, Part III covers the most important categories of shots that are bound to show up on a table near you.

Part IV: The Games You'll Play

You might think of pool as 8-ball or 9-ball, but a pool table can host a wide array of different games. In this section, I go into detail on the games of 8-ball and 9-ball — by far the most popular disciplines. But I also run through some other games that you may find fun to try. No matter what your taste, you shouldn't have any trouble finding a game for you.

Part V: Gearing Up

In this part, I handle some of the peripheral aspects of the game. Pool is full of accessories and tools and equipment. Picking a cue out of the rack at your local pool hall seems so easy, but you need to know what to look for when it comes to the hardware side of the sport. Also, Part V deals with the mental side of the game. You're hitting a cue ball that's completely stationary, so it's not about reaction time or instinct.

Part VI: The Part of Tens

This is the part that all *For Dummies* books are known for — the cool lists of things in the back of the book. In this part, I include lists of ten trick shots that can help you show off for your friends and ten common problems that you may be able to troubleshoot.

Icons Used in This Book

Throughout the book, you come across icons in the margins. These little symbols alert you to specific information. Here's what each icon means:

You can avoid some of the common mistakes made by developing pool players in a number of ways. When I've got a particularly useful suggestion that may help you avoid a frustrating situation, I flag it with this icon.

Because you were nice enough to open this book, I'll soothe your worries: You're not gonna be tested on anything in any of the 26 chapters. This book is only a reference. Occasionally, I do come up with something that's worth remembering. In this case, I mark it with this icon.

Pool is a game that is wrought with trouble — or at least situations that can be a problem for the uninformed player. So when I put a little Warning! icon on the page, take note. Check out these warnings to keep yourself and your cue in line.

The bits of information marked with the Technical Stuff icon are facts that you may find interesting but don't need to know. Feel free to skip over the text marked with this icon if you're not interested in the topic.

Where to Go from Here

This book is a reference, which means you can jump around to whatever section you want. If you're wondering how to aim a particular shot, check out Chapter 4. If you're looking for the basics behind the game of 9-ball, flip to Chapter 19. If you're sick of picking up a house cue at the pool hall and want to get one of your own, Chapter 21 can help. The point is that you're welcome to flip around the book to where you wanna go.

Finally, send me an e-mail with some feedback or a photo as proof that your pool game is on its way up. You can reach me at nleider12@hotmail.com.

Icons Used in This Book

Because you were nice enough to open this book, I'll soothe your worries: You're not going to be tested on anything in any of the 26 chapters. This book is only a reference. Occasionally, I do come up with something that's worth remembering. In this case, I mark it with this icon.

Where to Go from Here

Part I
Fundamentals of Pool

The 5th Wave   By Rich Tennant

"Now here's what you call a reeeeal cue ball!"

In this part . . .

Within this book, you have all the information necessary to develop into a pretty solid pool player. But if you're completely new to the sport of pool, this part is where you want to start. In this part, I start with the fundamentals involved in pool. I show you how to get into a comfortable stance, how to hold the cue, how to aim, and how to stroke the cue so that you'll be pocketing balls in no time. Finally, I also cover basic etiquette so that you'll know your place around any pool table.

Chapter 1

Arriving at the Pool Party

The game of pool is all about knowing where you are and where you want to go. You make one shot with an eye on the next one and the one after that one. To that end, you should start your venture into the world of pocket billiards with a roadmap. The sport of pool and billiards is something that can be a lifelong passion that combines physical exercise and substantial hand-eye coordination in a rather social game that is just plain fun. I've written this book to be your guide to take all the mystery and mythology out of pool so that you can get the straight story. So when you're ready, take your cue and start playing.

In this chapter, I get you rolling on the path to a greater understanding of the sport of pool, including stroke fundamentals, strategy, etiquette, and equipment.

Introducing Games You Can Play

You've got plenty of options when it comes to what type of games you can play on a pool table. Some use all the balls, while others use just some of them. Some let you use all the pockets; others limit their use. But no matter your style, you'll be able to find a pool game that's right for you.

8-ball (see Chapter 18) and 9-ball (see Chapter 19) are by far the most popular games among amateur players. *8-ball* requires you to make one group of balls (either the stripes or solids) before making the game-winning 8. *9-ball,* on the other hand, requires only that a player hit the lowest numbered ball on the way to hitting the 9 ball into a pocket.

But besides these two games, you have a ton of options when it comes to the cue sport. You can play one-pocket, straight pool, and a plethora of multi-player games on a regular, old pool table.

On top of that, you can venture out to different takes on the traditional table. Three-cushion, a game played on a table with no pockets, requires you to hit one cue ball off three cushions and another ball before hitting the third ball.

Snooker, another pocket billiards game, is played on a bigger table (10 or 12 feet long) with smaller balls and smaller pockets. The goal is to accumulate points by alternatively making red and colored balls (which are then spotted).

See Chapter 20 for details on all these game variations.

Getting in Position

Knowing where you need to put your feet, your hands, and your eyes to give you the best chance at playing your best is absolutely vital. Working from the ground up, when you have a solid stance (see Chapter 2) you are able to

✔ Stay balanced when you're in your stance, with properly spaced feet.

✔ Feel comfortable while down on a shot.

✔ Know that you're positioned along the line of the shot.

But positioning your body and legs is one thing. Properly holding the cue with both your *bridge hand* (in the front) or *grip hand* (in the back) is a fundamental skill all pool players must have.

Learning how to handle the cue (see Chapter 3) means much more than just picking up the cue and putting its tip to the cue ball. You first have to establish a proper grip on the back end of the cue. You must find the middle ground where you're not squeezing the cue too tightly, while also not allowing the cue to move in your hand by holding it too loosely.

And when you start to work on your bridge hand — the one up front — you need to establish a firm bridge to allow for an accurate stroke. By growing familiar with open, closed, and many different special bridges that you may need in the course of a game, you'll be ready for any situation you might face.

TIP

Don't restrict your bridge practice to the table. You can practice forming a proper bridge almost anywhere. You can use a pencil or a straw or anything that will help your grow comfortable with forming a fundamentally sound bridge.

Also, in preparing to shoot, you should become familiar with your own preshot routine (see Chapter 2). This repetitive process of approaching a shot should

- ✔ Establish an order of going through necessary steps to plan for your next shot and getting yourself prepared for the shot at hand.

- ✔ Create a routine that will help you prepare for stressful shots because you're so used to the steps along the way.

- ✔ Regulate the number of practice strokes you take for each shot.

- ✔ Give you a final opportunity to check that everything feels as it should.

Aiming for Success

After you're down in position to pull the trigger — or, in this case, swinging the cue — you need to know where to aim to properly strike an object ball so that it heads toward a pocket.

The most popular system for aiming is known as the *Ghost Ball System* (see Chapter 4). By connecting the centers of the object ball and the cue ball at impact, a line is formed that should point to the pocket. The important idea is that you see where the cue ball should be at impact and then send the cue ball on such a path where it can strike the object ball in the correct spot.

Any aiming system that sounds too good to be true probably is. Aiming is one of the most contentious areas of instruction in pool, with plenty of people claiming to have a secret to repeatedly pocket balls.

Stroking the Cue

Developing a smooth, even stroke not only looks good but is an important step to becoming a consistent pool player (see Chapter 5). When you want to deliver the cue tip to the cue ball in the best way possible, heed these tips:

- ✔ Keep your cue as level as it can be for a given shot.

- ✔ Move your body as little as possible, allowing your back arm from the elbow down to do the work of swinging the cue back and into the cue ball.

- ✔ Establish an even acceleration from the end of your backswing through contact with the cue ball.

- ✔ Keep your grip hand relaxed as it holds the cue on its way through the cue ball.

✔ Understand that the follow-through is an essential part of the stroke, and an abbreviated follow-through can lead to accuracy problems.

✔ Keep your back elbow in the same position throughout your stroke to minimize movement.

✔ Staying down after your follow-through can prevent you from jumping up during a shot, which will lead to accuracy problems.

Controlling the Cue Ball

Control the cue ball, and you will control the game. It's easy, right? Knock the cue ball off the object ball (which then goes into the pocket) and then leave the cue ball exactly where you want it to stop for your next shot.

Speed is an important factor when trying to control the cue ball. By understanding how much speed is necessary, depending on the distance the cue ball must travel and the angle it is going to hit the object ball, you can develop a feeling for hitting the cue ball at the correct distance.

Players have a tendency to *overhit* shots — that is, to use too much power on a specific shot. Don't be afraid to hit a ball with barely enough speed to get the cue ball in shape for your next shot. You'll find that you will underhit a shot far less than you overhit the same one.

A second way to control the cue ball is by understanding what happens when you hit the cue ball in different places (see Chapters 7–10). If you hit the cue ball above center, it will behave differently than a cue ball hit to the left of center. Understand and control the spin of the cue ball, and you'll be a long way to knowing where the cue ball's going to stop.

It's also important to know *why* you want to use spin during a shot. The ultimate goal is to change the cue ball's path before and/or after contact with the object ball so that you can get a better angle at the next ball.

Using any kind of spin on the cue ball to pocket a ball is rarely a good idea. Hitting away from center complicates a shot, which you don't want to do unless absolutely necessary.

Here are a few things to know when you're hitting the cue ball:

✔ If you hit the cue ball below center, it will begin to move toward the object ball while spinning backward. Conversely, a cue ball hit above center will quickly begin to roll.

✔ When the cue ball has no spin at impact, it will head in a direction 90 degrees in the opposite direction from the object ball's path. If the cue ball hits the object ball fully, it will stop in its place.

✔ If you hit a cue ball away from its vertical axis, the cue ball will move off of its line in the opposite direction (to the left if hit on the right).

✔ A side spin will pull the cue ball back to the other direction.

Top spin and back spin change the cue ball's path both after impact with the object ball and after contact with the rail. Side spin, meanwhile, can have a dramatic effect on the cue ball's path after hitting a rail. You can use a combination of these spins to achieve the desired path for your cue ball.

Seeing Shots

Playing your best is as much about execution as it is planning. Along with the physical process of putting cue to cue ball, you need to be able to see certain shots that you can make and see certain ways of getting in position for your next shots.

You could play pool for your whole life and see a particular shot only once. But other shots will pop up time and time again (see Chapter 13).

✔ **The break:** The *break shot* is a way of starting a game (see Chapter 11). In 8-ball and 9-ball, the break shot means hitting the cue ball into a stack of balls at a rather high speed. In Chapter 11, you discover how to develop a solid break that will give you a good chance of winning any game you play.

✔ **The straight shot:** Even when a ball is lined up perfectly with the cue ball and a pocket, the shot may not be so easy (see Chapter 13). When faced with a perfectly straight shot, you have to focus on your fundamentals. By minimizing the possibility for an error in aiming (you know exactly where the cue ball must go), missed straight shots often expose errors in your stroke.

✔ **Angled balls:** From a straight shot to one that is as angled as can be, you'll face a large amount of shots at plenty of angles. Over time, though, you'll begin to see certain shots that look similar. Grouping certain shots together allows you to get a feel for that particular set of angles.

✔ **Hanging balls:** When an object ball is sitting right near a pocket, you still have plenty of planning to do. You need to make the shot and figure out exactly where the cue ball will go.

Shots using multiple balls may give you an opportunity to pocket a ball when it may otherwise look like you can't. Combinations (see Chapter 14), kisses and caroms (see Chapter 15), and kicks and banks (see Chapter 16) are just a few ways to make balls that are more complicated than just hitting a cue ball into an object ball into a pocket.

When using these types of shots, you have to plan accordingly:

- ✔ Because these shots often involve more variables than a simple one-cue-ball, one-object-ball shot, these shots are often difficult to position with the cue ball.

- ✔ Aiming shots with multiple balls is similar to aiming regular shots. The only difference? Usually, multiple-ball shots require you to take an extra step to go from the cue ball to the ball that will be pocketed.

- ✔ Understanding which multiple-ball shots are makable is important. Often, these shots can be fairly easy if laid out in a certain way.

Playing for Your Next Shot

Making the shot at hand is one thing, but you also need to plan ahead for the next shot (see Chapter 12). When you're figuring out how to plan for your next few shots, these tips can help you develop a proper pattern:

- ✔ **Minimize cue-ball movement.** You'll be best served by minimizing the distance the cue ball moves. Usually, a player gets in trouble when the cue ball has to travel a significant distance. When you can, keep the cue ball on a short path from one ball to another.

- ✔ **Limit the speed.** Similarly, you don't want to use extra power when a soft hit on the cue ball will work. Hitting the cue ball hard increases the chances that it might get out of line.

- ✔ **Plan three balls ahead.** You want to plan to pocket the ball you're aiming at so that you can get a good position on the next ball and then the third ball. Always play three balls ahead, planning to pocket each ball in a way that keeps you at the table.

- ✔ **Avoid other balls.** When possible, you want to avoid sending your cue ball into other object balls (other than the one you're trying to pocket). Hitting other object balls only makes position play more difficult, so try to avoid them if possible.

Playing Defense

You need to play defense (see Chapter 17). Forget anything you've heard about defense and safety play as the wrong way to play. Playing effective safeties can keep you in control of the table and in control of the game.

When you don't have a viable option to pocket a ball, here are some ways to keep the cue ball in a spot that will tie up your opponent:

- ✔ **Blockers:** Try to put an object ball between the cue ball and your opponent's object ball. This blocker ball(s) can keep your opponent from hitting the ball directly.

- ✔ **Distance:** If you can't put a ball between the cue ball and the object ball, distance will make any shot more difficult.

- ✔ **Obstacles:** An obstacle can be a rail or a ball your opponent has to cue over, making a particular shot more challenging.

One way to play defense is by imagining where your opponent would have a difficult time hitting one of his object balls. If you can put the cue ball in this safety zone, you should be in good shape.

The goal is to make the game more difficult for your opponent. Combining any or all of these safety guidelines can help you stay in control of the table, so always look for new and different ways to put your opponent in jail.

Gearing Up

When you walk into a bar or pool hall, you need to find a house cue that works for you. Here are a few hints to help you pick a winner:

- ✔ **Look for a one-piece tip, not a plastic tip that is slipped on over the edge of the tip.** A one-piece tip will give you a more solid hit.

- ✔ **Try to find an evenly rounded tip.** You want one somewhere between the curve of a nickel and a dime.

- ✔ **After you find a quality tip, test the cue to see whether it's straight.** Roll it on the table. If it jumps around at all, it's not very straight.

- ✔ **Observe whether the cue feels heavy or light in your hand.** Cues come in many weights, usually from 18 to 21 ounces. Experiment with different weights until you find the number of ounces that works best for your game.

Should you ever be in the market for a table, you need to consider several factors:

- ✔ The size of the room you have available dictates the size of table you can fit. Tables come in 7-foot, 8-foot, and 9-foot models. Seven-footers are common in home rooms, simply because of spatial constraints.

Tables in pool halls tend to vary, with many establishments offering a few different sizes.

✔ Be sure you know what thickness the slate is on the table. Anything over an inch should last for as long as you'll play on it.

✔ Pockets can either be *drop pockets* (balls stay in the pocket) or *ball-return* (balls funnel back down to a collection area). Home tables are more likely to feature drop pockets (which usually make for a less expensive table). Tables at the local pool hall, though, will probably have return systems.

✔ A table's cloth will be important to the quality of play. Look for professional-grade worsted wool cloth.

✔ Tables come with a ton of accessories, including cue racks, table lights, bar stools, chalk, and matching furniture. Be sure you know what you'll need before buying premade packages.

For more on purchasing equipment, see Chapter 21.

Playing Nicely

Pool comes with its own set of social conditions (see Chapter 6). Here are a few of the common no-nos on and around a pool table:

✔ Agree to any special rules before a match begins. Clearing the air early keeps you and your opponent on the same page.

✔ If you don't know, ask. Ask a ref, another player, or your opponent if you have any questions about a rule or situation.

✔ Steer clear of drinks or food on or near the table. A table's cloth can be pretty expensive, so you don't want to drop a pizza slice on it.

✔ Avoid distracting your opponent in any way during a match. When one player does anything to get an opponent's mind off the match, it's considered a high crime.

✔ Respect the table and cues. Don't dump a full tray of balls on the table and don't use a cue for anything but hitting the balls as intended.

✔ When in doubt, try using a little common sense. Social graces go a long way at the table.

Chapter 2

Getting Down: Building a Solid Stance

In This Chapter
▶ Developing a consistent routine for every shot
▶ Placing your feet for a comfortable, stable stance
▶ Learning how to look at a shot and where to look during a shot

*T*he stance certainly isn't the most glamorous or exciting aspect of pool. It's not going to help you hit game-winning shots or play like the next world champion. But if you have any flaws in this fundamental area, you'll hinder the development of your game.

And here's the tricky part: No one stance is completely and absolutely correct. It's not as simple as saying your feet should be 18 inches apart, and your knees should be bent at a 15-degree angle. Considering the wide variety of people (and body types) that play pool, it's no surprise that no two stances are exactly the same.

As you read this chapter, realize that finding a comfortable and effective stance is more about knowing what it should do — provide balance, comfort, and consistency — and incorporating your own personal style in the whole process.

This chapter outlines the basic steps to creating a fundamentally sound stance — estimations on where your feet should go, how to lower your upper body over the table, and where to look when you're ready to shoot. This process, known as the *preshot routine,* is a vital step in becoming a pool player, rather than someone who just bangs balls around the table.

Keeping Your Preshot Routine Consistent

From the time you select a shot to the (hopefully) successful completion of that shot, you should have a consistent way of approaching the task. Developing a preshot routine you can trust will go a long way toward you becoming more comfortable at and around the table. A preshot routine can also help you develop a rhythm, allowing you to tackle any and all shots with a consistent way of doing business.

Approaching and stepping into the shot

After you choose which shot you're going to attempt, keep your body on the *shot line* — a straight line drawn through the middle of the cue ball to the exact point you want it to hit the object ball you're aiming at. Keeping your body and eyes on this line allows you to completely focus on the intended target.

As you can see in Figure 2-1, you can extend the shot line past the table. By visualizing this line and standing on it, you can keep your focus on where the cue ball should go so that it will lead to a successful shot.

Figure 2-1: The shot line is a straight line drawn through the middle of the cue ball to the exact point you want it to hit the object ball you're aiming at.

While on this shot line, chalk your cue, which should be done before *every* shot. Gently brushing the cube of chalk against the tip of your cue deposits an even surface of chalk to the tip. Layering the tip with chalk helps avoid *miscues,* where the cue tip slips off the cue ball instead of hitting through the intended point of contact.

After your cue is ready to go, it's time to step into the shot. With your body still on the shot line, place your back foot (which is the right foot for right-handed players and the left foot for lefties) on the shot line. Judging from where the cue ball is located, you should place your back foot so that it is perpendicular to the shot line.

After you have your back foot set, you can set your front foot. No set rule dictates the placement of your front foot. A good starting point is at a 45-degree angle from the shot line (see Figure 2-2). This angle opens up your body slightly to the shot, though not completely, so that you're perpendicular to the shot line.

Figure 2-2:
Correct placement of your front foot depends on the individual player, but a 45-degree angle from the shot line is a good starting point.

 Placing your front foot at a 45-degree angle is only a starting point. While plenty of players have an *open stance* in which their body faces the table, most players keep the front foot closer to the cue, often just a few inches from the shot line. Don't be afraid to experiment with what feels the best for you.

Stances are unique. Try different angles for your body, taking note of where you're more comfortable and successful. In recent years, the general trend among many professionals has been to have the front foot much closer to the shot line, sometimes just a few inches off the shot line. Wherever you decide to settle, be sure that the cue has plenty of room to move back and forth and that you feel comfortable and loose in the stance.

 Figure 2-3 shows one of the most common mistakes that beginners make: The player has his feet much too close to one another. Think about the goals of a stance: comfort and balance. Would you really be balanced if your feet were just a few inches apart? Probably not, so spread your feet a bit and get into a solid position.

With your feet a comfortable distance apart, you should be balanced evenly between your back and front feet. Don't put all your weight on one foot because that can keep you in a state of permanent imbalance. With a slight bit of pressure on your *bridge hand* (the hand on the table holding the tip-end of the cue), you should feel like a pool-playing tripod. Most of your weight will be on your feet, but with this bit of pressure on your hand, you'll be as sturdy as you need to be.

Figure 2-3: A common mistake is crouching, which works against the goal of comfort and balance.

As for your knees, think about the type of ready position that people assume in other sports. When tennis players are ready to return a serve or baseball players are ready to steal second base, they have a slight bend in their knees. This concept is a good starting point for your pool stance.

So begin with a slight bend in your knees. This slight bend is probably as low as you should go. Any changes to your stance should err on the side of straightening your legs. In fact, in a classic pool stance, the back leg is locked in place, which is perfectly acceptable if this position is comfortable for you.

If you want to get lower than you can with your current stance, don't bend your knees more. Instead, try widening your feet to get you down to where you want to be. Often, beginners get into the habit of squatting down to shoot. Not only is this position uncomfortable, but it's sure to lead to more misses.

To be comfortable and balanced, you'll need to be able to assume your stance for an extended period of time. If you're standing as you would for a shot and something feels out of line, it may be a hint that you're not as comfortable as you need to be. For example, if one of your legs begins to ache after 30 seconds or so, you're putting too much weight on that foot.

Lowering into your stance

Before I cover gripping both ends of the cue (see Chapter 3), I want to show you how you should lower your upper body into a shot. With your bridge hand on the table and your feet in the proper position, you are ready to lower yourself down on the shot by bending at the hips.

The most important thing to remember regarding this step of your preshot routine is that you need to keep your head and the entire cue on the shot line. Placing your cue on the shot line, your grip hand extends into the proper position while your torso drops into place.

So how low do you want to go? Again, like placing your feet for your stance (see the preceding section), this answer is open to some debate. Some players prefer a more upright stance, while others want to get down to the point where the cue is literally rubbing the bottom of their chin.

For most normal pool shots — meaning you're not stretched out over the table or the cue ball isn't up against the rail — you have enough space to keep your body position fairly consistent.

Some players prefer to assume a more standing position, as shown in Figure 2-4. This type of stance allows you to keep perspective on the table, though you should never be more erect than what you see in Figure 2-4.

Figure 2-4:
An upright stance lets you see the table well.

A lower stance, shown in Figure 2-5, is becoming more and more popular. Here, the player is so low that his chin will rub against the cue. This stance allows you to get as close to the cue as possible so that you can see exactly where your cue is going to contact the cue ball.

Regardless of the angle of your upper body, try to keep your back as close to straight as possible, while still being comfortable, of course.

Minimize the adjustments you make when you're down on a shot. A little tweak of your foot or body position is fine, but you want to be comfortable throughout your preshot routine. If you need to change something in your stance, get up and approach the shot again. You need to be confident with what you're doing, so you want to be at ease throughout the preshot routine.

Figure 2-5:
A chin-on-cue stance enables you to get as close as possible to the cue and gives you a great perspective of the cue ball's path.

Keeping your eyes in line

One of the most controversial topics in pool is where to place your eyes over the cue. A widely discussed belief is the *dominant eye theory,* meaning that you place your dominant eye directly over the cue. But these days, the consensus among pool instructors and professionals seems to be that you should stick with whatever works, obviously within reason.

If you want to use this technique, here's how to find your dominant eye. With your arm fully extended, use your finger to hide a spot on the wall. Close one eye at a time. If you have one eye open and the spot is still hidden by your finger, that is your dominant eye. When you have your other eye open, you should be able to see the spot.

Assuming that the right eye is the dominant eye for the player shown in Figure 2-6, he is using the dominant eye theory. As you'd guess, the cue stick is directly below the right eye.

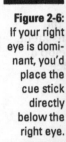

Figure 2-6: If your right eye is dominant, you'd place the cue stick directly below the right eye.

If you sight a shot with your chin directly on your cue, you're using a centered alignment with the cue between your eyes (see Figure 2-7). In fact, this centered approach has a secondary benefit: Many players know they're centered when they get in this type of stance because the cue can be "grooved" against the center of your chin.

Figure 2-7: Example of a centered cue.

No matter how you view shots, just remember that delivering the cue on a straight line to the intended point of contact is the most important thing. With this point in mind, be sure that wherever you sight your shots, be consistent. If you feel most comfortable with your left eye over the cue, stick with it — for every shot.

The most important thing, whether it be the placement of your feet, the angle of your upper body, or the placement of your eyes, is to be consistent. Keeping the same body position from shot to shot will help you develop a repeatable stance that will become second nature with a little practice.

Eying a Shot

After you get down into your stance, with your cue and body in line, you're close to being ready to shoot. But one of the most important — and often overlooked — aspects of the preshot routine is visually checking and rechecking your alignment.

Just as it's important to keep your stance consistent, you must have a process of eye movements that ensures that you're properly prepared to go ahead and pull the trigger.

Checking and rechecking your line

From the moment you choose the shot you want to attempt, you should always keep yourself in line with the shot line. (For more on the shot line, see the section "Keeping Your Preshot Routine Consistent," earlier in this chapter.) After you assume your stance and lower yourself into the proper position, you're ready to check and recheck your alignment.

With your cue tip just a half inch or so from the point where you want to make contact with the cue ball (Part II covers the contact point), you should be able to see and feel that everything is in line.

A popular training technique for keeping your stroke fundamentals in order involves videotaping yourself at the table. Set up the video camera at eye level (when you're down on a shot). Record yourself hitting ten shots with the camera at each of the two locations, as shown in Figure 2-8.

While down in your stance, you want to see that the contact point on the cue ball will send the cue ball along the shot line. Move your eyes from the contact point on the cue ball to the intended contact point on the object.

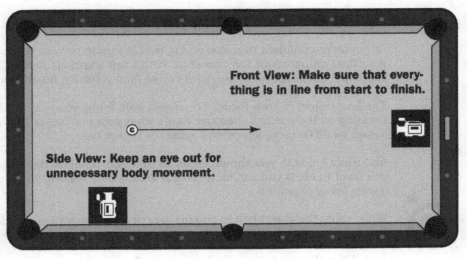

Figure 2-8: Recording a video of you shooting from two angles gives you a better understanding of what's happening during your stroke.

Front View: Make sure that everything is in line from start to finish.

Side View: Keep an eye out for unnecessary body movement.

When you're all set, you should have nearly every moving part in line with the shot line. As shown in Figure 2-9, you can see that your bridge hand, the cue, your upper arm, your forearm, and your back foot are all on the shot line.

Figure 2-9: When you're aligned properly, your bridge hand, cue, back arm, and back foot should all be on the shot line.

If one piece of this puzzle is off line, you risk throwing everything out of whack. While you may be able to make some shots while your forearm or eyes stray off the shot line, you'll be well served to drill yourself on these fundamentals early in your development as a player.

Final focus? The object ball

After you're confident that everything is as it should be, you're ready to make your final preparations for your shot. With a few warm-up strokes, double and triple-check the shot line, until you're finally, finally, finally ready to go.

The final object of your focus? The object ball. While you may think that focusing on the cue ball (because that's what your cue is going to hit) makes sense, you'll be more successful eying the object ball.

And while I'm at it, you should focus on the *exact* point on the object ball that you want to hit. If you aim for a general area, you're leaving yourself open to a wide array of results.

While eying the object ball as you hit the cue ball is always ideal, a few shots require you to keep your focus on the cue ball:

✔ When the cue ball is up against the rail (or cushion), you may have only a small area where you can hit the cue ball without miscuing. In this case, you want to focus on the point where you must hit the cue ball.

✔ Similarly, when you have to hit the cue ball when it's right in front of another object ball (see Figure 2-10), the margin for error is small, so you need to focus on making a good hit on the cue ball.

✔ Until you get comfortable with your break, focus on the point on the cue ball you want to hit (usually in the middle of the cue ball just below center).

Figure 2-10:
Up against
another ball.

Chapter 3

Handling the Cue

You can hold a cue in a million ways, though only a few of these options are correct. Whether squeezing the butt end of the cue to sawdust or building an unstable channel for the cue's shaft, players have to learn and relearn how to get a proper grip on the stick.

Surprisingly, while gripping the back end of the cue may seem like second nature, many players of all skill levels struggle with this apparently simple task. The truth is that holding the cue isn't as easy as gripping it and ripping it.

It may not seem like much, but a solid bridge (the position of your front hand) is one of the most important fundamental lessons in pool. With a few pointers to get you start, you should be on your way to establishing rock-solid bridges as you shoot from anywhere on the table.

Then there's the mechanical bridge. This poor piece of equipment faces more scorn and spiteful wrath from many bar-room shooters than any bit of pool gear. But you'll be quick to accept that not only is the mechanical bridge necessary, it's absolutely critical that you grow to reach a comfort level with this tool.

In this chapter, you not only see how to get a handle on the cue, but also what *not* to do when you're trying to establish a solid foundation for your cue.

Holding Back: The Grip Hand

How you hold the back of the cue, known as the *butt*, isn't really an exact science as much as it is a certain feel that's right. That being said, you can be on your way toward getting that right feeling by following a few guidelines:

- ✔ **Don't grip it to death.** The most common mistake made by all players with respect to the grip of the cue is too much tension! Relax a bit. You don't need to strangle the back of the cue. In this case, the harder you squeeze, the less control you'll have on the cue at impact.

  This advice is a little counterintuitive, but by releasing the cue and gently cradling it before, during, and after your stroke, you'll increase your accuracy. You need to trust the cue to do what it is supposed to do (which is hit the cue ball at the exact contact point).

- ✔ **Find a comfortable spot to grip the back end of the cue.** Where you grip the butt of the cue is not as important as where you grip the cue *in relation to your bridge hand.* To find the correct spot for your grip hand, get down in your natural stance. With the tip of the cue near the cue ball, check the position of the forearm of your grip hand. Is it perpendicular to the ground? If not, move your grip hand (while the cue remains still) so that your forearm is at a 90-degree angle to the ground. After you find the right angle for your back forearm, you know you're gripping the cue in the right spot.

In addition, pay attention to your finger and thumb placement. Also, make sure that you don't clench. (See the next two sections for detail.)

Forming a ring with two fingers and a thumb

When you get down in your stance, ready to stroke the shot, the cue should rest gently in your back hand. Most of the cue's weight should fall on your index and middle fingers, leaving your ring and pinky fingers to rest on the cue.

As you can see in Figure 3-1, you should have some space between the top of the cue and your hand. This little sliver of air is an easy way to keep your grip loose. If you don't have a little sliver of space, you might inadvertently start gripping the cue tighter and tighter without consciously trying to do so.

Looking at the grip from behind (see Figure 3-2), you can see how the majority of the cue's weight falls on the index and middle fingers. Also, your palm shouldn't be pressed against the cue, which would be yet another sign that you're gripping the cue too tightly.

Putting your thumb on top of the cue may feel natural. You may feel like you can really guide the cue where you want it. No matter how comfortable this position may seem, it's a bad habit that can cause complications and inconsistency. Really concentrate on these fundamentals now so that you're practicing good habits from the get-go.

The ideal position for your hand is dangling from your wrist, neither cocked out or wrapped under your forearm. Your hand should be in line with your forearm, while your thumb points directly at the ground.

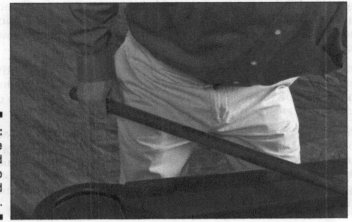

Figure 3-1:
Notice the ring formed by your two fingers and thumb.

Figure 3-2:
There should be some space between the cue and your palm.

Here are a few checkpoints to help you find the proper grip:

- ✔ Check to see whether your thumb is pointed straight down at the floor to make sure that your hand isn't out of line and that your wrist is nice and loose. If your wrist is at an angle, your thumb will be at an angle.

- ✔ While your thumb points down, it will rest on the side of the cue, still letting the cue rest on your index and middle fingers.

- ✔ You might have to change your thinking on how you grip a pool cue. It's not like holding a bat in baseball, where you have to *drive* the bat through the ball. Instead, you should think of your grip hand as carrying the cue to impact. You don't need to grip and push the cue through the cue ball with a bunch of tension in your grip hand. Instead, let the cue's momentum do the majority of the work.

- ✔ If you can lift the cue tip off the table using only your grip hand, you're squeezing *way* too tightly. If you lift the cue with only your back hand, the tip of the cue should stay on the table because the cue's weight is in front of your grip hand.

- ✔ Your thumb and index and middle fingers should stay in relatively the same position on the cue while you stroke the cue. The two fingers continue to be the weight bearers, and your thumb keeps the cue from wavering from side to side.

- ✔ The rest of your hand will move as you complete your entire stroke — going from still to backswing to foreswing and into your follow-through. For example, the tips of your ring and pinky fingers barely touch the cue when you're transitioning from your backswing into your stroke (see Figure 3-3). At the end of your follow-through, though, your cue should finish near the base of your fingers (see Figure 3-4).

Figure 3-3:
Your thumb and first two fingers should remain looped around the cue.

(Still) no clenching

Keeping an easy grip on the cue may feel a little strange at first, especially if you've been squeezing the life out of it for some time. And while I describe some methods of checking yourself, you need to take extra caution that you don't clench up *during* your stroke.

Figure 3-4:
At the end of your stroke, the cue should still be resting on your index finger and thumb.

Here's a mistake I still make to this day: I will be free and easy during my warm-up strokes, perfect during my backswing, but then I suddenly wrench the cue with my grip hand while executing the stroke. Often, this mistake is caused by a lack of trust in your plan. I'm not alone in making this mistake, though. This error is common when faced with a difficult shot because you're not completely convinced that what you're doing is correct.

But if you clench up, you're shooting yourself in the foot. The tension in your hand, especially because it's so sudden and just before contact, can jerk the cue off line, resulting in some inaccuracy when you strike the cue ball.

This habit isn't easily broken. You have to take special care to keep your grip relaxed, no matter what shot you're faced with. The most effective way to train yourself to stay loose during your stroke is to drill it into your subconscious when you're practicing. You have to make staying loose second nature, which takes some time, but it will be well worth it when you know you can trust your grip.

Building Bridges

The bridge is one of the most overlooked elements among beginner players. No matter how true your stroke is, you will be inconsistent without a steady bridge that can deliver the cue to the intended contact point on the cue ball.

I break this topic into three parts to make it easily digested. You can use two types of bridges — the open and closed bridges — on your run-of-the-mill shots with no obstacles or distractions. From there, you can take a look at some of the special cases, where other balls or rails (or both) get in the way of your bridge hand.

Spread or palm down?

An *open bridge* is one where your hand does not encircle the shaft of the cue. Instead of wrapping a finger around the top of the shaft, you leave the top of the shaft untouched, meaning you can sight right down the line of your cue to the intended contact point on the cue ball.

Open bridges can be used for just about any shot, except for a few tricky spots where you have to maneuver around blocking balls. But open bridges are especially effective for shots that require an exact hit on the cue ball. Because you're able to sight right down the shaft of your cue, you can get a great look at the cue's path and the whole shot line.

Also, you should use short bridges on shots that require a soft hit on the cue ball. Because you're not putting a lot into your stroke, you don't run the risk of the cue moving around in the open bridge. At the same time, the increased visibility helps you line up the shot.

You can use two types of open bridge:

- ✔ The fist bridge
- ✔ The spread bridge with an open hand

The fist bridge

While some bridges are rather complex exercises of finger yoga, the fist bridge, shown in Figure 3-5, is a starter's dream. It's simple, it's effective, and you can use it in many situations.

In a few steps, you can start using this fist bridge:

1. **Make a fist with your bridge hand (the left hand for righties and the right hand for lefties), putting your thumb between the first and second knuckles on your index finger.**

2. **With your palm down, place your fist on the table, roughly where you want your bridge to be.**

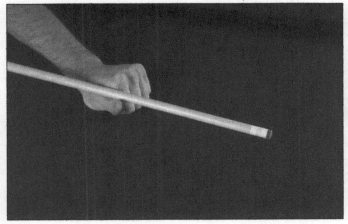

Figure 3-5:
The fist bridge is a good start for open bridges.

3. **Raise your thumb so that you're pressing the inside of your thumb against the first knuckle in your index finger.**

   It's absolutely critical that you firmly plant your thumb against your hand. This step is the point where the cue will be grooved, so you want to make sure that your thumb is pressed firmly against your fist. In most cases, tension and pressure are things to be avoided, but you do want to press your thumb up against your hand in this step.

I talk about the stance in Chapter 2. In order to steady your whole body, including your bridge hand and arm, put some weight forward on your bridge hand. Your bridge hand is what's controlling the tip edge of the cue, so you want to be sure that it's as sturdy as possible.

The spread bridge with an open hand

When's the last time you saw a coffee mug that had a base substantially smaller than it's rim? If you can remember, it may be around the same time you had to get a big coffee stain out of your shirt.

The point here is that a nice, wide base keeps things from tipping and turning. The same is true for bridges. One way to improve on the fist bridge, described in the preceding section, is to open your hand, spreading your fingers across the table to widen the base of your bridge. While this bridge is a little more complicated than the fist bridge, you should be able to grow comfortable with it after a little practice:

1. **Start with your hand completely flat against the table, with your fingers spread wide, but not overextending yourself (see Figure 3-6).**

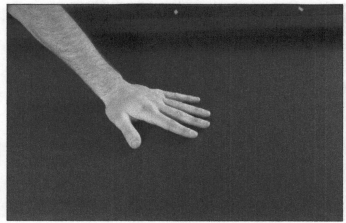

Figure 3-6:
Lay your
hand flat on
the table.

2. **Without lifting your fingers or palm off the table, try to raise the first row of knuckles while keeping your fingers straight and sliding the tips of your fingers across the cloth toward your palm (see Figure 3-7).**

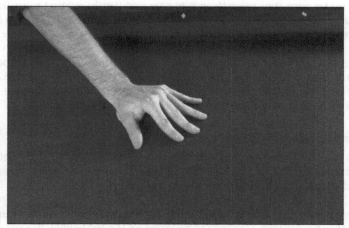

Figure 3-7:
Raise the
middle of
your hand
up a little.

3. **Lift your thumb, pressing it against your index finger between the first and second knuckles, as shown in Figure 3-8.**

The cue grooves at the point where your thumb and index finger meet.

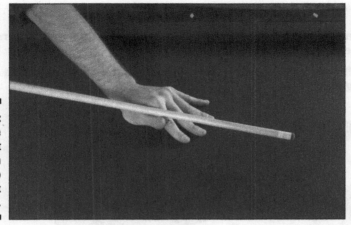

Figure 3-8:
The cue slides right between your thumb and index finger.

What's important with this bridge is that your finger tips and the butt of your hand are firmly planted on the table. With a little weight pushing forward on your bridge hand, you should have close to the same amount of pressure on each finger, which gives you the most stability.

And again, as with the fist bridge, be sure to keep your thumb pressing against your hand. If you let your thumb move up and down or forward and back, you'll unintentionally move the cue, leaving you with an inaccurate hit on the cue ball.

Closing the bridge

Unfortunately, no matter how well you plan, you're going to be left with some long shots that require a firm stroke. In such a situation, you need to maximize your control of the cue. One way to do so is to use a *closed bridge* — one where you wrap your finger around the top of the shaft so that you've got it completely surrounded — eliminating the possibility that the cue might jump up during the stroke.

When you first start using a closed bridge, it may feel a bit awkward, either because you've never done it or you've been using an incorrect version of a closed bridge. But it's imperative that you get the hang of it because you'll use it quite a bit.

Here's a step-by-step guide to getting started:

1. **Start by placing your hand on the table, relaxing your fingers so that there is no tension.**

2. **Lift your index finger so that it points in the air, as shown in Figure 3-9.**

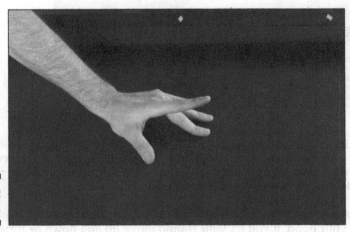

Figure 3-9:
Finger up.

3. **Slide your thumb over so that it touches your middle finger (as shown in Figure 3-10).**

   When you move your thumb, the middle part of your hand should rise off the table, as shown in Figure 3-10.

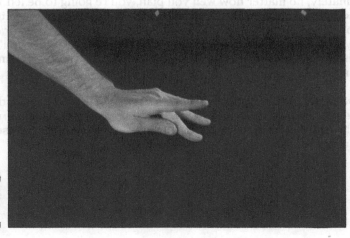

Figure 3-10:
Thumb over.

4. **Place the shaft of your cue in the groove between the tip of your thumb and middle finger (see Figure 3-11).**

Figure 3-11:
Cue in.

5. **Close the loop around your cue's shaft by touching the tip of your index finger to the tip of your thumb and the side of your middle finger, as shown in Figure 3-12.**

Figure 3-12:
Loop your index finger around the shaft.

While the closed bridge is more complex than the open bridges I describe in the previous sections, you can lose some stability if you don't plant the heel of your hand on the table. And like any bridge, you need to put some pressure on the fingers that are touching the table. This pressure keeps your hand from teetering back and forth while you stroke.

Think of the loop around the cue as a safety net that will keep the cue down during your stroke. While it may slightly touch the cue's shaft, it should never hinder the cue as it's sliding back and forth through your hand.

Bridge adjustments for special cases

The standard open and closed bridges described in the preceding sections are good for all normal shots, but you're not always going to be able to lay your hand flat on the table when you're about to stroke the cue ball. Sometimes a rail will get in the way; sometimes another ball will block your shot. No matter what the problem may be, you have to be able to form a well-constructed bridge that will let you cue the cue ball with consistency.

It's not uncommon for the cue ball to come to a rest near a cushion, leaving you no choice but to place your bridge hand on the rail of the table. In these instances, you still have some options for what type of bridge to use.

Open rail bridge

Open bridges are best for shots where you're looking for a soft, precise hit on the cue ball. The same conditions for deciding between open and closed bridges still apply when you're cueing from the rail.

In Figure 3-13, imagine the cue ball is close enough to the rail that you can't place your hand directly on the table. In this case, you want to hit the cue ball with as level a cue as possible (see Chapter 5). As you can see, the open bridge consists of your hand flat against the edge of the table, which will keep the cue almost parallel to the table.

Scrunch your index finger so that the second knuckle juts into the air an inch or so. Your raised knuckle is one side of the groove for the cue. The other side is your thumb, which you press against the corner of the table with the tip rising above.

With this bridge, you can sight right down the line of the shaft, giving you a perfect perspective of the contact point on the cue ball. As the cue is grooved between your thumb and index finger, keep the cue as level as possible — or as level as the shot will allow — to maximize accuracy.

This bridge is ideal for situations where the cue ball is frozen to the rail. Because only a small fraction of the cue ball will be exposed over the top of the rail, you need to see as much of the ball as possible.

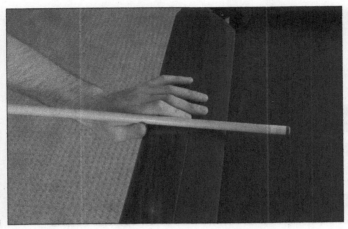

Figure 3-13: With your hand up against the side of the table, the cue slides between your index finger and thumb.

Closed rail bridge

Using a closed bridge from the rail is a bit different than a normal closed bridge, described earlier in this chapter. You still have a finger wrapped around the top of the shaft, effectively closing it off, but you make the table's rail work for you.

1. **Just as you would with a normal closed bridge, start with your hand flat against the rail.**

   Does it seem like you're always starting with a relaxed hand? Well, you are. You want to get the maximum amount of stability without over-straining, so you start with as little tension as possible.

2. **Lift your index finger in the air, while you slide your thumb over so that it makes contact with your middle finger.**

   Just as you did for the closed bridge, your thumb should be pressed against your middle finger. But unlike in a closed bridge, you should keep your thumb flat against the rail so that it can guide the shaft as it slides along the rail.

3. **With the cue in place, wrap your index finger over the top of the shaft.**

   The shaft should also be touching the tip of your index finger so that you have total control of the cue. Figure 13-14 shows the correct way to position your index finger so that it's touching the other side of your cue's shaft.

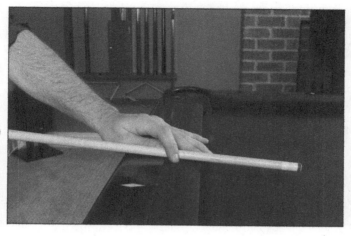

Figure 3-14:
Let your
index finger
loop around
the shaft.

Along the rail

Bridging along the rail can be a whole different beast than bridging across the
rail. In this situation, you're sliding your cue along the line of the rail, leaving
you in an awkward position with your bridge hand. While every situation is
different, Figure 3-15 shows a common bridge used along the rail.

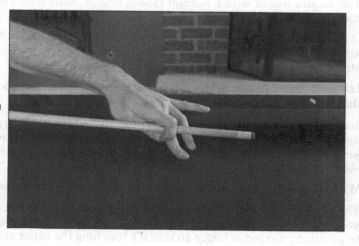

Figure 3-15:
Place your
palm on
the rail to
establish a
firm base for
your bridge.

Similar to the closed rail bridge, described earlier in this chapter, you're still
sliding the cue between your thumb and ring finger on one side and your
index finger on the other. In this case, you want to keep your palm on the
rail, with your fingers forming a loop for the cue, just like a standard closed
bridge. In Figure 3-15, your middle finger will balance your bridge between
the table and rail.

This rail bridge has plenty of variations because you may be bridging in a pocket or over another ball. After you have experience with the various bridges, you should be able to form a solid foundation, no matter what's in your way. Just remember that you want to keep your hand as firm as possible so that the cue has a steady bridge as it hits the cue ball.

Elevated bridges

If the rails prevent you from stroking with a level cue, another obstacle may be an object ball. Sometimes you're forced to cue over an object ball, which requires another kind of bridge — an elevated bridge.

For simplicity's sake, try to think of an *elevated bridge* as a slightly modified open bridge. (For more on open bridges, see the "Keeping it open" section earlier in this chapter.) Create a normal open bridge, with your fingers and hand on the table. Then lift your wrist in the air, as if you are tipping the bridge forward. Your finger tips are the only parts of your hand that touch the table, so keep pressure on them so that you'll have a sturdy base. Figure 3-16 is an example of a bridge that helps you avoid a blocking ball.

Figure 3-16:
Tip your normal open bridge forward.

The cue still goes between your thumb and index finger, though it will be at a much steeper angle toward the cue ball because you've got to clear the obstacle.

Grasping mechanical bridges

The mechanical bridge is often derided among bar-room shooters as a *cheater's stick* or, for the not-so-PC players, the lady's cue.

But watch any professional match in just about any discipline, and you'll see the mechanical bridge make an appearance. The fact is this tool is absolutely critical. You'd be best served to get used to a mechanical bridge early because it will come in handy when you're out of place.

Put it down!

First things first: Put the bridge down. Some players insist on holding the mechanical bridge in the air as they hit the cue ball. This approach is one way to greatly increase the probability of the bridge moving during a shot, which isn't what you want to happen.

Keep the mechanical bridge flat against the table, using your bridge hand to hold it in place. You want to reduce the number of variables, and keeping the bridge flat against the table is much better than having it floating in mid-air during your shot.

The elbow's action

You want to normalize your stroke when you use the mechanical bridge. While a shot with the mechanical bridge is certainly a different activity than a normal stroke, you can keep relatively the same action when it comes to your elbow.

Grip the butt of your cue with your thumb and first two fingers, just as you would normally (shown in Figure 3-17). Now, don't move your upper arm or torso. You want to keep your whole body still, stroking the cue using only your forearm — again, just as you would for a normal shot.

Figure 3-17:
Sight down
the cue with
a gentle
grip of two
fingers and
your thumb.

With an easy, controlled stroke, accelerate through the cue ball. During a normal stroke, you do not move your body and head (see Chapter 5). With a shot using the mechanical bridge, the same holds true. Move only your back arm from the elbow down, using the same stroking action you would for any other shot. Follow-through, at least as much as the shot allows without hitting any object balls. You can see in Figure 3-18 that everything remains relatively still, except for the back arm that strokes the cue through the cue ball.

Figure 3-18:
Keep your body still and let your back fore-arm, wrist, and hand do the work.

Chapter 4

On Target: The Science and Feel of Aiming

In This Chapter
▶ Looking at the basic fundamentals of aiming
▶ Understanding the important difference between the contact and aiming points
▶ Using the Ghost Ball System as a basic aiming system
▶ Peeking at more complex aiming systems

*I*n baseball, the thwack of a fastball hitting the sweet spot of a bat is unmistakable. That one sound is a *part* of the game. For pool players, no pleasure is as sweet — and simple — as the sound of a ball smacking the back of the pocket before dropping in the hole.

From the first time you hit a ball, whether you're the best player in the world or the only player in your basement, that sound will become a part of the experience. It will signify success, because a ball is no longer on the table and you're the one that made it disappear.

What goes into creating this pleasant little piece of audio? Sure, a straight-in shot is a piece of cake. But what about the infinite variety of cut shots that force you to hit the ball at any and every angle?

This chapter starts off with a quick overview of the science of aiming. From there, you can get to the table and see what really goes into pocketing a ball. I start with the Ghost Ball System — don't be scared, it's easy! — while taking a glance at a few other systems for aiming.

Staying Centered: The Line of Centers

Want to know the easiest way to make shots? The *Line of Centers* (see Figure 4-1) is your ticket to success. This line connects the center of the *object ball* (the one you're aiming to make) and the center of the cue ball with the pocket intended for the shot.

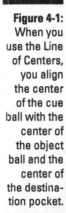

Figure 4-1:
When you use the Line of Centers, you align the center of the cue ball with the center of the object ball and the center of the destination pocket.

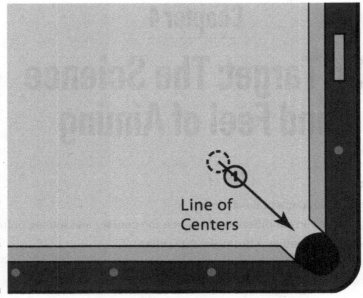

Line of
Centers

As you can see in Figure 4-1, the 1 ball is being struck by the cue ball to the right and into the corner pocket. In order to hit the 1 ball at the angle necessary to complete this task, the cue ball must be in line with the pocket when it contacts the 1 ball. Do this alignment, and you'll make the shot.

Understanding the Line of Centers is a great way to start picturing the intended target for the cue ball. For starters, think about a straight-in shot. What makes this relatively easy? Part of it has to do with the Line of Centers. For a straight shot, the center of the cue ball, the center of the object ball, and the pocket are all in one line. You don't need to picture a crooked line connecting all three; it's just a matter of keeping everything on that one line.

The Line of Centers is important because you can apply it to all shots: As long as the centers of the cue and object balls are lined up with the pocket when they collide, you will make the shot. Before you get into your stance and begin your preparations to shoot, walk over and put your cue in line with the Line of Centers. By placing your cue on this line, you can visualize the angle of the shot.

Shots at an angle (referred to as *cut shots*) are far more common than straight-in shots. And for the nearly infinite variety of cut shots, the Line of Centers helps you figure out where the cue ball must be to pocket the object ball.

Ready, Aim, Shoot: The Contact and Aiming Points

The Line of Centers concept (see preceding section) is a great way to "see" how a shot is made, but you need to be familiar with a few more points. The distinction between the contact point and the aiming point is a big step in developing a reliable sense of aim. The difference between these two points is also one of the most misunderstood aspects in the game of pool.

As you would expect, the *contact point* is the exact spot where the cue ball and object ball touch at impact. The *aiming point*, meanwhile, is where you focus on sending the cue ball so that it hits the object ball at the intended contact point.

Figure 4-2 shows the simplest example: a straight-in shot. Here, the contact point and aiming point are at the exact same location on the object ball. You're hitting the cue ball in the same exact direction you want the object ball to go after impact.

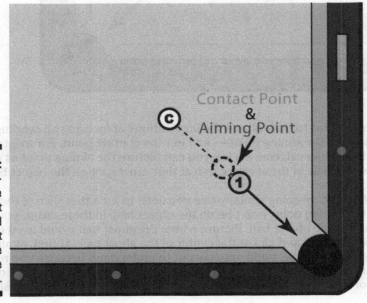

Figure 4-2:
In a straight-in shot, the contact point and aiming point are at the exact same location.

Contact Point & Aiming Point

But once the cue ball strays from a straight-in shot, no matter how small the angle, the contact point and aiming point are no longer the same. In Figure 4-3, a simple cut shot shows how these two points are vastly different. If you were to aim at the contact point, you would miss the shot to the left of the pocket every time. Instead, you have to aim to the left of the contact point, allowing the cue ball to strike the 1 ball at the correct contact point.

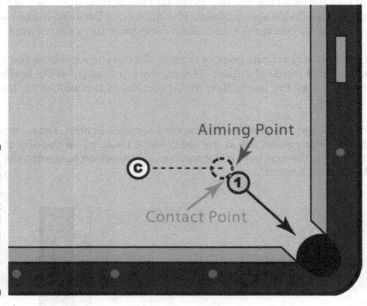

Figure 4-3:
For angled shots, the contact point and aiming point will never be the same.

It is important to understand the implications of focusing on sending the cue ball toward the aiming point — and not the contact point. For most shots (all but those at an extreme angle), you can picture the aiming point as a spot on the object ball. In these cases, aim at that *exact* spot on the object ball.

For *thin cuts*, meaning shots where you need to hit a thin slice of the object ball, the aiming point won't be on the object ball. In these cases, you must not aim at the object ball. Picture where the ghost ball would need to be to pocket the shot and aim at the center of the ghost ball. At first, aiming for these shots may be a difficult concept to understand because you're not aiming at the ball you intend to pocket. But with experience, you'll develop a feel for where the ball must be in order to execute the shot successfully.

The contact point is exactly that — a specific spot on the object ball. Because both balls are round and very hard, the point of impact is quite small. Regardless of the difficulty of a shot, take aim at a precise point, instead of relying on generalities when it comes to the end result.

As the angle of a shot increases (which means the cut shot becomes *thinner*), the shot becomes more difficult. This difficulty has to do with the growing distance between the aiming point and the contact point. Unlike a straight-in shot, where you don't need to aim the cue ball to contact the object ball at another point, a thin cut shot creates a large disparity between where you aim and the point that actually makes contact with the object ball.

But all is not lost. If you can understand the difference between these two points, you're on the road to improvement. Remember, you can quickly understand the concept of aiming, but it takes a lifetime to master.

Did You See That? The Ghost Ball System

The *Ghost Ball System* is not only one of the easiest aiming systems to understand, it's also among the most popular and effective ways to aim.

The Ghost Ball System is simply picturing where the cue ball must be when it collides with the object ball for a successful shot.

When you're looking at any shot, you can work in the Ghost Ball System with a few quick steps:

1. **Looking at the object ball, draw a line straight from the center of the pocket through the center of the object ball.**

   The point where this line intersects the object ball on its side farthest from the pocket is the contact point.

2. **After you know where the cue ball has to hit the object ball, imagine a ball that is on that same line from the pocket through the object ball.**

   This imaginary ball is the Ghost Ball.

3. **Aim at the center of the Ghost Ball.**

   The center of the Ghost Ball is your aiming point because it's where you're going to hit the center of the cue ball, resulting in contact at the intended contact point.

It is important to remember that, for any specific shot, the contact point on the object ball will stay the same no matter where the cue ball is located (see Figure 4-4). Whether the shot is straight in or the thinnest of cuts, the object ball's contact point will not change. The aiming point, however, is dependent on the location of the cue ball. Because you have to deliver the cue ball to a specific contact point on the ball you intend to pocket, your aim will change with different cue-ball locations.

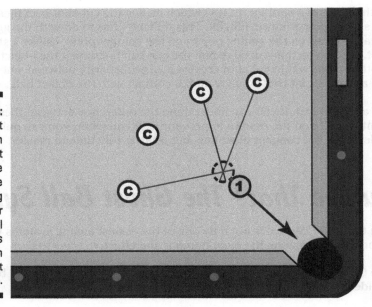

Figure 4-4:
The contact point on the object remains the same, while the aiming point for the cue ball changes with each different angle.

As a mental exercise, look at the variety of shots in Figure 4-4. You can see that each shot has a unique aiming point, while the contact point remains the same. Being able to picture where these two points are for each and every shot is absolutely vital to refining your aim.

No matter what kind of shot, this system gives you an idea of what is necessary to pocket a ball.

Like everything in pool that sounds so simple and easy, the Ghost Ball System has a slight — emphasis on *slight* — imperfection. The Ghost Ball (or the imaginary location of a cue ball that is in perfect line with the object ball and pocket at impact) will not always send the object on that exact line for the center of the pocket.

Throw is a term for a phenomenon that describes a slight alteration of the object ball's path after being hit by the cue ball. When the cue ball collides with the object ball, the two spheres are in contact for a tiny amount of time. During this brief instant, friction causes the object ball to be *thrown* off of the ideal line (see Figure 4-5).

While this effect is often unnoticeable, it does occur, usually in the area of 1 to 3 degrees. So the Ghost Ball System might not be *exactly* as it seems, but most players subconsciously compensate for the tiny change due to throw.

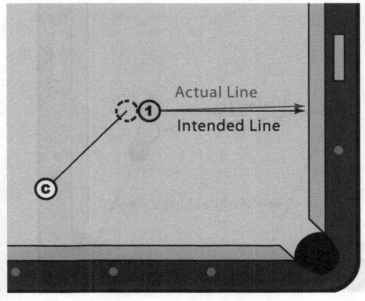

Figure 4-5:
Friction
affects the
course of
the object
ball.

Many different variables affect the amount of throw in a given shot. The spin
and speed of the cue ball can increase or decrease how much (if at all) an object
ball deviates from the ideal shot line. The table's cloth and the condition of the
balls can also affect throw. In general, an object ball may be thrown offline by 1
to 3 degrees, with the most amount of throw topping out at 6 degrees.

With a Little Geometry: Aiming with Parallel Lines

While the Ghost Ball System (see the preceding section) is definitely the most
widely practiced method of aiming, it's certainly not the only way to line up
shots. The Parallel Lines System is another popular method of aiming.

Looking at the shot diagrammed in Figure 4-6, you can see how this system
works step by step:

1. **First, visualize a line that goes from the middle of the pocket right
   through the middle of the object ball.**

   This step is quite similar to the first step when aiming with the Ghost Ball
   System, described in the preceding section. (As a guide, the object ball
   has a red ring around it, to highlight the correct angle to the pocket.)

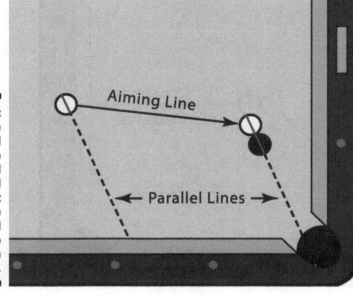

Figure 4-6:
When the parallel lines on the object ball and cue ball line up at impact, the object ball will stop where you want it.

When you need to "see" lines on the pool table, use your cue. Even the best players in the world will line up shots using their cues as guides. So don't be afraid to put the tip of your cue in the pocket and hold it over the object ball to make sure that you're seeing a perfectly straight line from ball to pocket.

2. **Look at the cue ball and imagine a line parallel to the one that connects the object ball with the pocket.**

   Like the object ball, the cue ball is shown with a red circle around it, emphasizing the correct angle.

Mosconi and the Fat Man:

The Parallel Lines System of aiming was popularized by Willie Mosconi, who may just be the greatest player to ever pick up a cue. While Minnesota Fats (Rudolf Wanderone) is certainly the most well-known name in pool, Mosconi is widely acknowledged as a far superior player.

While Minnesota Fats is widely regarded as the prototypical hustler-type, preferring gambling matches to tournaments, Mosconi was an unparalleled tournament player. During a career that spanned four decades, Mosconi won a total of 15 world titles. He also holds one of the most famed records in all of pool. He pocketed 526 consecutive balls playing straight pool (see Chapter 20), which is the highest run ever.

While certainly a capable player, Fats was more known for his personality than his playing. Mosconi, meanwhile, was the biggest star in the universe of pool. He won 15 world titles during his career, which spanned four decades.

3. **With the two lines perfectly parallel, hit the cue ball so that it strikes the object ball with the red ring in perfect line with the object ball's red ring.**

   By connecting these two rings at the intended contact point, you can aim even the toughest cuts with a little geometry and imagination.

From Thin to Full: Aiming with the Fractional Ball System

I use the term *full* to describe a straight-in shot (where the cue ball *fully* hits the object ball). The Fractional Ball System is a way to approach certain shots by how full the cue ball strikes the object ball.

Unlike the Ghost Ball System, where you focus on aiming and contact points, the Fractional Ball System deals only with the aiming point. Instead of factoring in the aiming point, you focus on how much of the cue ball overlaps with the object ball at impact.

The Fractional Ball System is a great way to summarize a shot at first glance. For those just beginning to play pool, this system gives you a way to group certain shots together. While experienced players can use a form of this method to aim just about any shot, I cover this system as a way to keep certain shots organized in your memory.

Figure 4-7 shows the four main cornerstones of the Fractional Ball System.

- **Cornerstone 1:** Full-ball hit. At the moment of impact, the cue ball completely covers the object ball (from your perspective). Because the cue ball is hitting the object ball straight on, the cue ball fully overlaps with the object ball.

- **Cornerstone 2:** 3/4-full hit. This measurement is for slight angles, where the cue ball nearly covers the entire object ball.

- **Cornerstone 3:** Half-ball hit. Half the cue ball overlaps with half the object ball. For all half-ball hits, you aim the center of the cue ball to the outer edge of the object ball.

- **Cornerstone 4:** 1/4-full hit. This is the thinnest of the four shots that you need to know for the Fractional Ball System. In fact, the 1/4-ball hit is so thin that the aiming point is no longer on the object ball. Instead, you must aim at a point on the side of the ball opposite the direction you intend the object ball to travel.

Shown from the perspective of the shooter, the shots range from full ball (left; where the cue ball rolls directly into the object ball) to the 1/4-ball hit (right; where only one quarter of the cue ball overlaps with the object ball at impact).

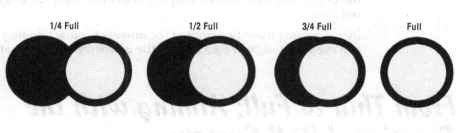

1/4 Full   1/2 Full   3/4 Full   Full

While the Ghost Ball System (see the section "Did You See That? The Ghost Ball System," earlier in this chapter) is applicable to every shot you can face on a table, the Fractional Ball System is a great way to characterize shots. Look at the half-ball hit as an example. Figure 4-8 shows a half-ball hit. The center of the cue ball is in direct line with the upper edge of the 2 ball, meaning half of each ball overlaps.

Figure 4-8:
A half-ball
hit will send
the object
ball in
roughly a
30-degree
angle from
the aiming
line.

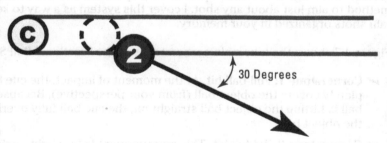

30 Degrees

Now, geometry tells you that the 2 ball will be sent in a direction 30 degrees off of the cue ball's initial line. (You get the same result using the Ghost Ball System because the center of the outlined cue ball lines up with the center of the 2 ball and the arrow.)

To set up a half-ball hit, all you have to do is aim the center of the cue ball for an outer edge of the object ball. Start with the cue ball just a foot away from the object ball. It will take only a few hits for you to become familiar with the object ball's angle of deflection. It may take more practice before you use a half-ball hit in a game, but it helps to become familiar with this shot, as it's right in between a full ball hit and the thinnest cut.

Knowing that the half-ball hit is 30 degrees, look at the other two cut shots. Hitting just 1/4 of the object ball (meaning a 1/4-ball hit) will result in the object ball being deflected by roughly 45 degrees. A 3/4-ball hit, meanwhile, will send the object ball in a direction 15 degrees from the cue ball's line.

These figures are by no means necessary to memorize in order to play pool. In fact, the Fractional Ball System is a great way to *characterize* shots. You might not aim at a shot a certain way if it's close to a half-ball hit, but you can remember how you approach cut angles near half ball.

Chapter 5

Hit It: Creating a Solid Stroke

. . . .

In This Chapter

▶ Warming up in a consistent manner to build rhythm

▶ Starting your final backswing in a controlled fashion

▶ Easing into your final stroke and accelerating through the cue ball

▶ Following through and staying down during the shot

. . . .

F inding a proper stroke involves a lot of doing — something that you can't achieve by reading a few pages of a book. Describing the fluid, controlled, graceful display that a perfect pool stroke can be isn't easy. The perfect pool stroke has something almost artistic to it — the rhythm, the ease, the timing of countless parts of the body working together to lead to a perfect conclusion. It's a mysterious property — the "it" factor of a pool stroke — that one player will have and another won't.

And while the execution of a stroke, from backswing to follow-through, may be a visual art, you can still pick up a lot of information from these pages that will allow you to replicate such a stroke. This chapter gives you a sort of road map that will keep you on the path to building a fundamentally strong stroke. You find out what you should do, including where all the major body parts should be at different points of your stroke. You also discover a few don'ts that may function as red flags, keeping you from veering off the road to establishing a visually pleasing and — still more important than anything else — effective stroke.

The start of the final stroke really begins with the warm-up strokes. During your warm-up, you get a chance to verify that everything is in line, while acquainting yourself with the motion of the cue from start to backswing and back. I then take you through the final stroke, from the moment you pull the cue back all the way through contact with the cue ball and past the point your cue stops after the follow-through. If you know the fundamentals of the stroke, you're on your way to building a beautiful stroke.

Practice Time: Warming Up

Just like a runner doesn't roll out of bed into the starting blocks, a pool player needs to warm up — and warm up before every stroke. By taking a few practice strokes before each shot, you're allowing yourself to check how everything fits together.

You should need only a few warm-up strokes — three, four, or five — to know whether everything is clicking together. And while this last check may not be a conscious thing, like you do when you're running down a checklist of what things should be where, it is a chance to get comfortable with your stance and what is going to happen in the ensuing stroke.

Figure 5-1 is a proper setup. To stroke the cue the correct way, you have to keep a lot of different body parts in line. Here are a few points (going from the toes on up) that may cause you to break from your stance and start all over:

✔ **Balance:** Do you feel comfortable with the way your weight is distributed? Are you in an athletic stance (see Chapter 2)? Are you leaning to one side or the other?

Figure 5-1:
When you're focused on the shot, everything should be in line and ready to go.

- **Body position:** Is your upper body close enough to the cue ball so that you can comfortably pull the cue back on your backswing? Do you have enough space for your cue to swing back and through the shot?

- **Bridge:** Is your bridge hand firmly planted on the table? Is there any sign of movement in your bridge hand when you're going through your warm-up strokes?

- **Cue:** Does the cue remain on the shot line the entire time? Does the cue stay on the same line as you pull it back and bring it forward?

- **Aim:** Are you locked in to where you want to hit the cue ball? Is the cue gliding toward the cue ball in a straight line?

- **Eyes:** Can you keep your head still while the cue swings back and forth? Does your upper body move, thus moving your eyes, at any point in your warm-up?

Seems like a lot, huh? Well, it may be if you're mentally checking off each point on every stroke. But a natural, fundamentally sound stroke is also comfortable, so you should let your body tell you whether something is askew.

While you should plan the shot when you're standing and execute it when you're in your stance, right after your final practice stroke is the final chance to rethink your plan. If you're practice stroking and you doubt yourself or your plan, stand up and start over. If you're not 100 percent sure that you're ready to make the shot at hand, it's time to stand up and go at it again.

Getting Comfortable: Rhythm and Routine

The time between getting in your stance and pulling back the cue for the final stroke can be valuable for more than just troubleshooting. These few seconds can help you establish a rhythm and a routine. You can take this time to make sure that you're comfortable with your environment, which will only lead to better results.

Finding your rhythm

Your practice strokes can help you establish your rhythm — whether that means the pace of a hare or the pace of a tortoise is up to you. While there is no set pace for your warm-up strokes, I can confidently say that a huge majority of players are best served by controlled, measured strokes.

If you really have to lay into a shot, you might pick up the pace just a bit; and if you have to lightly tap the cue ball, you might ease back a bit. But in general, you want to find a nice, even, easy rhythm.

Making it routine

Chapter 2 details the importance of building a reliable preshot routine. Your warm-up strokes are one of the last pieces to that puzzle. Try to find a routine that you can stick to with a majority of your shots. Most players recommend taking at least three strokes, just to give yourself an opportunity to make sure that everything fits together as it should. Conversely, I'd advise against making it common practice to stick to any number of strokes over eight. After all, you'll spend more time counting to whatever number is your routine instead of focusing on pocketing the ball.

This advice doesn't mean you should *never* use more than eight strokes. For some tricky shots, whether you're bridging over a ball or you have to lean over the table a certain way, you may want to take a few extra strokes to make sure that you're comfortable with how you're situated and what you've got to do. (On the other side of that coin, it's never advisable to go below your standard number of strokes.)

After you're confident that you're in line and you're situated correctly, you're ready to pull the trigger on your final stroke.

Starting the Stroke with the Backswing

The backswing is an oft-overlooked part of the stroke. It's not so much a part of putting the cue to the ball as it is getting the cue *in the right position* to do so. And although you can easily underestimate its importance, the backswing is vital to a fluid, controlled stroke.

Just as your warm-up should have a comfortable rhythm and pace (see the previous section), your backswing should also have a comfortable tempo. Figure 5-2 shows what your general position should be right before you're ready to pull the cue back.

In Figure 5-2, notice how the player's back arm is perpendicular to the cue. Your back arm should be at a right angle to the cue at the beginning of the stroke (and at impact). Also, the player is fairly centered over the cue, not stretching in one direction.

Start your stroke by slowly pulling the straight cue back, keeping the cue on the shot line, at a nice, easy tempo until you've reached the point where you're ready to swing the cue forward.

Figure 5-2: This is the starting point for the back-swing — comfortable and in line.

I have no golden rule to offer you when it comes to the pace of your backswing, but a player may take as much as a few seconds to complete the backswing. Familiarize yourself with this tempo by stroking the cue without aiming at a ball. Just swing the cue back, counting "one Mississippi . . ., two Mississippi." This tempo should be a good starting point for building a smooth backswing.

Staying still

A thousand pool players have a thousand unique ways of stroking, but the easiest way to build a fundamentally sound stroke is to limit necessary movement and eliminate unnecessary movement.

From the point where you start your backswing, the only part of you that should move is your back arm, from the elbow down. Your body should remain perfectly still. Your head should stay centered on the shot. Even your back arm, from the elbow to the shoulder, should not move at all.

You can see in Figure 5-3 how little has changed from the starting point of the stroke to the end of the backswing. All that has moved is the back forearm, wrist, and hand. If you can eliminate all other movement, you're on the fast track to a dependable, repeatable stroke.

Figure 5-3:
At the end of the backswing, everything has remained still except for the lower half of the back arm.

Keeping the cue level

At all times, no matter what shot you're looking at, you want to keep the cue as level as possible. Know that you can't keep the cue completely parallel with the ground; you have to raise the back end of the cue a smidge so that you don't smash your hand or butt of the cue into the rails or table bed. But the goal is to keep your cue parallel to the ground.

The primary reason you want to keep the cue on the level is to avoid unintentional movement of the cue ball after contact. When you raise the butt of the cue — called *jacking up,* in pool-speak — some of the force of your stroke will push the cue ball into the table, which can impart some unintentional spin on the cue ball. Jacking up leads to a hit that isn't as smooth as a hit with a level cue. So as a rule, always check yourself to make sure that you're holding the cue as level as possible.

Some shots dictate that you jack up — such as when the cue ball is up against the rail and you want to hit below center. Even in these situations, minimize the angle your cue deviates from parallel. You have to do what you have to do, but don't unnecessarily jack up your cue.

Making Contact: Swinging through the Ball

After the backswing is over, you have only one place to go: straight for the cue ball.

For many players, moving from the backswing toward the cue ball can lead to inaccuracies in the delivery of the cue. The change in momentum can cause the back hand to fall off of the shot line. For the best way to make the transition, you can choose between two different schools of thought:

- ✔ **To pause:** Some players (including Hall of Famers like Allison Fisher and Buddy Hall) like to pause at the moment between backswing and foreswing. The pause may be for just an instant, but it can help you slow yourself down after the backswing.

- ✔ **Not to pause:** Plenty of other players prefer to seamlessly transition from the backswing into the forward stroke. Again, the pause may be more suitable for you to slowly stop your backswing and then immediately move forward toward the cue ball. This transfer is certainly more fluid, which may or may not benefit you.

A disclaimer: Neither of these choices is the "correct" way; play with both and see which you prefer (which may just be the one that leads to more successful shots).

Accelerating into the ball

After you're ready to move the cue toward the cue ball, the cue needs to accelerate from the start of your swing until you make contact with the cue ball (at which point the cue will slow down due to the collision). No matter whether you're barely brushing the cue ball or smashing the rack on the break, you want to keep the cue tip accelerating toward the cue ball.

It's all too easy to start your final stroke by throwing the cue toward the cue ball in a jerky fashion. Remember, you want to start slow and slowly accelerate into the cue ball. Practice a controlled start to your final stroke; you'll be surprised how you can still hit the ball firmly when you start at a snail's pace.

Keeping control

Just as the backswing is an exercise in minimizing movement, you want to remain in complete control from the end of your backswing and into and through contact with the cue ball. Here are some quick pointers to keep your stroke in line and in control:

- ✔ **Stay relaxed.** You can easily tense up during your final stroke. Your grip on the back of the cue should remain relaxed throughout the stroke. Tensing up only steers the cue off line.

- ✔ **Imitate a pendulum.** Just like during your backswing, the only part of your body that should move is your back arm from the elbow down. Think of your back forearm as a pendulum, swinging back and forward. The path of your hand, wrist, and forearm should be the exact same in both directions.

You can see in Figures 5-4 and 5-5 that the upper arm remains still while the forearm swivels from forward to backward to forward.

✔ **Don't steer.** One sure way to miss a shot is by steering the cue ball to the left or right with your cue tip. Instead, visualize the cue moving straight through the cue ball.

Figure 5-4: The upper arm stays in place, while the forearm moves forward into the stroke.

Figure 5-5: At the moment of impact, your forearm swings forward.

Hitting the cue ball

Although I certainly wouldn't recommend thinking about information in this section *during* your shot, you want to know what your stance should look like at the moment of impact. Figure 5-6 is a photo taken at the point of contact between the cue and cue ball.

Figure 5-6: Look familiar? Your position at impact should be about identical to your position at the start of your stroke.

Again, your body should be still and centered over the cue. Your elbow should be back near its starting position perpendicular to the ground. As long as you stay balanced throughout your stroke, you should be able to keep still while your back arm does all the work.

Grand Finale: Following Through

Contact has been made, but you aren't done yet. The follow-through is just as important as any other component of the stroke.

A smooth stroke continues into and through the cue ball. Just as you started your backstroke with a slow pull of the cue, you want to end your stroke by gradually decelerating the cue until it comes to a complete stop. Figure 5-7 is a shot of the cue almost at the moment of impact with the cue ball.

Figure 5-7: Here's the cue at impact.

Figure 5-8 is a shot of the cue after completing a healthy follow-through. On the average stroke, the cue should travel anywhere from 6 to 18 inches forward after impact. Extending the stroke into a long follow-through only helps to remove any jerky movements, which can include a clenching up of the cue at impact.

Obviously, if a ball or a rail is in the path of your follow-through, you can't drive your cue into that obstacle. In these cases, you need to stop the cue a little short, but for your run of the day shots, make the most of your follow-through.

Figure 5-8:
See how far
it extends
forward?

Holding the elbow in place

To let your cue continue forward past the point of contact when you're using the *pendulum stroke,* your grip hand will come up toward your torso, which forces the tip of your cue downward. Some players and teachers believe that you must drop your elbow after contact with the cue ball to allow the cue to follow through naturally. But in order to produce the most consistent stroke possible, you should try to keep your elbow in the same position for the entire stroke, from backswing on through contact.

In an effort to limit the number of moving parts during your stroke, focus on keeping your back elbow in place. If you can keep your elbow still, you're limiting the movement of your stroke to the back forearm down. Staying still also helps you keep your back shoulder and upper arm on the shot line, which increases accuracy.

Check the video

Even the most intelligent player in the world needs a stroke that will let him execute a game-winning plan. Thankfully, we live in an era where a video catalog of the fundamentals of the pool stroke is as close as the nearest computer. Plenty of resources online show what a proper stroke should look like.

Dr. Dave Alciatore, a mechanical engineering professor at Colorado State University and reviewer of this book, is a leader in online resources for pool players. His Web site (`http://billiards.colostate.edu`) has a load of instruction videos for almost any topic on the game.

Also, many online pool stores offer a large collection of instructional DVDs, which are fantastic when you want to *see* the proper fundamentals of the stroke.

Many players have a tendency to drop their elbows during powerful shots, allowing a natural follow-through (because the forearm and cue have a significant amount of momentum). But even in special circumstances where you really need to hit the cue ball hard, the elbow shouldn't drop more than a few inches.

Look at the two photos in Figures 5-9 and 5-10. The first shot is the elbow during a normal stroke. The forearm is the only part of the body that's moving and the upper arm hasn't moved. In Figure 5-10, after contact has been made, the back elbow remains in the same position, with the back hand bringing the butt of the cue through the cue ball.

Figure 5-9: During the stroke, the elbow remains steady.

Figure 5-10:
After your
follow-
through,
the elbow
drop should
remain near
the same.

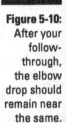

Staying down

If you ask a professional player to list her top ten bad habits, chances are good that she lists one of them as "coming up too soon" or "not staying down." Just as the follow-through is a continuation of the stroke, so is the part of the shot where you stay in your post-stroke position.

The best way to show the importance of staying down is with a golf analogy. When you're on the tee lining up your drive, you want to stay focused on the position of the ball before, during, and after you swing the club. Right when you smack the ball, you don't lift your head to see where the ball is headed. You keep your head down so that you can deliver an effective stroke. (After all, does a drive go farther when you're watching?)

Well, the same is true in pool. Keep your body down with your cue held still in its finishing position. Let the balls travel where they may while you stay still. Most teachers recommend staying in your stance until the balls come to a rest. (With the exception being if a ball is heading toward you. In this case, getting up is okay. I wouldn't recommend taking a foul because the 7 ball bounced off your arm.)

Chapter 6

Playing Nice: The Etiquette of the Game

....

In This Chapter

▶ Discovering the subtle guidelines of table-side behavior

▶ Understanding how pool players interact

▶ Defining what is and what is not sharking

▶ Treating the equipment with respect

....

I may not need to blather on and on about how pool is a cerebral game, best appreciated by the socially refined, but a certain code goes along with the game. The unwritten rules of the poolroom are many, though not totally extraneous to the game, but you should be fine if you read through this chapter once.

Golf is a game that is repeatedly compared to pool — both games require quiet concentration on a stationary target. And just as you can commit social suicide on a golf course (for example, by walking through another player's putting line), you will have plenty of opportunities for faux pas at the pool table.

Besides the specific situations I talk about in this chapter, just remember to be a good sportsman and use common sense. This advice may sound like a no-brainer, but you'd be surprised how many disputes arise from completely avoidable circumstances.

In this chapter, I talk about some general dos and don'ts. From there, I get into the subject of sharking — deliberately distracting your opponent. And finally, I run through a checklist of things you need to know about the equipment you're handling.

Competing Graciously

While hundreds of entries in the rulebook dictate what you can and can't do with the cue ball, very few outline how you're supposed to interact with your opponent. In the following sections, I offer some clarification on these unwritten social niceties.

The best way to end misunderstandings is to avoid them all together.

Set the record straight

Whether you're competing in a friendly game in your basement or in a weekend tournament at your local hall, you *need* to be absolutely clear on the rules that are in effect for your game. To this end, a few rules are constantly changing, depending on where and with whom you're playing. Before you get to lag for the break, make sure that you know the answer to these questions:

- ✔ **Is the table open after the break?** Sometimes, if you make one stripe, you're stripes. Other times, the table is still *open* (stripes and solids have yet to be assigned to players). Make sure that you know how pocketing balls on the break will affect how you choose your balls. (See Chapter 18 for detailed info on the break.)

- ✔ **What needs to be called?** Many leagues dictate that you need to call which ball is going into which pocket. Other leagues let you count *slop* — unintentionally pocketed balls. Know what you need to call so that you aren't called for a foul.

- ✔ **Do three consecutive fouls result in a loss?** In many amateur leagues, this rule doesn't apply, but it's worth asking.

- ✔ **Are there any house rules?** It seems every table has its own set of rules. Ask whether the house has any special rules outside the ordinary. You may be surprised how often you discover a rule you wouldn't have thought of.

Ask when you don't know

So what if something pops up while you're in the middle of a game, and you're not exactly sure how to handle it? Simple; just ask.

In Chapter 22, I talk about the importance of carrying yourself with confidence. When you're at the table, you have to come across as someone in total control. Well, here's an exception — don't just assume you know the proper ruling for one thing or another.

If you have any doubt about a certain ruling, just ask your opponent. Double-checking before you shoot ensures that both you and your opponent are on the same page.

Some league systems allow for another player on your team to coach you at the table. While asking for a clarification of a rule usually doesn't constitute a coach, you should avoid asking your teammate a question because others may construe it as asking for advice on the shot.

Get extra eyes for close calls

If you or your opponent line up a shot that may lead to controversy — for example, if the cue ball may hit the intended ball first — asking for somebody to watch the shot is perfectly fine. Usually, you can find an experienced player in the pool hall who can give you an unbiased pair of eyes. Ideally, this person is a certified ref, but you're not going to see too many of those wandering around your pool hall or your basement.

For an example of when you may want to ask for a third party to watch, look at Figure 6-1. You're stripes, and you've got the 11 ball in your sights. Because you're going to shoot the 11 in the corner pocket, you could possibly hit the 4 ball first. The dotted line ball shows about where the cue ball will need to be to pocket the 11, which is in close proximity to the 4.

In this case, have somebody watch so that she can act as an arbitrator should any dispute arise.

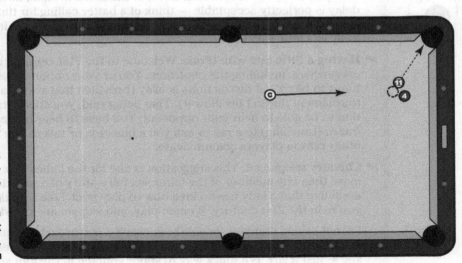

Figure 6-1: Hitting the 11 ball into the pocket without hitting the 4 ball first may be a tricky enough situation to warrant extra eyes.

Other little things . . .

Whether you're in competition or just hitting balls on a Friday night, you should be aware of a few other social graces. While these tips are more suggestions than absolute rules, you should be perfectly fine if you use a little common sense and old-fashioned manners.

- ✔ **From the peanut gallery:** Like golfers, pool players can be pretty prickly about being told how to do something — even if it's clear they are doing something incorrectly. Take caution when you offer suggestions.

  Even if you're 100 percent sure that you can help another player, try to offer comments or suggestions as a question. "Have you ever tried . . . ?" or "Do you think . . . ?" may be good icebreakers if you want to talk shop with a fellow player.

- ✔ **Slowing it down:** Chances are you can go a very long time without playing in a match that has a shot clock. Playing without a shot clock gives you the freedom to line up your shot, take your time to get comfortable, and pull the trigger when you're ready. Just don't abuse this freedom.

  You likely won't hear this complaint if you take a minute or two to line up a particularly difficult shot. You will hear some groans (or snoars?), though, when you get up from your stance four times to pocket a *hanger* (an object ball hanging an inch or two from the edge of a pocket). As always, a little common sense can help you avoid any complications with an antsy opponent.

  If you get in too much of a rhythm, though, your opponent may try to cool you off by slowing herself down at the table. In small doses, this delay is perfectly acceptable — think of a batter calling for timeout in baseball. But again, five minutes for a straight-in shot from 6 inches away is a little excessive.

- ✔ **Having a little tact with iPods:** Welcome to the 21st century. iPods are everywhere, including the poolroom. You or your opponent using some tunes to block out distractions is okay (provided that your league or tournament doesn't disallow it). That being said, you should take caution to be able to hear your opponent. You have to hear him call a ball *frozen* (touching) to a rail or ask you a question or talk to you for any other reason players communicate.

- ✔ **Chivalry misplaced:** This suggestion is one for the ladies. I've heard more than one member of the fairer sex tell a story of a would-be suitor assuming that a lady has no idea how to play pool. Like with the iPods, you're in the 21st century. Women play, and women are knowledgeable.

  I'm not saying that you *shouldn't* approach a player just because she's female. I'm just guessing that assuming that a woman is clueless because she's "just a girl" is a quick way to shoot yourself in the foot socially.

For almost any situation you encounter in a pool hall or someone's home game room, you can draw a parallel to another sport. Just remember the general standards of sportsmanship — honesty, politeness, and fairness — and you'll be in good shape.

Sharking

When you think of pool, you think of *sharks* as predatory hustlers feeding on the bank accounts of inexperienced players. But a more common definition in pool is someone who intentionally, though not explicitly, distracts or throws off his opponent.

Unfortunately, *sharking* is a too-common activity among pool players. Pool requires a ton of quiet concentration, so distracting a player in pool is relatively easy as compared to a sport like basketball, where 20,000 fans scream during a free throw.

You can shark an opponent in many ways. You may even shark without knowing it. The following list offers a rundown of common ways players shark one another:

- ✔ **The in-the-line shark:** You're about to nail the game-winning shot when your opponent appears in your line of sight. He's sliding his cue from hand to hand like it's on fire, all while you're trying to concentrate. He's trying to shark you. After all, if you concentrate more on his unsportsmanlike conduct and less on the shot in front of you, he's already at an advantage, right?

  While some less than scrupulous players may try such a tactic, you should avoid doing so. The chance such an action will increase your odds of winning isn't worth the trouble it'll cause.

  So, be mindful of where your opponent is aiming. If you can avoid being directly in her line of vision, that's great. If you can't, or if she's aiming directly at you while you're sitting harmlessly in your chair, just sit still and let her shoot.

- ✔ **The timing shark:** Another way a player may try to knock you out of your rhythm is with a seemingly random sound effect right when you're about to pull the trigger. Some players have been known to drop cues during their opponents' backswings, letting the thwack of the cue against the ground knock a player out of rhythm. Then there's the sneeze or cough or laugh, but that one's a little tougher to hide as accidental.

- ✔ **The subtlest of sharks:** "Wow, you really are stroking straight today!" Sounds innocuous enough, right? Well, opponents can use these seemingly harmless observations as psychological grenades. The thinking is that if you point out something specific in your opponent's game, he'll start focusing on that particular aspect. If your opponent comments on your straight follow-through, you may get stuck thinking about it.

All in all, it's just another way to get you out of your rhythm and comfort zone. But it's worth noting, especially for this example, how you can partake in this type of sharking without even knowing it. You can shark an opponent without intending to do so. Whether you're playing a friend or someone you've never met, try to avoid making specific comments during play — if it's competitive, that is; you can chatter all you want if you're just knocking balls around for fun or practice.

So what do you do about a shark? Well, you have a few options because every situation is a little different.

The first school of thought says that you can be sharked only if you *allow* yourself to be sharked. Simply put, don't let the distractions bother you. Zone out all the noise in the poolroom or whatever is going on beyond the table in your line of sight. While you probably won't be able to ignore an opponent armed with an air horn, do your best to ignore it, if possible.

Next, ask your opponent to stop doing whatever he's doing to distract you. Sounds easy, but this can be kind of a sticky request. But if your opponent is doing something out of the ordinary, you have a right to ask that he cease and desist.

In the end, do whatever you think is best for you. The goal is to stay focused on the game, not the accompanying antics, so whatever allows you to do so is the best bet.

Respecting the Tools

Chapter 21 talks all about how quality pool equipment can last forever — if it's treated right, that is. Part of the etiquette of pool is learning how to look after all the tools you'll be handling during play. The following list gives you a few tips for taking care of your pool equipment:

✔ **No dumping:** It's a small thing, really, but it isn't all that hard to remember. Ask a pool player to name his biggest pet peeve, and two out of ten will say, "Players who dump the balls all over the table."

When you get to the table, *place* the 16 balls on the cloth. You're not going to crack an inch-thick slab of slate by tossing a ball a few inches, but you can lightly damage the cloth. After a few hundred heave-hos, the cloth can bunch up (or *pill*) and result in uneven play. And if there's one way to raise the ire of pool players, it's a healthy *table roll* — meaning the ball doesn't roll in a straight line, as it should.

✔ **Clear it out:** Another no-no around the table is putting your frosty cold beverage on the rail or (God forbid) on the playing surface. While some bar-room tables look like they've been mistaken for a recycling bin for the last two decades, you should keep drinks, burgers, and smokes away from the playing surface.

Your spilt gin and tonic can scar any table that is kept in decent condition. Not to mention that cigarettes can do some hefty damage to cloth and wooden rails.

✔ **Leave it up:** Try to equate the chalk on the rail of the table with a toilet seat. Just like men have been leaving the toilet seat up for centuries, pool players have mistakenly left the chalk *down* for just as long.

While you're going to get a certain amount of chalk on your hands, you can limit the blue stain of an afternoon spent at the pool hall by leaving the little cue of chalk with the exposed side facing up.

If you leave it facing down, you'll leave a whiff of blue on the rail. Bend over this part of the rail for a shot, and now you've got a nice splotch of aqua on your pants or shirt. While erroneously leaving the chalk down instead of up seems like a minor point, it's a peeve of more than a few pool players. So, that's toilet seat down, chalk up. Got it?

✔ **Massés and jumps:** Many rooms disallow jump and massé shots because of a slight chance that these attempts can do some damage to a table's cloth. But, in reality, tables — both private and public — can survive the occasional tricky shot.

That being said, if you're going to go for a jump or massé, you should have some familiarity with the shot before you pull it out on another person's table. If you aren't sure that you're capable of executing the shot safely, it's best to err on the side of caution.

Part II
Controlling the Cue Ball

The 5th Wave — By Rich Tennant

©RICHTENNANT

"I'm gonna play the 7 ball off the 3 ball, bank it into the side pocket, and position the cue ball so I can talk to that girl at the end of the bar."

Part II

Controlling the

Cue Ball

In this part . . .

This advice sounds so simple, but the most important aspect of quality play is how to control the cue ball. Keep the white ball obeying your every wish, and you'll be surprised how easy the game can be. In this part, I cover the different ways of manipulating the cue ball — from hitting it so that it stops dead in its tracks after colliding with another ball to making it dance around the table in ways thought unimaginable. The information in this part is crucial to increasing your understanding of the game by knowing what to do with the cue ball and how to do it.

Chapter 7

Getting Control and Stopping the Cue Ball

. . . .

In This Chapter

▶ Keeping the cue ball under control

▶ Understanding what effect the cue-ball contact point has on the cue ball

▶ Starting to control the cue ball with stun shots

▶ Seeing the options for position that open up with stun and stop shots

. . . .

From the oldest of old-timers to the youngest sharks-in-the-making, any pool player worth her weight in chalk will tell you that making the shot is all about controlling the white ball. With a little practice, almost anyone can make a shot here and there. But to know exactly where the cue ball's going to go after that shot? That's the sign of a pool player —not just someone banging balls around the table.

It's pretty cool, really, when you think about the amount of control you can have on the cue ball. When things are working perfectly, the cue ball is at your complete mercy — *on a string,* in poolspeak. Speed, spin direction, angle . . . everything needs to be aligned if you want to keep your cue ball in line.

This chapter is your introduction to understanding how to shoot the cue ball so that it will do as you wish before and after impact with the object ball. I also cover the *stun shot* — one of the most important concepts when it comes to cue-ball control — along with the angles of deflection for stun shots so that you can get a working familiarity with the cue ball's reactions. Getting started with stun and stop shots is a great way to begin working on position for your next shot.

Going Out from Center

Everything starts in the center of the cue ball. It's almost like the default setting on the cue ball because you want to hit every shot either at center ball or as close as possible.

First, just to be perfectly clear, *center ball* is a term that refers to where the cue tip strikes the cue ball. From the perspective of a shooter lining up a shot (see Figure 7-1), center ball means any point along the ball's vertical axis, which keeps you from putting *English* (sidespin) on the cue ball. (See Chapter 5 for more information on the proper stroke.)

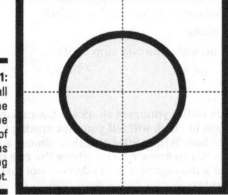

Figure 7-1:
Center ball refers to the point in the middle of the ball as you're lining up the shot.

Striking the cue ball in its center is the easiest way for the cue ball to begin rolling naturally. When you strike on center, you shouldn't have any sidespin that might cause the ball to roll anything but straight.

If your stroke is accurate and your contact point is on the vertical axis, the cue ball should roll in a straight line. Here's how you can check whether you're striking the cue ball along its vertical axis:

1. **Set up the cue ball on the *footspot* (the point in the middle of the table lengthwise, two diamonds from the bottom rail).**

   See Figure 7-2 for an example.

   As a way to accentuate the spin of the ball after contact, use a striped ball as the cue ball. Line up the stripe so that it's vertical and pointing in the direction you're aiming. If you strike the ball properly, the band of color shouldn't move as the ball rolls to and from the rail.

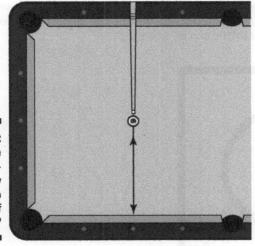

Figure 7-2:
Is the cue ball coming directly back to the tip of your cue?

2. **Hit the cue ball.**

   When you hit the cue ball, it should roll to the long rail and directly back to the footspot.

   If you're hitting the cue ball with any sidespin, it should be fairly apparent by the ball's path. If it doesn't go straight to the rail or if it rebounds from the rail at an angle, you're unintentionally hitting the cue ball with spin.

3. **(Optional) As a way of upping the difficulty, try hitting the cue ball down off the head rail and back.**

   The longer distance means more room for error. So if you're executing the shot perfectly, you're that much more in line!

The beginning pool player shouldn't deviate from center-ball hits. This simplifies pocketing balls and getting a feel for executing a proper stroke. Only when you're completely comfortable with a center-ball hit are you ready to venture outward.

After you master the center-ball hit, you're ready to look at what you can do by hitting the cue ball away from center. Putting spin on the cue ball can greatly increase the options you have for your next shot. But spin also increases the complexity and difficulty of a shot, so you should venture from center only when it's absolutely necessary.

Not only can you hit the cue ball off center, you can venture a good distance toward its outer edge. As a general rule, think of the cue ball's *miscue limit* — that is, the farthest from center you can strike the cue ball without having the tip slip off the ball — as one half of the ball's radius.

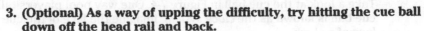

As you can see in Figure 7-3, you have a lot of real estate to work with on the surface of the cue ball. But like I said before, the farther from center, the more complications you introduce into the shot.

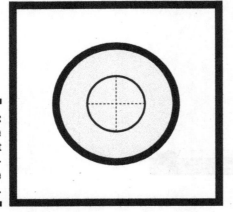

Your goal in any shot is to keep control of the cue ball before, during, and after impact with an object ball. A center-ball shot is the easiest option, but it's not always possible. Sometimes you need the cue ball to react in a different fashion, which is when you'll stray from center.

Take a look at the cue ball in Figure 7-4. One way pool players talk about the cue ball is known as the *clock system*. Imagine the face of the cue ball as the face of a clock.

As you can see, a hit at 6:00 is on the vertical axis and below center. A hit at 9:00 is on the horizontal axis and to the left of the vertical axis. The clock system is an easy way to picture contact points and a great way to discuss shots with other players.

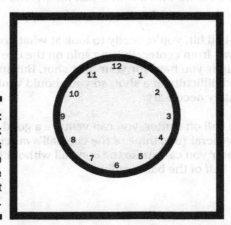

Figure 7-4:
The clock system is one way to describe a contact point.

Working the Angles in a Stun Shot

When it comes to controlling the cue ball, nothing is as important as the *stun shot,* which means leaving the cue ball with no spin at the point of contact with the object ball.

When the cue ball hits an object ball with no spin, it deflects at a right angle from the direction of the object ball. No matter the angle or speed, a stun shot will deflect in the opposite direction at an angle of 90 degrees (along what is known as the *tangent line*). Now, because this angle is a constant, the stun shot is a great way to get started in understanding the principles of cue-ball control, a major component of position play (covered in depth in Chapter 12).

Finding the angle

To start with a stun shot, look at the example in Figure 7-5. Figure 7-5 shows a fairly straight shot on the 6 ball in the corner pocket. If you can deliver the cue ball to the 6 so that it has no spin at impact, you can predict exactly where the cue ball will hit the rail.

When you're at an angle, it's tough to know for sure that the cue ball has no spin. You'll know the cue ball has no spin when it deflects at a right angle from the direction of the object ball.

At the moment of impact, the cue ball's and the 6 ball's centers should be in direct line with the pocket (as described in Chapter 4). Now, because the cue ball has no spin, nothing changes the angle of deflection from 90 degrees.

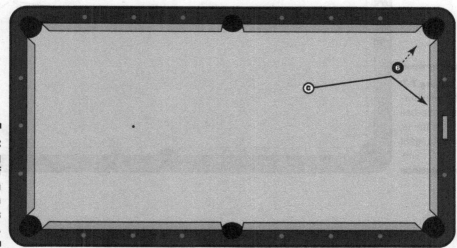

Figure 7-5:
Calculating
the angle of
deflection
using the
object ball's
path.

If you draw a line at a right angle from the two centers, as shown in Figure 7-6, you know the line the cue ball will take after impact. The line drawn from the center of the cue ball is the *90-degree rule* — one of the most important fundamentals of cue ball control.

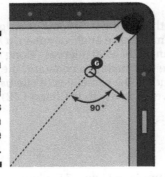

Figure 7-6:
In a stun shot, the cue ball will always deflect at a 90-degree angle.

The 90-degree rule holds true for all different angles. Figure 7-7 shows three different cue-ball positions for the shot on the 6 ball into the corner pocket.

But no matter where the cue ball is before the shot, if it hits the 2 ball (from the left side), the cue ball will deflect along the same line.

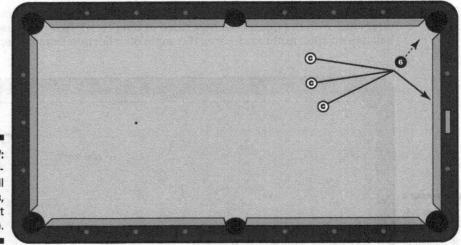

Figure 7-7:
Three different cue-ball locations, one tangent line.

Using the angle for position

Because this angle is so easy to determine, stun shots are a fantastic way to *play position,* which just means putting the cue ball in a perfect spot for your next shot. If you need to play position along the so-called tangent line, position is just a matter of speed control because the direction is solely dependent on you hitting the cue ball so that it has no spin at impact with the object ball.

Using the tangent line is a great way to know where the cue ball is going, so if you plan accordingly, you're often able to use the tangent line to your advantage. Look at the example in Figure 7-8 (from a game of 9-ball). If you're wondering how to play position from the 7 ball to the 8, you can use the 90-degree tangent line to make things easy on yourself.

If you can pocket the 7 ball with a stunned cue ball, you'll be in good shape to drift into position for the 8 ball on the opposite side. If the cue ball travels at a right angle from the path of the 7 ball, you should get on the side of the 8 ball that will allow you to get position on the game-winning 9 ball.

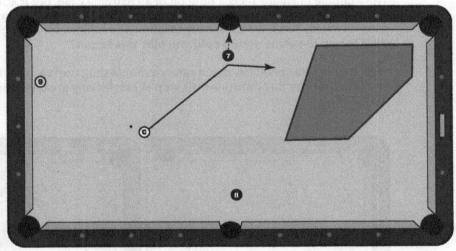

Figure 7-8:
The tangent line points to position for the 8 ball.

Making the Stop Shot: Straight and Stun

One stun shot in particular is exceptionally important to understand. When you're faced with a straight-in shot, you can completely *kill* (or stop) the cue ball at impact. This type of stun shot is known as the stop shot. A *stop shot* is a specific kind of stun shot where the cue ball has no momentum after impact, so it won't veer to the right or left.

When the path of the cue ball and the direction of the object ball are virtually overlapping, the cue ball will stop at impact. Because the cue ball is hitting the object ball completely full, all the cue ball's forward momentum will be transferred to the object ball. So instead of moving along a tangent line, the cue ball will sit right where it hits the object ball.

Sitting for position

Just as the stun shot is useful because you can easily predict the cue ball's path, the stop shot is a specific kind of stun shot where no movement occurs after impact. Often, you'll be able to stop the cue ball directly behind one ball and have position on another. Because the cue ball doesn't move after impact with the object ball, this shot is a simple and effective way to play position.

The example in Figure 7-9 is a little bit of an extreme case, but it still shows why the stop shot is a great weapon to have. Here, you have ball in hand in a game of 8-ball. You have three stripes left on the table before you can make the 8 to win the game. How would you play this layout?

Well, before you spend too much time contemplating the many variations, you can clear the three stripes with stop shots, leaving great position on the 8 ball.

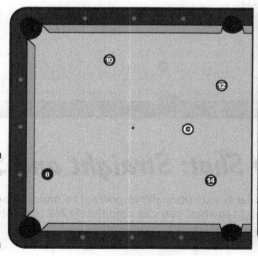
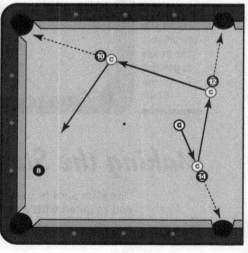

Figure 7-9:
See how the
stop shot
simplifies
matters?

Kill the cue ball after putting the 14 in the side and then put the 12 in the other side. Now all you have to do is stop the cue ball behind the 10 for your shot on the 8 ball.

Stopping for safety

The stop shot is also a great way to play defense. Because you know exactly where the cue ball should stop, you can plan to hide the cue ball behind any blocking balls that may be around.

Figure 7-10 shows one example of how stopping the cue ball can put your opponent on the run. (See Chapter 17 for details on safeties.) In Figure 7-10, you're solids. You don't really have an open shot to run the table, but there is a great safety you can play. If you hit the 4 ball with a stop shot, you can tuck the cue ball behind the 8 ball, leaving your opponent without an option.

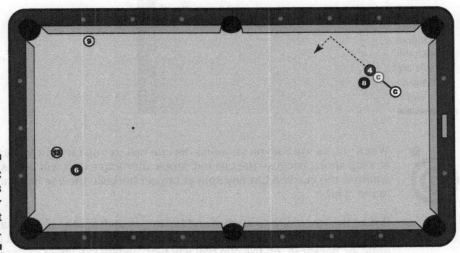

Figure 7-10:
The 4 ball is perfect for a stop shot safety.

Shooting Stun Shots

Seeing and doing are two very different things. Unfortunately, executing a stun isn't as easy as hitting the cue ball in the center.

A number of variables are involved with stun shots, including the effect of *drag* (the friction between the cue ball and cloth after the cue ball is struck), the speed of the cue ball, and the angle of the cue ball and object ball at impact.

Drag

When the cue ball is struck, it skids along the cloth for a certain distance before the friction between the ball and cloth causes the cue ball to roll forward. This drag is why center-ball hits don't always work for stun shots.

Instead, you often have to compensate for drag when you're aiming a stun shot. As the distance between the cue ball and object ball increases, the cue ball has more time to give in to drag and start rolling forward.

When the cue ball is close to the object ball (see Figure 7-11), you can kill the cue ball at impact with a center-ball hit. With medium speed, the cue ball won't have time to start rolling forward, so it should stop at impact.

Figure 7-11:
A center-ball hit should work wonders when the balls are relatively close.

When you're working on stunning the cue ball, set up straight-in shots (known as stop shots, because the cue ball stops after impact). It will be easier to tell whether the cue ball has any spin at impact because the cue ball shouldn't move at all.

But as the cue ball gets farther and farther away from the object ball, you have to compensate by hitting the cue ball below center. Putting a bit of *draw,* or backspin, on the cue ball will help negate the effect of drag.

In Figure 7-12, the cue ball is 2 diamonds away from the 9 ball. This distance isn't very large, but it's enough to cause a cue ball hit with medium speed to start rolling forward. In order to keep the cue ball from moving forward after impact, hit a bit below the horizontal axis on the cue ball. Aim for a spot about one cue tip's width below center (or *one tip* of draw), as shown in Figure 7-13.

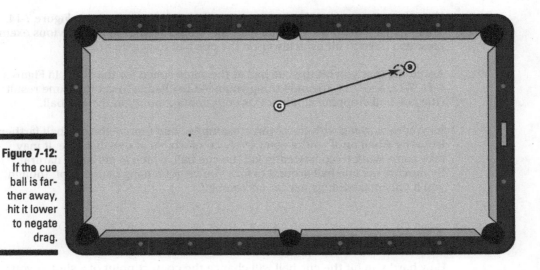

Figure 7-12:
If the cue ball is farther away, hit it lower to negate drag.

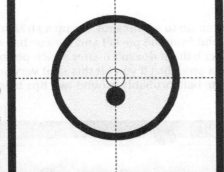

Figure 7-13:
One tip of draw should work for this shot.

If you hit this shot with just enough speed for the 9 to get to the corner pocket (known as *pocket speed*), you should be able to stop the cue ball at impact, as shown by the dotted cue ball in Figure 7-12.

Equipment can vary, so there's no exact science to how far below center to hit the cue ball. With a few attempts on a table, though, you should get an idea of where you need to hit the cue ball to make it stop at impact.

Now move the cue ball farther away from the 9 ball, as shown in Figure 7-14. This time, if you hit the cue ball with the same speed as in the previous examples, you have to hit even lower on the cue ball to negate drag.

Assuming that you hit the cue ball at the same speed for the shots in Figures 7-11, 7-12, and 7-14, the only thing you need to change to get the same result (the cue ball stopping at impact) is your contact point on the cue ball.

As you're working with these three examples, don't move the cue ball farther from the 9 ball until you're completely comfortable at one distance. It may take some work to consistently kill the cue ball, which is perfectly natural. By moving the cue ball around before you've got a hang of one shot, though, you'll only make things harder on yourself.

Change of speed

How hard you hit the cue ball will change the contact point of a shot. If you lightly tap the cue ball toward an object ball, it will start rolling almost immediately. A softly hit cue ball doesn't have the same forward momentum as a speeding-bullet cue ball.

To get an idea of what speed can do to a stop shot, set up a straight-in shot with the object ball one diamond from the pocket and the cue ball another three diamonds from the object ball. (It doesn't matter which pocket you're aiming at, as long as the shot is straight.) If you hit this shot very softly, you'll need to hit fairly low on the cue ball, probably around two tips below center."

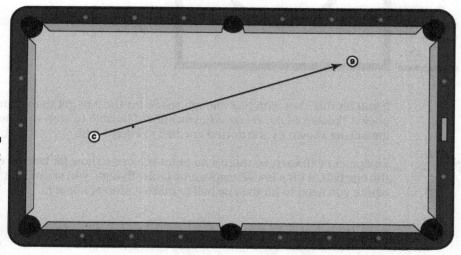

Figure 7-14:
The cue ball has to travel farther, so you have to hit lower.

However, if you hit this shot with a firm stroke, you can hit closer to center. The forward momentum of a solidly struck cue ball will keep it sliding over the cloth, instead of rolling like a soft hit.

It's important to get a feel for both the distance of a shot and the speed needed to stop the cue ball. There is no clean-cut method of calculating how much speed and how low you have to hit the cue ball, but you should be able to develop a feel for it with some practice.

Incorporating an angle

When — and only when — you think you have a good feel for stop shots, you can start shooting stun shots (that is, stop shots at an angle). By shooting stun shots in a controlled environment (not in a match), you can start to see the cue ball head along the tangent line.

The shot shown in Figure 7-15 is at a slight angle. If you hit the 9 ball into the middle of the pocket with a cue ball that has no spin, it will travel along the tangent line shown in Figure 7-15.

To know whether you're executing this shot properly, put a piece of chalk on the rail where the cue ball *should* hit. This trick will help you gauge how you're doing.

If the cue ball is hitting the rail to the left of the chalk, the cue ball is rolling forward at impact. Either hit the cue ball lower at the same speed or hit the ball at the same point with more speed.

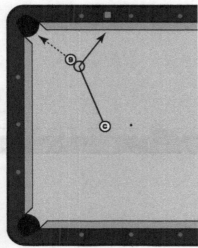

Figure 7-15: Here's an easy way to see whether the cue ball has spin at impact with the object ball.

If the cue ball is hitting the rail to the right of the chalk, the cue ball has draw (backspin) on it at impact. Try hitting the cue ball softer at the same point or a touch higher at the same speed.

The speed of the cue ball dictates how low you hit the cue ball. But one factor that can affect how hard you hit the cue ball is position for your next shot.

Obviously, all things being equal, the harder you hit a stun shot, the farther the cue ball will travel. Before you get into position for a shot, you want to know exactly where you want the cue ball to come to a stop. After you establish this point, you can plan to use the correct amount of speed to put the cue ball where it's supposed to be.

Looking at the shot in Figure 7-16, you can see how the cue ball will continue along the tangent line. You have to determine how far you want the cue ball to roll after impact with the 3 ball. You can stop the cue ball anywhere on this line, depending on how hard you hit the cue ball.

The cue ball's speed doesn't affect stop shots (straight-in stun shots) because the cue ball will stop immediately after impact. This section refers to angled stun shots only.

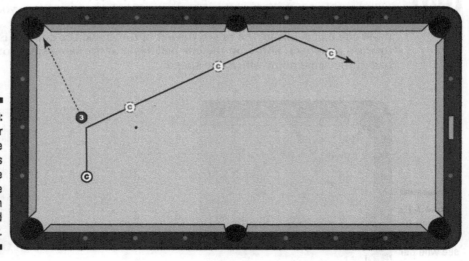

Figure 7-16:
How far
the cue
ball travels
down the
tangent line
depends on
how hard
you hit it.

Chapter 8

Aim High: Incorporating Follow

- -

In This Chapter

▶ Understanding what can happen when you hit the ball above its horizontal axis

▶ Incorporating the effects of follow into your plans for position

▶ Seeing how speed can change the path of a cue ball with follow

▶ Experimenting with force follow

- -

I'll bet if you haven't done it, you've seen someone do it. There it is, the game-winning 8 ball just sitting in the corner, looking like it's just going to tip over and fall in the pocket. The cue ball comes to a stop, and you're one easy — okay, *super* easy — shot from winning the game. The game is so over your opponent's already walking to the bar to buy you the beer he's about to owe you.

Without even a second thought, you hit the cue ball straight into the 8, knocking it into the pocket. But then, alas, the cue ball follows the black ball right down the hole. Grabbing defeat from the jaws of victory, you scratched on the 8 ball.

While you certainly didn't mean for the cue ball to follow the 8 ball into the pocket, this shot is a perfect example of what you can do when you put top-spin, or follow, on the cue ball.

In this chapter, you find out how to incorporate follow into your game. Starting with some basic position play, you discover when and how to use follow.

Starting on a Straight and Narrow Roll

Follow is *topspin*. If you gently push a ball across the table with your hand, the ball will begin rolling naturally. Think of a tire on a car driving along the highway. It doesn't skid or slip, but it rolls along the pavement. A cue ball naturally rolling along the cloth is acting in a similar way.

Besides the stun shot (see Chapter 7), another fundamental building block for controlling the cue ball is the rolling cue ball.

Hitting the cue ball well above center on its vertical axis is the fastest way to get the cue ball rolling naturally. Now, to be perfectly clear, a *naturally* rolling cue ball is just what you'd think it is: The cue ball has no spin besides that which is rolling perfectly along the table. It's rolling without skidding or dragging on the cloth. Many shots in pool incorporate a rolling cue ball.

As a reference point, set up the shot in Figure 8-1. The 8 ball is on the *footspot* (along the center of the table, two diamonds off the bottom rail), and the cue ball is in line with the corner pocket. Now, hitting the cue ball exactly at its center, try to pocket the 8 ball with *pocket speed* — the minimum speed required to get the 8 ball into the pocket.

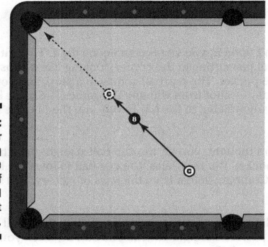

Figure 8-1:
Here's your starting point. Hit the center of the cue ball with pocket speed.

If the cue ball hit the 8 ball and then followed it toward the corner pocket for a bit, great! You've used follow to make the cue ball move forward of the contact point. That situation is an example of what can happen when the cue ball has topspin at impact. It *follows* the object ball, which can open up a world of possibilities for positioning the cue ball for your next shot (see "Playing Position with Follow").

Unlike stun, where the cue ball completely stops at the moment of impact because it has no spin, a naturally rolling cue ball will stop momentarily, but then regain some forward momentum thanks to the spin. This topspin will cause the cue ball to grab the cloth, and the ball will continue rolling.

Now, if the cue ball didn't follow the 8 ball at all, it had no topspin when it contacted the object ball. You might be hitting the cue ball below center. Try to hit the cue ball at its exact middle. If you still can't get the cue ball to roll forward after hitting the 8, aim a tiny bit above center (half the diameter of the cue tip or so).

To start, hit this shot with pocket speed — just enough speed to get the 8 ball to the corner pocket. Speed is an important factor in using follow, so try to keep things consistent as you get started.

Rolling Askew

After you get the hang of some straight-in shots with a rolling cue ball (see the preceding section), it's time to get to the interesting stuff — the angled shots. When a rolling cue ball hits an object ball, it will retain some of its natural topspin. This means the cue ball will almost *want* to keep rolling forward because it was spinning in that direction before impact.

Set up a shot like the one shown in Figure 8-2. The 8 ball is one diamond off each rail with the cue ball at a 30-degree angle or so. Again, try to make this shot with pocket speed, hitting the cue ball at its absolute center.

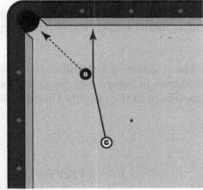

Figure 8-2:
At an angle, the cue ball heads off in a different direction.

This spin is *the* difference between a rolling cue ball and a stunned cue ball (see Chapter 7). A cue ball with stun (no spin at impact) will always deflect off at a 90-degree angle to the object ball, as shown in Figure 8-3. This tangent line is no longer in play when the cue ball is rolling forward. Now, the cue ball will deflect at an angle closer to the path of the object ball.

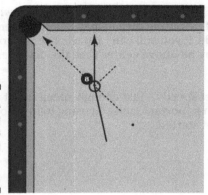

Figure 8-3: A rolling cue ball moves forward of the tangent line.

The exact angle of the cue ball after impact depends on the cue ball's approach angle toward the object ball. For example, a cue ball that hits the object ball completely full will follow the exact path of the object ball. Conversely, an object ball that is hit at an extreme angle (a thin cut) will deflect at an angle closer to the 90-degree tangent line.

When you thinly cut the object ball, only a small amount of energy is transferred from the cue ball to the object ball. This means the cue ball will be affected less than if it hits a ball completely full. The thinner the cut, the less a rolling cue ball will deviate from the tangent line.

Fortunately, due to some complex physics involved in two spherical bodies coming into contact with one another, many angled shots have surprisingly similar angles of deflection.

For shots between *one-quarter* and *three-quarters full* (the overlap between the object ball and cue ball at impact, shown in Figure 8-4), you can assume that the cue ball will be redirected somewhere in the neighborhood of 30 degrees from its original path.

Figure 8-4: Hit the object ball between these two extremes, and you'll have an idea of where the cue ball will be headed.

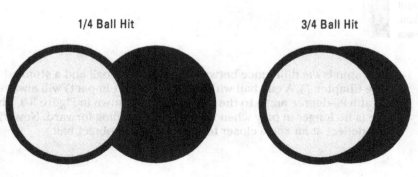

1/4 Ball Hit

3/4 Ball Hit

Figure 8-5 shows an estimation of the direction the cue ball will take after impact with the object ball for any hit between one-quarter and three-quarters. If you can gain an understanding of this rule, you'll be well on your way to predicting where the cue ball will be headed.

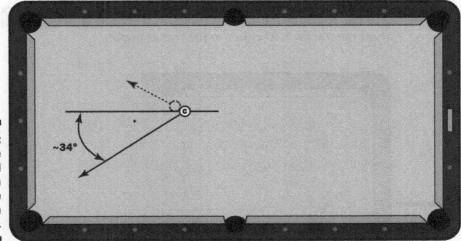

Figure 8-5:
The cue ball will deflect at a 34-degree angle in a half-ball hit.

For nearly full hits, a rolling cue ball won't be redirected much (compared to half- or three-fourths-ball hits). You should be able to make a very educated guess after you get some practice with a rolling cue ball. The cue ball will follow the object ball on a totally full hit, so calculate the small angle from the object ball's direction as you deviate from straight-in.

Playing Position with Follow

With follow, you can do some pretty neat things with the cue ball. But, you may wonder, "Why do I want to complicate matters by hitting the cue ball anywhere but center?" The short answer: Sometimes you'll be forced to if you want to make more than just the shot you're looking at.

It would be great if you could hit the cue ball in the center for every shot, but it's not going to happen. You'll quickly see that you need to be able to control the cue ball's angle after impact with one ball, so you'll be in good shape to pocket the next.

Follow allows you to move the cue ball off of the tangent line. How much it deviates from the tangent line depends on how much follow is on the cue ball at impact.

The shot in Figure 8-6 isn't very interesting if you're just looking to pocket the 4 ball. But when you start to look at what you can do with follow, you'll see the effect topspin can have on the cue ball. Instead of following along the tangent line (the dotted line in the diagram), a cue ball with topspin will hit the short rail (on the left) closer to the corner pocket.

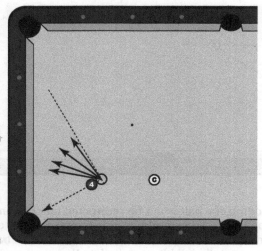

Figure 8-6:
Just four of the many options when you use follow.

Doesn't look like much, but now look at that shot in a game of 8 ball. In Figure 8-7, you're solids, and you're one ball from a shot on the game-winning 8. If you pocket the 4 with a stunned cue ball, you run the risk of running into the 11 ball. But if you use a bit of follow, the cue ball will drift down to the short rail, in perfect position to make the 8. This situation may be simple, but it's exactly what you can do with follow.

To get position on the 8, you can hit the cue ball with a bit of follow to ensure that it'll be rolling by the time it hits the 4 ball. Also, a soft, center-ball hit may work because the cue ball will begin rolling by the time it hits the 4.

Hitting Above Center

To make the cue ball begin rolling directly after contact, you have to hit higher on the cue ball's vertical axis, as shown in Figure 8-8. (See Chapter 7 for a discussion on the different spots on the cue ball you can hit to change its spin.)

You can't realistically create more topspin than a naturally rolling cue ball. But with an above-center hit on the cue ball, you can control the amount of topspin the cue ball has when it hits an object ball.

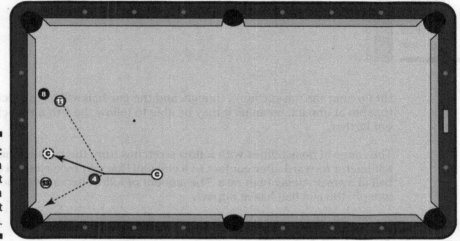

Figure 8-7:
You need a follow shot here for a chance at the 8.

Figure 8-8:
Hit the cue ball in the shaded area for straight follow.

The higher you hit on the cue ball, the quicker the cue ball will begin rolling. Provided you keep everything else (speed, direction, contact point on the cue ball) constant, you can greatly change how much follow the cue ball will have after impact with an object ball.

For simplicity's sake, I use a straight-in shot as the starting point. In Figure 8-9, you're hitting the 3 ball into the corner pocket. If you hit this shot with medium speed, just barely above center, the cue ball will follow the 3 for a few inches, maybe as far as halfway to the pocket.

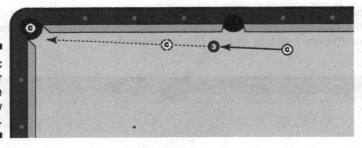

Figure 8-9:
The higher
you hit, the
more follow
you'll see.

Hit up near the miscue limit, though, and the cue ball will have much more topspin at impact, meaning it may be able to follow the 3 to the pocket — if not farther.

The range of possibilities with follow stretches from the cue ball moving a millimeter forward after contact to a cue ball that can race after an object ball at a surprisingly high rate. The amount of follow depends on how much topspin the cue ball has at impact.

Speeding Along

The example in Figure 8-9 is a great starting point to see how speed affects different shots with follow. (The previous section discusses what happens when you hit above center.) But you can also experiment with different speeds.

Dragging you down

The friction between a spinning cue ball and the table's cloth — called *drag* — comes into play in every pool shot, including follow shots. Hitting above center on the cue ball, you're trying to control when the cue ball begins rolling and how much roll it has.

Because of this effect, you need to consider distance when you're trying to use follow to change the cue ball's angle of deflection after it hits the object ball. Figure 8-10 shows two different shots — one with the cue ball very near the 9 ball and another with the cue ball fairly far from the 10 ball.

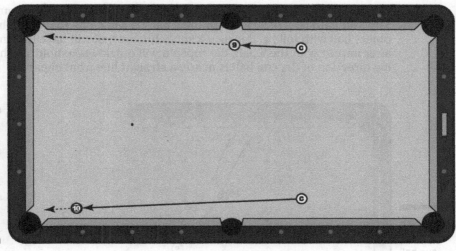

Figure 8-10:
You need to think about the distance the cue ball travels before impact.

Start with the shot on the 9 ball. When the cue ball is close to the object ball, there is less distance (and time) for the cue ball to begin rolling. For this shot, if you hit near the miscue limit on the cue ball (half way from the center and the top), you'll be able to make sure that the cue ball is rolling by the time it hits the 9.

But with the shot on the 10 ball, the cue ball has to travel more than half the length of the table. From this distance, you shouldn't have any problems delivering a rolling cue ball to the 10. The cue ball has a longer distance to begin rolling, so a center-ball hit is fine.

Taking time to take

For shots at an angle, speed will change how quickly the cue ball begins to move forward from the tangent line. When the cue ball strikes an object ball, it will head along the tangent line immediately after impact, regardless of what spin (if any) the cue ball has when it hits the object ball. But at a certain point, the cue ball's spin will take over and change the course of the cue ball.

When the cue ball hits the object ball without much speed, the spin will almost immediately take and cause the cue ball to veer off the tangent line. But when you firmly strike the cue ball, it redirects along the tangent line for a longer time.

In Figure 8-11, you can see two different cue ball paths from the same shot. The first path (the one closer to the 5 ball) is a cue ball that softly hits the object ball with follow. Because a softly hit cue ball will have less momentum after impact with the 5 ball, the topspin will quickly take hold, so the resulting direction of the cue ball is nearly a straight line from impact.

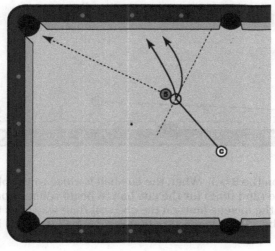

Figure 8-11:
A softly hit cue ball will follow the object ball quicker than a firmly struck ball.

When you strike the ball with some speed, though, the cue ball's momentum will carry it along the tangent line for a greater distance. In this case, the cue ball continues along this line for a few inches, while the cue ball spins on the cloth without changing the ball's course. Once the force of the cue ball's topspin becomes greater than that of its momentum along the tangent line, though, it will bend forward in a line almost parallel to the softly hit ball.

You can use this phenomenon for your benefit, should you find yourself in a position where you have to avoid another ball. In Figure 8-12, you are a ball away from the 8. This shot is not by any means easy, but it shows a special option that you can use with follow.

A fairly hard hit cue ball with follow can curve around the 13 ball so that it will head to the lower-left corner, bounce around, and come to a stop with a great line on the 8 ball.

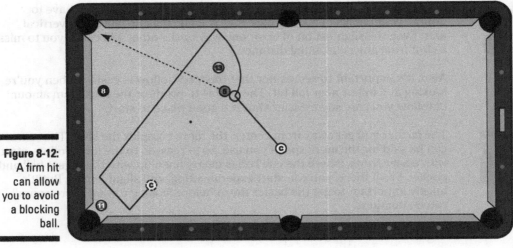

Figure 8-12:
A firm hit can allow you to avoid a blocking ball.

Experimenting with force follow

Certainly there is a limit to how much follow you can impart on the cue ball. If you hit the cue ball at the highest point possible (without a miscue) and with the most power you can generate, you'll be using the maximum amount of follow, which is known as *force follow* (see Figure 8-13).

During this shot, the cue ball will have such topspin that it will hop up into the air after impact with the cue ball as a result of the cue ball becoming airborne after it was struck by the cue. When the cue ball lands on the table, it may spin for a fraction of a second before taking off in a direction close to the angle of the object ball's path.

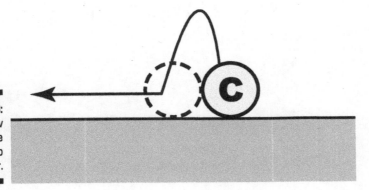

Figure 8-13:
Force follow may pop the cue ball into the air.

It's no secret that you gain power at the cost of accuracy, so you have to double your efforts of making sure that you cue the cue ball on its vertical axis. Even the slightest bit of error one way or the other will cause you to miss a shot from any substantial distance.

Also, it's important to remember that the force follow is easiest when you're looking at a full or near full hit. The goal is to produce the maximum amount of follow you can, so an easier shot is a good place to start.

The farther you get away from center, the more complex the shot. The same can be said for the more speed you use. So in regards to the force follow, start with easier shots, where the cue ball is nearly lined up with the object ball and pocket. From there, you can start experimenting with slight angles. But it's hugely important to get the basics down before looking toward more complicated situations.

Chapter 9

Using Draw: Putting Backspin on the Cue Ball

Manipulating the movement of the cue ball is one of the most important lessons a player can learn when beginning to play the game of pool. Hitting the cue ball so that it spins this way or that way can leave the cue ball circling the table like it's got a mind of its own. But, for the experienced pool player, the cue ball's movements are all choreographed down to the smallest detail.

Hitting the cue ball so that it spins backward while traveling to the object ball is a very common way to manipulate the cue ball. But a cue ball with backspin is also one of the most misunderstood concepts in pool.

In this chapter, I cover the subject of draw in three phases: what happens during a draw shot, how to create draw, and what practical advantages draw can have.

Figuring Out What Draw Is

Draw, or backspin, on a cue ball can lead to rather surprising results for a pool newbie. After all, a cue ball with backspin is rather unnatural. A ball moving in one direction will roll in that same direction. A cue ball with draw is moving in one direction and spinning in the other.

So when a cue ball with a ton of draw fully hits an object ball, it can react in a pretty incredible fashion. The cue ball will stop at impact and then the backspin will take effect, pulling the cue ball straight back in the direction it came from.

While this effect may seem pretty cool at first, learning to draw a cue ball is one of the most important lessons for a developing pool player. It can open up a world of possibilities, most of which deal with getting in position for the next shot.

And hopefully, with a little practice, you won't see draw as all that unnatural.

Looking at Full Hits

A simple example shows what happens during a shot where a cue ball with back spin hits an object ball. To put draw on the cue ball, you have to hit low on the cue ball, below the horizontal axis on the cue ball.

While I talk about hitting to the right or left of center in Chapter 10, I want to focus on draw alone in this chapter. To create backspin, you have to hit the cue ball somewhere in the shaded area on the cue ball, as shown in Figure 9-1.

Figure 9-1:
For straight draw, hit below center on the cue ball.

To see what happens when you hit below center, line up a straight-in shot, like the one shown in Figure 9-2. Practice pocketing the shot by hitting the center of the cue ball. With a center-ball hit, you should pocket the 6 and leave the cue ball at about the point of contact. When you can make this shot four or five times in a row, you should be comfortable enough to start working with draw.

Here's how to add draw to your shot:

1. **Without changing your stroke or stance, aim to hit the cue ball just below center, about the width of your cue's tip.**

2. **Hit the cue ball with a medium stroke, keeping your cue as close to level as possible.**

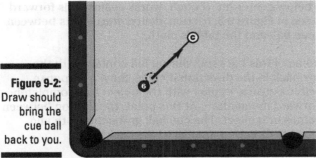

Figure 9-2:
Draw should
bring the
cue ball
back to you.

3. **Pay attention to your follow-through.**

A proper follow-through is absolutely vital to produce a tangible amount of backspin. Because a draw shot involves hitting the cue ball lower than normal, many players won't properly follow-through, opting instead for an abbreviated punch stroke. But you need to accelerate into the ball as normal, and a proper follow-through can help you do so.

Double- and triple-check that you have a sturdy bridge before, during, and after you hit a draw shot. If you're not confident in your draw stroke, you might allow your bridge hand to relax during the shot, which is counterproductive and can lead to dismal results.

The cue striking the cue ball below center should produce enough backspin to pocket the 6 ball and have the cue ball come back straight toward you, just as the arrow shows in Figure 9-2.

When the cue strikes the cue ball below center, the forward force moves the cue ball in one direction while it spins in the other, as shown in Figure 9-3.

Figure 9-3:
A ball with
draw will
move in one
direction
while
spinning in
the other.

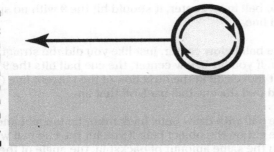

The spin caused by the below-center hit, though, works against this forward momentum. As you can see in Figure 9-3, friction, called *drag,* exists between the backward-spinning cue ball and the table's cloth.

A cue ball that retains some of this backspin during full contact with the object ball will then draw back in the direction it came. Such a response from the cue ball is possible because impact with the object ball completely stopped the cue ball's forward momentum. At this point, the friction between the cue ball and cloth comes into effect. The cue ball grabs the cloth and begins moving in the opposite direction, thanks to the backspin.

Drawing Cut Shots

Things change a bit when you move from hitting the object ball full to cutting it to one side. The cue ball still retains some of its forward momentum, so that the cue ball's angle after impact isn't as simple as the cue ball coming straight back toward you.

In Chapter 8, I go into detail about stun shots, which is where the cue ball hits an object ball with no spin. In these cases, the cue ball then deflects off the object ball at a 90-degree angle from the direction of the object ball. This 90-degree line is known as the *tangent line.*

The reason I mention the tangent line is because a cue ball with draw will deviate from this right angle. And this change to the cue ball's path after contacting an object ball is the whole point of using draw on a shot.

Set up a shot like the one in Figure 9-4. The 9 ball is one diamond from the short rail, and you have to cut it a little to the left into the corner pocket. First, hitting the cue ball at its absolute center, try to make this shot with just enough power to put the 9 in the pocket and send the cue ball off the long rail. If you hit the cue ball in its center, it should hit the 9 with no spin and hit the rail at the dotted line.

This time, hit the cue ball below center, just like you did the straight-in shot from the last section. If you hit below center, the cue ball hits the 9 with some draw. And as it moves off in the direction of the tangent line (the dotted line), the spin should pull the cue ball back off that line.

Just how much a cue ball with draw pulls back from the tangent line depends on the fullness of the cut on the object ball. If you hit the cue ball with the same speed and with the same amount of backspin, the angle of the cut is the determining factor.

If the cue ball hits an object ball nearly full, a good chunk of the cue ball's forward momentum is transferred to the object ball. With the cue ball losing most of its forward momentum, the backspin can then take hold of the cue ball. Conversely, a cue ball that hits only a small fraction of the object ball will retain much of its forward momentum, so the draw won't have as much of an effect.

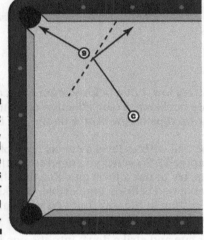

Figure 9-4:
At an angle, draw will change the cue ball's angle after hitting a ball.

Understanding Drag

Understanding drag — the friction between a backward-spinning cue ball and the table's cloth — is an important step in being able to draw the cue ball. Here are the two major factors when it comes to drag:

✔ **Distance:** The goal is to hit the object ball with the cue ball while it's still spinning backward. To achieve this goal, you must hit the cue ball with enough draw to overcome drag. And because drag is a table-versus-cue-ball force, it only follows that you create more draw as you get farther from the object ball.

Line up a straight-in shot with the cue ball one diamond away from the object ball. Try to draw the cue ball back to its original starting point. Try the same shot, only with the cue ball three diamonds from the object ball. If you hit this shot with the same contact point on the cue ball and the same speed, you should see the cue ball draw back much less (if at all). You can see the effect of distance on a draw shot.

✔ **Speed:** A second variable involved with drag is the speed at which you hit the cue ball. If you lightly stroke a ball, it has less forward momentum, meaning the table will work against the cue ball's backspin much quicker than a firmly struck cue ball.

For the large majority of shots that involve draw over distance (more than, say, two feet between the cue ball and object ball), you can stave off the effects of draw by either hitting lower on the cue ball or hitting the cue ball harder.

Stroking with Draw

A draw shot is more than just hitting low, but a below-center hit is a good place to start to see how to create backspin. To be effective creating draw, here are a few tips for when your tip dips below center on the cue ball:

✔ **Keep a level cue.** Hitting the ball with as level a cue as possible is always a good idea (see Chapter 5). So when you need to hit the cue ball below its horizontal axis, try to use a level cue. Keeping the cue completely parallel to the table bed is likely impossible, thanks to the rails and/or your grip hand getting in the way, but you will maximize the amount of draw on a shot by leveling off your cue as much as you can.

Don't lift up the butt of your cue and strike down into the cue ball. It's a bit of a myth among some players that a quick jab stroke with an elevated cue can create more backspin. But remember: It's a myth.

Try to keep your bridge as low as you can for a shot that requires draw. No matter whether you're using an open or closed bridge, flatten your hand on the table. Lowering the bridge helps lower the cue, which is a good thing.

✔ **Follow through.** A second important aspect to the draw stroke — and possibly the one that's most often overlooked — is the follow-through. Because you have to hit low on the cue ball, you may give in to the temptation of punching the cue ball with a short, quick stroke with little to no follow-through. This approach is not only wrong, it's counterproductive.

Trust your stroke. Trust that you can let your cue hit *through* the cue ball and follow forward just as you would any other shot. Focusing on a fluid stroke that continues through the ball may be difficult at first. Whether you're afraid of hitting the table or popping the cue ball up by cuing too low, you must follow through if you want to develop a reliable draw stroke.

One of the keys to a fluid stroke is accelerating through the cue ball. When you're lining up a draw shot, especially one that may require a firmer stroke, don't forget that you want the cue to be accelerating from the start of your stroke and into impact with the cue ball.

✔ **Hit where you aim!** Another common problem with drawing the cue ball can be a bit mysterious. You may aim well below center on the cue ball with your cue tip returning to the correct point on the cue ball to create draw on each practice stroke. Then you pull the trigger and . . . nothing. The cue ball doesn't draw like you told it to.

Often, this issue is a case of the cue tip coming up during your final stroke and hitting the ball above your original aiming point. Overcoming this problem takes a little self-awareness, but you must hit the cue ball where you're aiming. Whether you're unsure of yourself or something physical in your stroke is forcing the tip of your cue up, you have to put the cue's tip at the correct point on the cue ball.

This drill is practice only, but try to hit the cue ball as low as you think you can. Try to find the miscue limit by *trying to miscue*. If the cue tip slips under the ball, and you miscue with the cue ball jumping up, you've gone too low. Try the same shot moving up a smidge. If you aren't miscuing, move your cue tip lower and lower until you do. The point here is not to have you hear the horrible sound that accompanies a miscue; it's to help you get to know the answer to the question, "How low can you go?"

Playing Position with Draw

Draw is a great weapon when you're trying to kill — or at least maim — your bad habit of losing control of the cue ball. And while learning how to draw the cue ball is no piece of cake, you've got a lot of possibilities as far as position after you learn how.

Outside of a straight-in shot, where the cue ball returns in the exact opposite direction from which it came, draw is used to change the angle of the cue ball after it contacts an object ball.

In Figure 9-5, the cue ball will go along the dotted line if it has no spin when it hits the 8 ball (which is a stun shot, described in Chapter 7). But if it has backspin (draw), it can go along any of the gray lines, depending on how much it's spinning. The more draw the cue ball has at impact, the more it will deviate from the tangent line, which is 90 degrees from the direction of the cue ball.

The different paths in Figure 9-5 show what is meant by changing the angle. If the cue ball has backspin at contact with the 8 ball, it will travel in a different direction than a cue ball with no spin (or topspin, as described in Chapter 8).

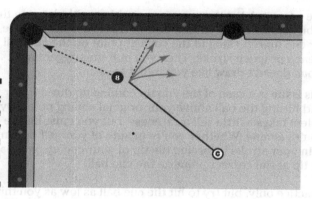

Figure 9-5:
Here are just a few options you have with draw.

Pulling the cue ball back

Making the cue ball jump back after hitting an object ball sounds neat, but you're not going to have gray lines (refer to Figure 9-5) on the table when you're playing a game. In this section, I give you concrete examples of how draw can help you play proper position.

The situation in Figure 9-6 is a perfect example where you get to show off your newly discovered draw stroke. You're playing a game of 9-ball and are two shots from victory. With the 8 ball so close to the 9, you're restricted with regard to the paths the cue ball can take.

If you hit this shot with follow, you'll run into the 9, and most likely be left with a difficult shot on the 9 (if any angle at all). If you hit the 8 ball with stun (no spin), the cue ball will travel along the dotted line, which leaves you in a tough spot to make the 9.

But hit the 8 with a cue ball with draw, and you can leave yourself with a perfect angle on the game-winner. As you can see, the cue ball will roll back toward you and into the middle of the left side of the table.

The draw helps pull the cue ball off the tangent line (the dotted line) and back toward you. Hit the cue ball as low as you can with a soft stroke, and you should be in good shape.

Similarly, you can use draw to play a safety. You may be in a situation where a light draw shot can tuck the cue ball behind a blocker, leaving your opponent in trouble.

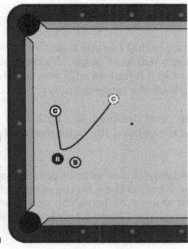

Figure 9-6:
Simplify
position play
by drawing
the cue ball
back.

The 2 ball in Figure 9-7 is a natural blocker for a safety on your opponent. If you can softly hit the 3 ball so that the cue ball draws back between the 2 ball and the rail, the only thing keeping your opponent from fouling is a miracle shot.

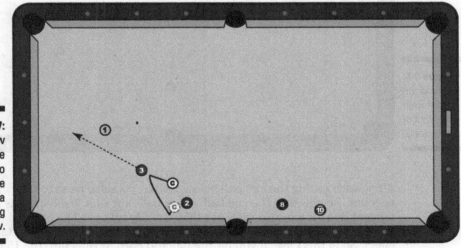

Figure 9-7:
Aim low
and stroke
softly to
hide the cue
ball with a
safety using
draw.

Bending the angle

One of the neat things with using draw is that the cue ball won't always travel in a straight line. When you're cutting a ball at an angle, the cue ball wants to travel along the tangent line, as it would if it had no spin. But eventually, the spin grabs the cloth and pulls the ball off the tangent line.

You can use draw, just like follow, to bend the cue ball's path. And you may even find yourself in a spot where you can bend the ball around a blocking ball.

You are solids in Figure 9-8. The bad news is that your opponent has a wall of balls blocking your route from the 7 ball to the 5 on the other side of the table. The good news? With the right amount of draw, you can bend the cue ball's path so that it slides right through the 15 and 10 balls on its way up the table for position on the 5.

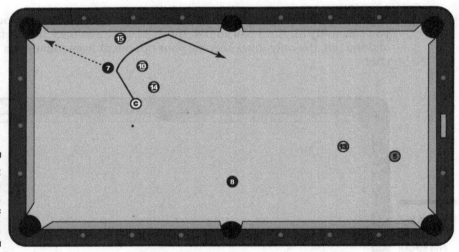

Figure 9-8:
Bend the ball through the wall of blockers.

Along with hitting the cue ball below center, you also need to take into account the speed of the cue ball. A cue ball that's hit firmly travels along the tangent line for a longer distance than a softly hit ball. The forward momentum keeps the cue ball on the tangent line until the cue ball's spin takes effect. So in this case, if you hit the ball too hard, it runs into the 15 ball. Hit it too soft, and it collides with the 10.

In Figure 9-9, you can see how the cue ball's path will change depending on the speed of the shot. A firmly hit ball will continue along the tangent line for a greater distance before the draw takes, and the cue ball comes back off the line (see line A). Conversely, a softer hit ball will deviate from the tangent line quickly because the cue ball will have less momentum heading in the direction of the tangent line (see line B).

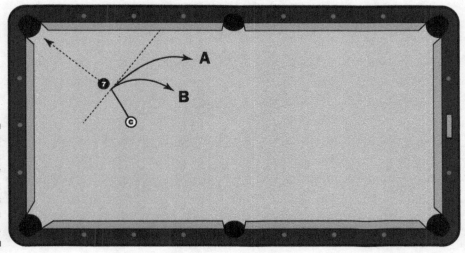

Figure 9-9:
Speed will change how quickly a ball draws back off the tangent line.

But if you can find the right speed and spin, the cue ball can go right through the gap, leaving you in good shape for the 5 ball.

Getting comfortable with curving the cue ball takes a bit of practice. Experiment with different speeds and cue-ball contact points so that you can start to get a feel for the cue ball's path. Concentrating on shorter shots, where the cue ball doesn't have to travel very far until it's out in the open, is also a good idea.

In Figure 9-8, you can see how the cue ball's path will change depending on the speed of the shot. A firm hit ball will continue along the contact line for a longer distance before the draw takes and the cue ball comes back off that line (see line A). Conversely, a softer hit ball will draw back off the tangent line quickly, so the cue ball will have less momentum heading in the direction of the tangent line (see line B).

But if you can find the right speed and spin, the cue ball can, for right through the gap, leaving you in good shape for the 5 ball.

Getting comfortable with curving the cue ball takes a lot of practice. Experiment with different speeds and cue ball contact points in this section so that you can start to get a feel for the cue ball's path. Concentrating on shorter shots, where the cue ball doesn't have to travel very far until it scoots in the right is also a good idea.

Chapter 10

The English Effect: Using Sidespin on the Cue Ball

In This Chapter

▶ Seeing what happens to the cue ball when it's hit with sidespin

▶ Discovering what you can (and can't) do with English

▶ Seeing how a spinning cue ball can affect an object ball

▶ Using English in a safe way

1 start this chapter with a disclaimer that I wish I could have heard when I started using English (the term for imparting sidespin on the cue ball): This ain't going to be easy.

I don't say this warning to scare you. Really. But before you incorporate the information in this chapter into your game, you have to be fairly confident in the development of your skills. You have to feel like you've got a firm grasp on hitting the cue ball in its center (see Chapter 7).

The reason? English is a tricky son of a gun. Most players (myself included) enter a world of confusion when trying to understand English. A lot happens when the cue tip deviates off the vertical axis of the cue ball.

But before you rip these pages out of the book and set them on fire, you should know that you can do some fantastic things with English, when you use it properly. You can control the cue ball, sometimes in fantastic fashion. Harness the power of English, and you're in good shape.

Getting to Know English

Simply put, *English* means putting sidespin on the cue ball. In the previous two chapters, I cover follow (topspin) and draw (backspin). Well, English is the wide range of possibilities of hitting the cue ball to the right or left of center.

As you can see in Figure 10-1, English implies a hit anywhere off the vertical axis. Even the slight movement, maybe just an eighth of a inch, is considered an off-center hit.

Figure 10-1:
Deviating from the center line (hitting the cue ball in the gray area) means using English.

Draw is commonly referred to as *bottom English,* and follow as *high English.* And this terminology isn't technically wrong, but the modern connotation to English is that it's hitting the ball to the left or right of center.

Because I talk about how English can be a rather tough nut to crack, the natural question is, "Why the heck complicate matters by introducing sidespin to a shot?" Well, the potential to change the cue ball's path is why English is used by many and so important to those who can use it properly.

Using sidespin can greatly increase your control of the cue ball. Sidespin can dramatically change the angle of the cue ball as it hits a rail. It can also change the speed a ball has after hitting a rail. It can also change the path a cue ball takes after contact with the cue.

English can change the cue ball's angle after hitting a cushion. In the vast majority of cases, you should avoid using English to pocket a ball. So, if you're loading up on English, be sure that you're going to pocket the ball. After all, if you miss the first shot, it won't matter much where you leave the cue ball.

Experimenting with English

Talking about what English can do and showing you are two very different things. A lot happens when you hit the cue ball to the right or left of center. One simple shot can go a long way to showing you the different concepts involved with English.

The following process is a simple way to get acquainted with English:

1. **Put the cue ball on the headspot and line up so that you're aiming directly at the middle of the far end of the table.**

2. **Aim to hit the cue ball on it's horizontal axis, but with one tip of right English.**

   One tip means the diameter of the cue's tip. As you can see in Figure 10-2, one tip of English refers to the distance from center you hit the cue ball.

3. **Strike the ball with an easy stroke, hitting it just hard enough that it will hit the far rail and stop before it comes all the way back to you.**

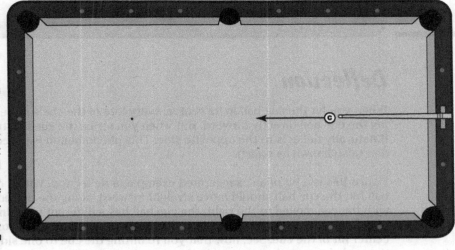

Figure 10-2: Using one tip of right English, hit the cue ball toward the center of the far short rail.

If you hit the cue ball with a bit of right English, you should notice that the cue ball takes a bit of a curved path to the far rail. But maybe the first thing you noticed was how the cue ball hit the rail and, instead of coming straight back toward you, veered off to the right.

Try the same shot, but hit the cue ball even farther to the right, while making sure that you're still stroking through the cue ball and not trying to steer it with your cue.

Figure 10-3 shows how English can greatly change the behavior of the cue ball, as compared with a shot where you hit the cue ball in the exact center. To break down what is happening here, the following sections go through the differences involved with a cue ball that's loaded with sidespin.

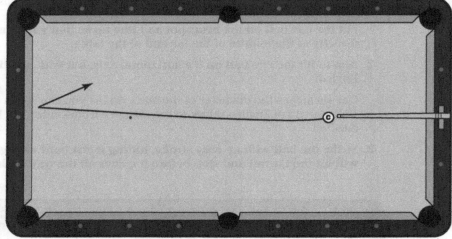

Figure 10-3:
Instead
of going
straight to
the rail, the
cue ball will
take a
longer
route.

Deflection

When you hit the cue ball in its center, every iota of the cue's force is pushing the cue ball directly forward. But when you strike the cue ball to one side, it naturally deflects to the opposite side. This phenomenon is called *deflection* (also known as *squirt*).

Figure 10-4 is a bit of an exaggerated example of deflection. With a centerball hit, the cue ball should move straight forward, along the dotted line. But with the cue moved to the right, the cue ball has a different path. Instead of moving directly ahead, the cue ball deflects to the left because of the off-center hit of the cue. See, now that you're hitting the cue to one side, part of the cue's force pushes the cue in the opposite direction.

Figure 10-4:
Deflection
pushes the
cue ball
off the line
straight
toward your
target.

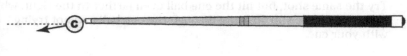

The farther you hit from center, the more the cue ball will deflect to the opposite side. Because deflection is a result of the cue hitting the cue ball off center, its effect on the cue ball will be a direct result of how much English you use on a particular shot.

Changes in your stroke or the playing conditions, such as the condition of the balls or the cue you're using, can give you different results. If you remove all these variables, deflection becomes a matter of how far from center you hit the cue ball.

Swerve

The cue ball initially moves in the direction away from the side you hit the cue ball, but another force is at play. As the cue ball rolls forward toward the far rail, the sidespin starts to grab the cloth, pulling the cue ball in the opposite direction. So a ball hit with left English will immediately deflect to the right, but the left spin will gradually move the ball back to the left.

Unfortunately, this spin doesn't stop working when you get back to the line straight from the cue ball to the center of the far rail. Instead, it can cause the cue ball to actually hit the rail on the left side of center. Swerve, this curving of the cue ball's path, is affected by speed. A firmly struck ball will have more forward momentum and thus less of an opportunity to grab the cloth and curve the cue ball. It also has less time to do so because the ball is moving pretty quickly.

And again, the amount of English on the cue ball will have a bearing on the amount the cue ball "swerves." The cue ball swerves because of the friction between a spinning ball and the cloth. The more the cue ball spins, the more it will swerve.

When you lift the butt of the cue up (meaning the cue will be hitting down into the cue ball), the shot has more swerve. So whenever possible, keep the cue as level to the ground as possible.

Note that the cue ball doesn't always end up hitting the rail directly in the middle. The combination of curve and deflection can steer the cue ball off this line, which is why aiming shots with English is tricky (and something I cover later in this chapter in the "Pocketing a Straight Shot with English" section).

Rebound angle

The reason that most all shots with English are hit off center is the cue ball's angle of rebound off the rail. The first few times you see a spinning cue ball hit a rail, it's actually quite surprising just how much a spinning cue ball will jump off the rail in the direction it is spinning.

A cue ball hit straight into a rail with follow (see Chapter 8) or draw (see Chapter 9) always rebounds on the same line it went into the rail. But add a little sidespin? Things can change. Drastically.

To see how English can affect the path of a cue ball that hits a rail, line up the shot shown in Figure 10-5. With the cue ball in the same spot as the first shot, aim for the diamond closest to the side pocket.

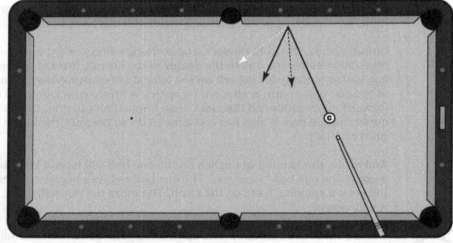

Figure 10-5: English can shorten or lengthen an angle.

With a center-ball hit, the cue ball rebounds at about the same angle it hit the rail (shown by the solid line). If you use right English, the cue ball rebounds at a steeper angle, almost coming back at you (shown by the black dotted line). Because the cue ball comes back at such an angle, you're said to have *shortened the angle*. This type of spin is called *reverse English*.

Conversely, a ball hit with left English rebounds at an angle toward the far short rail (the white dotted arrow), also called *lengthening the angle*. This type of spin is called *running English*.

I go into what happens when a cue ball with English hits an object ball in the next section of this chapter ("Pocketing a Straight Shot with English"), but the change in the cue ball's angle off a rail is the single most important reason to learn English. Learning to control English means you can do a lot of things with the cue ball that you couldn't do by just using draw or follow.

Pocketing a Straight Shot with English

Pocketing balls when you're using English involves many different factors. Again, I want to emphasize that this learning process can be rather arduous. You shouldn't start to mess around with English until you're confident that you're comfortable hitting the cue ball up and down its vertical axis. Only when you have a grasp on center-ball hits are you ready to start using English.

That being said, if you think you're ready to go, then you can introduce an object ball into the equation. Set up the shot shown in Figure 10-6. The cue ball is in line with the 9 ball into the corner pocket. This shot shouldn't be a problem with a center-ball hit.

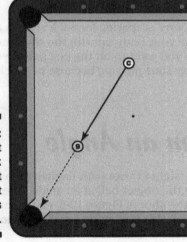

Figure 10-6:
This shot
may look
easy, but
see what
happens
with English.

After you pocket this shot five times in a row by hitting the cue ball in the center, try to make it with left English. Remember that the cue ball will deflect to the right and curve back to the left, so you must take this action into consideration when aiming.

After you can pocket this shot by using a tip's width of left English, try it with a tip of right English. Also, when you're starting out with English, try to hit the same shot with the same speed. After you can routinely pocket the shot with a right English and a medium stroke, see what happens when you use a firm stroke or a light stroke.

If you're struggling with this drill, shorten it up. Move the cue ball closer to the 9. Find a spot where you're able to make the shot at least once in awhile. The occasional success tells you what you did right, instead of seeing nothing but failure.

Unfortunately, when it comes to aiming, no surefire system exists for shots with English. Aiming isn't as simple as saying, "Aim three inches to the right when using left English." Things like distance between the cue ball and object ball, speed, and the amount of English make every shot unique.

Starting with a shot where the cue ball and object ball are relatively close (between a diamond or two away), you can adjust for deflection and curve, without those effects becoming too big of an influence on the cue ball.

Learn from your misses. If you're constantly hitting the 9 ball to the right of the pocket, you know you need to aim farther to the left. Don't just set up and hit the shot like a robot, thinking you'll eventually correct whatever it is you're doing wrong.

Swatting at the balls, instead of properly preparing for each shot, is easy to do. Every time you set up a shot, line your body up with the shot line and think of where you'll aim and where you want to hit the cue ball. If you don't focus on the individual shot, you may start missing because of a lackadaisical approach.

Coming at English from an Angle

When you can routinely pocket a straight-in shot with English (see preceding section), you can start approaching the object ball at an angle. The shot in Figure 10-7 is the same distance as the shot in Figure 10-6, just from a different angle. See whether you can pocket this ball, using what you know about controlling the cue ball with a straight-in shot.

This shot is a bit more difficult than the straight-in shot in the last section. However, if you can get to the point where you can pocket it with some consistency, shooting at an angle is a perfect way to demonstrate what you can do with English.

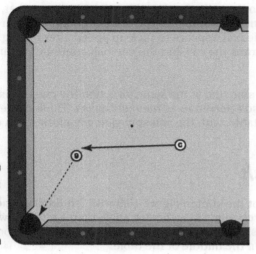

Figure 10-7:
Try cutting
a ball with
English.

Outside English

Figure 10-8 is an example of what's called *outside English*. In this case, you make the 9 ball in the corner by hitting the cue ball to the right of center. *Outside* refers to you cuing on the side of the cue ball opposite to the direction you're cutting the 9 ball.

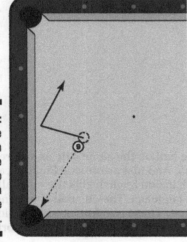

Figure 10-8:
Outside
English
causes the
cue ball to
rebound at a
wider angle
than normal.

As the cue ball heads to the rail, after knocking the 9 in the pocket, the spin makes the cue ball seem to *jump* off the rail at a wider angle (toward the other long rail). The cue ball appears to pick up speed after hitting the rail because the sidespin grabs the rail and the cue ball continues rolling toward the other long rail.

Because the cue ball is spinning in the same direction the cue ball is headed, this type of action is also referred to as *running English.* Think of the cue ball as running around the table, with the sidespin giving it a little extra oomph.

Inside English

Conversely, if you shoot the shot in Figure 10-9 with left English, the cue ball hits the short rail and rebounds at a shorter angle than a cue ball with no sidespin. The left English causes the cue ball to hit the rail and rebound heading nearly straight down the middle of the table.

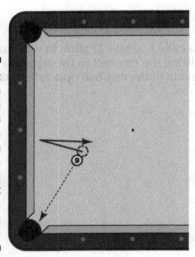

Figure 10-9: Inside English works against the cue ball's momentum, sharpening its angle out of the rail and slowing it down.

Here, because you're hitting the cue ball on the same side as you're cutting the 9 ball, you're using *inside English.* And just as outside English caused the cue ball to pick up speed off the rail, inside English kills the cue ball — or reduces its speed, in less violent language. The cue ball is moving to the right, while it's spinning to the left. These two forces work against one another, meaning the cue ball will come off the rail at an angle shorter than normal and with less speed.

Depending on the angle the cue ball takes to the rail, inside English can be either running or reverse English. Inside and outside English refer to the contact point on the cue ball relative to the object ball. Running and reverse English refer to the cue ball relative to the rail.

Throwing Object Balls

When a shot involves English, you'll have to pay great attention to the cue ball — where to hit it, how to aim it, how it reacts with rails. But English (and all cue-ball spins, for that matter) has a small impact on the object ball as well. At impact, the cue ball and object ball are only in contact for a fraction of a second. But even in that instant, the spin on the cue ball can affect the object ball's path. The change in the object ball's path is known as *throw*.

When the two spheres collide, the friction between a spinning cue ball and object ball *throws* the object ball a little off its normal line (which is the line of centers, as described Chapter 2). While throw occurs in almost every shot where the cue ball's spin and the cut angle don't mesh, the effect is usually negligible (or at least not noticeable because you probably subconsciously compensate for it in most instances). Figure 10-10 shows how a spinning cue ball can throw an object ball off line.

Figure 10-10:
A cue ball with English throws the cue ball in the direction its spinning.

But a cue ball loaded up with sidespin can change the angle of the object ball in a way that's significant. It can throw an object ball off the line of centers by a few degrees, which is something you may want to take into account when using English.

The shot in Figure 10-11 isn't an extraordinary shot, but it can show what throw can do. Say that you want to pocket the 3 ball in the upper-left corner using left English. If you hit it with pocket speed, the 3 ball can be thrown well off target — all thanks to the cue ball's spin.

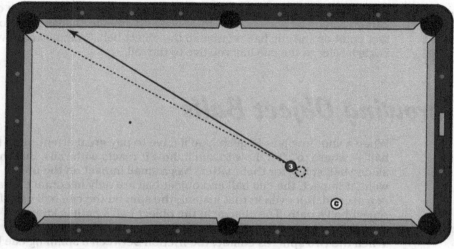

Figure 10-11:
Throw can become troublesome over long distances.

Finding New Opportunities for Position

You should use English only when absolutely necessary. If you can find a way to execute a shot without using sidespin while still achieving all the necessary goals, you should go with the center-ball hit.

But in certain situations, English can greatly improve your position for the next shot.

Shortening the cue ball's path

One way to make things easier on yourself is to find a shorter route to position on your next ball. If you restrict yourself to hitting the center of the cue ball, you're faced with tough shots when the cue ball is naturally headed in the opposite direction from your next ball.

In Figure 10-12, you can't get a good angle on the 9 ball with a center-ball hit. You can use follow to leave the cue ball near the footspot, or you can use stun to send the cue ball two rails. But both shots leave a tricky shot on the 9 ball.

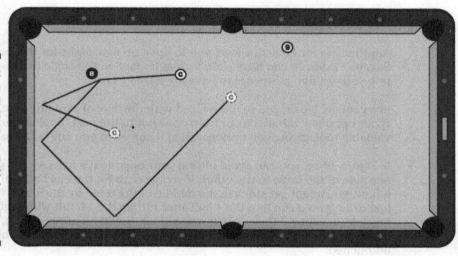

Figure 10-12:
With a center-ball hit, you'd either have to go multiple rails for pinpoint position or settle for a long, angled shot.

If you use maximum right English (inside English, in this case), however, you can alter the angle of the cue ball off the short rail, as shown in Figure 10-13. Now, the cue ball rebounds toward the 9 ball, heading nearly straight up the table, in perfect shape for the 9 in the top-left corner pocket.

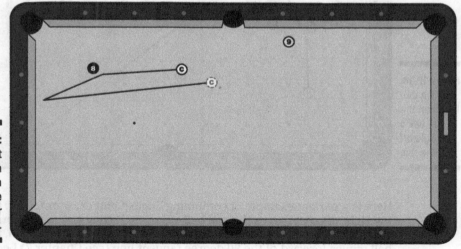

Figure 10-13:
Using right English can give you a better angle to your next ball.

Avoiding obstacles

Another use for English allows you to open up new paths for the cue ball. Because sidespin can have such a great impact on the angle of a cue ball off a rail, you can find new ways to navigate a tricky table.

In a game of 8-ball, you're often faced with the task of avoiding obstacles (your opponent's balls) to go from one shot to the next. English can be a valuable tool, giving you options when it comes to you cue ball's path.

In Figure 10-14, you can avoid hitting your opponent's balls as you go from one side of the table to the other. If you were to hit the cue ball with just follow, you might get stuck in the middle of the table by the 5 ball. If you use just draw, you'd run into the 4 ball after hitting the 14. But with high right English (meaning if the cue ball was a clock, you'd hit around 1:30), you can lengthen the cue ball's angle off the first rail so that it runs down the table untouched.

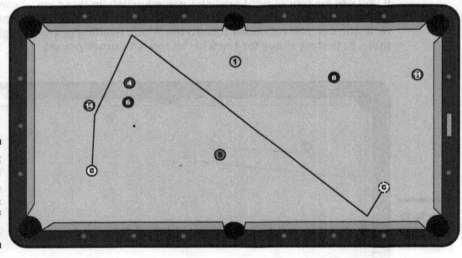

Figure 10-14: English can lengthen the cue ball's angle off the rail.

Here is a perfect example of combining English and draw or follow. Hitting to the right of center gives the cue ball sidespin. Hitting above the horizontal axis gives the cue ball topspin. So after impact with the object ball, the cue ball moves forward of the 90-degree tangent line (see Chapter 7) because the sidespin has little effect until it hits the rail.

But after the cue ball runs into the rail, the right English helps send the ball along its new path, between the blocking balls and the other end of the table, in line with the 14.

Combining English and follow or draw gives you two tools in one shot. Surprisingly, the combination of top or bottom spin with sidespin has little affect on each. The cue ball continues to spin to the side, even as it rolls forward or spins backward.

If a cue ball is spinning in the same direction it's moving as it hits the rail (has *running English*), it picks up speed at impact; a cue ball spinning in the opposite direction it's heading will slow down upon impact with the rail (*reverse English*). You can use reverse English to kill the cue ball, just as it did after the cue ball hit the second rail in Figure 10-14. The cue ball jumped off the first rail, but that same sidespin worked against the cue ball's forward momentum when it hit the second rail, helping the cue ball come to a stop in line for the 14 ball.

Part III
Taking Your Shots

The 5th Wave   By Rich Tennant

"That's the problem with asking a chiropractor to rack the balls. He has to manipulate and align them first."

In this part . . .

Controlling the cue ball is one thing (see Part II); making object balls is another. In Part III, I dive into the varied ways of sending object balls into pockets. For some players, just being able to see certain shots is half the battle. So in this part, I detail a bunch of different ways to execute shots so that you can stay at the table.

Chapter 11

Opening Shots: The Rack and the Break

- -

In This Chapter

▶ Racking the right way

▶ Cutting through fact and fiction about the break

▶ Generating the most power in your break shot

▶ Taking a look at specialty breaks

- -

The break shot in pool is an anomaly. For every second of every game, you need to be in complete control, using only as much power and speed as needed. A universal goal in pool is to reduce unwanted or unpredictable movements. So, instead of squeezing the cue to saw dust and drilling the cue ball into orbit, you're taught to relax and keep the cue ball's movements to the bare minimum.

Except during the break shot, of course. This opening shot, at least in the majority of pool's different games, is a combination of power and speed, all to create a collision that is as violent as possible.

But look underneath the surface of a skull-rattling break shot, and you'll see principles much more akin to the rest of the game. Accuracy must precede power. In the end, a great break shot is controlled chaos. You need to control the cue ball, while disrupting the rack as much as possible.

In this chapter, I look at how you rack for a few different games. I then go through the process of developing a powerful break, one that will do what needs to be done so that you can be in complete control of the table.

The Rack: Setting Up for the Break

Despite sharing its name with one of the more infamous torture devices of medieval times, the *rack,* shown in Figure 11-1, is a breeze to handle. A simple equilateral triangle, the rack is the tool that will get the balls set for nearly every game you play.

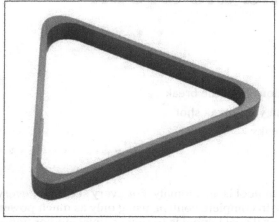

Figure 11-1:
The typical rack is a triangle made of plastic, metal, or wood.

Made of plastic, metal, or wood, the rack isn't exactly the most complex of sporting equipment. But before you throw the balls in it and claim you're ready to go, you need to remember a few key points when you set up your good rack (or triangle, as it may be called).

Location, location, location

For the majority of games you'll be playing, the head ball — meaning the one on the top of the triangle — should be directly on top of the footspot. Just as it is in Figure 11-2, the footspot is always in the middle of the table lengthwise and two diamonds from the bottom of the table. (For information on ball placement, see the next section.)

With the head ball on the footspot, you then need to arrange the triangle so that it's lined up with the table. To make sure that your rack isn't tilted, which can be perceived as a way of manipulating the outcome of the subsequent break shot, arrange the bottom of the triangle so that it's parallel with the short rails (at the top and bottom of the table).

If the head ball is on the footspot and the back of the triangle is parallel to the short rails, you have the balls in the proper position.

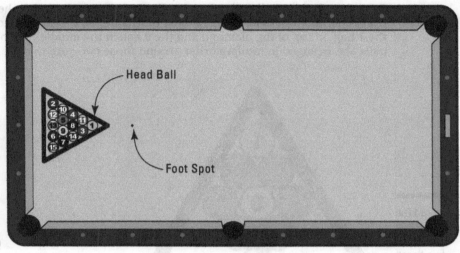

Head Ball

Foot Spot

Figure 11-2:
Keep the head ball on the footspot, and you'll be in perfect shape.

Tight is right

After you have the rack in the right spot, it's a matter of getting the balls in their proper place. The goal of the rack should be to leave all the balls touching their neighbors.

Because 8-ball uses all 15 object balls, you'll completely fill up the triangle. In most leagues, the rules about which balls go where are pretty limited. As long as the 8 ball is in the middle of the triangle, as shown in Figure 11-3, and there is one solid and one stripe in the bottom corners, the rack should be legal. (*Note:* Some players always rack with the 1 ball on the top, but most versions of the rules of 8-ball don't dictate which ball should be on top of the rack.)

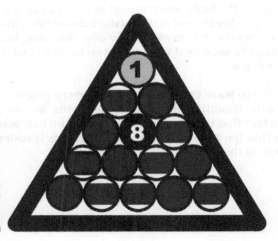

Figure 11-3:
An 8-ball rack is a five-tiered triangle of 15 balls.

Even though the 9-ball rack, shown in Figure 11-4, is a diamond, the normal triangular rack works just fine. In most tournaments, a legal rack consists of the 1 ball on top of the diamond and the 9 ball in the middle. The other seven balls are arranged in random order around those two sure things.

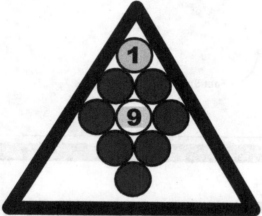

Figure 11-4:
A 9-ball rack is a five-tiered diamond of nine balls.

Just as in an 8-ball rack, the 9-ball rack must be in line and tight to maximize the chances of a successful break. (For more information, see the preceding two sections.)

With the balls positioned in their proper spots, push them up toward the head ball. The pressure of pushing into the balls will keep them pressed against one another, with the hope they will continue to be in contact when you lift the rack off of the balls.

If a rack has a few balls that are *loose* — meaning they aren't touching one or more adjacent balls — the balls won't spread as much as they would in a tight rack. The power of a break shot is diminished, decreasing the likelihood that balls go into the pockets and spread evenly over the table. In extreme cases, these racks, sometimes called *slugs*, will even leave a cluster of balls sitting around the footspot.

While you'd ideally like to leave every ball touching every neighbor, it may be difficult, considering the condition of the table, rack, balls, and so on. To that end, it is most important that the head ball is touching the two below it. This positioning ensures that the maximum amount of energy is transferred from the cue ball to the top of the rack of balls.

Many tournaments and leagues dictate that an opponent racks for the other player. During competition, it's not completely unheard of for a player to give his opponent a rack that is less than ideal. While most players try their best to create a good rack, some skip the sportsmanship to gain an advantage — or at least negate his opponent's advantage of having the break. If you suspect your opponent to be manipulating the rack illegally, inspect the rack to make sure that the balls are properly positioned before you break.

If you see something inappropriate, ask your opponent to rerack the balls. If it happens again, tell your opponent what isn't right with the rack. If it continues, notify a league official or tournament referee.

Every table is different. And, not surprisingly, not every table is in perfect condition. Sometimes, because of inconsistencies in the cloth, you'll have a tough time getting the top few balls to remain touching when you remove the rack. If you're finding it impossible to rack properly, consider *tapping* the balls in place, which means gently tapping the top of the balls with another ball. Tapping creates a tiny crater in the cloth, so the balls remain in place and in contact with each other. Tapping is common practice in most leagues; in tournament play, though, you should ask your opponent or a referee before you begin tapping balls in place.

The Break: Covering the Who, What, and Where

Sure, you can always flip a coin to decide who breaks first, but where's the skill in that? In most leagues and tournaments, the person who breaks first is decided by *the lag*.

When you and your opponent are ready to play, you both line up to shoot at the same time, as shown in Figure 11-5. All you want to do during the lag is hit the ball to the far end of the table and back, aiming to leave the ball as close to the short rail nearest to you as possible. The person whose ball is the closest to the short rail wins (regardless whether the ball hits the rail or not).

If you win, you get to choose whether to break or allow your opponent to break. In most games, including 8-ball and 9-ball (see Chapters 18 and 19), you'll want to break. But you may want to give the break to your opponent when you're playing straight pool (see Chapter 20).

With just a few minutes of practice, you should become at least competent with the lag. For simplicity's sake, hit the cue ball on its vertical axis, maybe just a smidgeon above center. This positioning allows the ball to gently roll after impact, instead of skidding on the cloth.

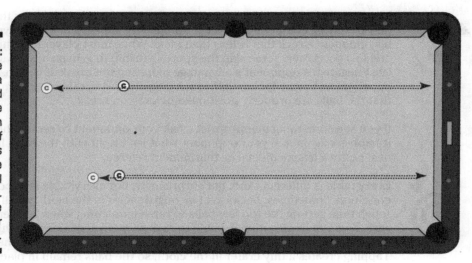

Figure 11-5:
During the lag, you hit a ball up and down the table with the aim of leaving it as close to the bottom rail as possible. Here, the top player wins.

Defining goals for each break

Before you start smashing open racks, you need to know what you want to achieve out of each break shot. The following guidelines keep you focused on breaking as best you can:

✔ **Making a ball:** In 8-ball and 9-ball, you desperately want to make a ball on the break. If you pocket at least one, you can continue shooting and establish control of the game from the start. (See Chapters 18 and 19 for full descriptions of what happens when you make a ball on the break for each game.)

✔ **Spreading the rack:** Power is the name of the game when it comes to breaking. If you can transfer a lot of energy to the rack, you'll be more likely to spread the balls all over the table. By distributing the balls evenly — or as close to evenly as possible — you decrease the chances for balls to stick in troublesome clusters.

The more balls roll, the more likely they are to find a pocket.

✔ **Controlling the cue ball:** Probably the most overlooked aspect to the break among amateur players is controlling the cue ball. Ideally, the cue ball will smack the head ball and bounce back toward the center of the table. Leaving the cue ball near the middle of the table increases your chances of having a clear shot after the break. Concentrating on cue-ball control will also reduce your odds of scratching.

In Figure 11-6, the best place to leave the cue ball is in the gray oval in the middle of the table. If you can stop the cue ball anywhere in this area, you'll probably have a shot to another ball. Also, notice how this area is a good distance from all six pockets, so scratching won't be a worry.

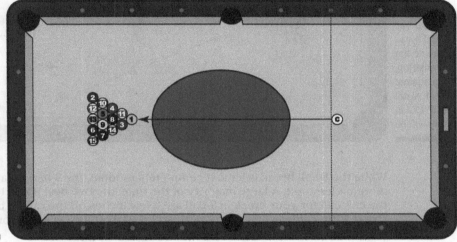

Figure 11-6: You want to keep the cue ball in the middle of the table after you break.

Positioning the cue ball

You can place the cue ball anywhere behind the *headstring* — an imaginary line running the width of the table and two diamonds from the top rail, as shown in Figure 11-7. So how do you decide where the best spot is? With a few tips, you can try out a few spots before settling into the placement that you're most comfortable with.

When you're starting out, the best area to place the cue ball for your break is near the center of the table (at the head spot, which is in the middle of the table along the headstring). Aiming from head-on allows you to exert the most force upon the rack.

Because making a ball on the break is so important, many professional players slightly change the placement of the cue ball in an effort to create different results.

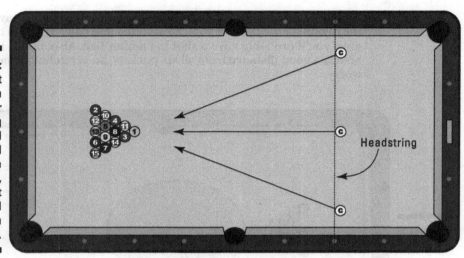

Figure 11-7:
The most
common
spots for
breaking
in 8-ball
and 9-ball
are on the
headstring,
up against
either rail
and right in
the middle.

While the 8-ball break is almost completely random, the 9-ball break is a little more understood. A large majority of the time, the two best spots to place the cue ball for your break in 9-ball are a few inches off the rail on the head-string. Either side is fine, so try both and see which one is more comfortable.

Recently, many professionals have experimented with a softer break stroke — one that will pocket one of the balls on the side of the diamond, while leaving the cue ball in the middle of the table. The so-called *soft break* is effective for the world's best players, but it's not ideal for developing players. The soft break takes a highly tuned stroke and consistently tight rack. For starters, you want to create as much motion as possible, so stick to cueing the cue ball near its center so that it strikes the object ball as full as possible.

Don't be afraid to change up your starting point, if you're having difficulty pocketing balls on the break. What works one day may not work the next. Pros often switch positions from one side of the table to the other in the middle of matches.

Want a hint on the best place to break? You may be able to find one on the table. If a particular spot looks particularly worn, it's probably because most players break from that spot. Keep an eye out for *track lines* from the head-string to the footspot. This tip isn't a sure thing, but those track lines may give you a starting point.

Gaining Power on Your Break Stroke

The break stroke is a bit different from your normal mid-game stroke (see Chapter 5). You need to generate a substantial amount of power, while staying in control, so take some time to make sure that you have a grasp on the fundamentals of the break stroke.

Before you even move the cue back and forth for a few warm-up strokes, you need to make the following physical changes in stance:

- **Narrow your stance.** Your stance during a normal shot is built for stability, with your knees slightly bent and your feet a little more than shoulder width's apart (see Chapter 2). Your break stance, however, should be a little narrower — like you're ready to jump as high as possible. (We talk about incorporating body movement into the break shot in the "Throwing your body into your break stroke" section of this chapter; for now, keep your feet just a touch closer.)

- **Bend your knees.** With your feet a little closer together, bend your knees a bit more than normal. You need to have a stance that is built for the quick snap of your break, so lower your center of gravity a bit.

- **Stand up . . . just a little bit.** You want to keep your head higher than on your normal stroke. If you normally have your chin on the cue during a shot, lift up so that your head is 18 inches above the cue. If you normally keep your head a foot above the cue, hold it 2 feet above it during the break.

  Having a more upright stance gives your back arm more room to operate. Because you're going to be swinging the cue forward much faster, you want to have plenty of space so that you can be free and easy.

With a proper stance (see Figure 11-8), you're ready to get the cue in motion.

Closing the bridge

Because you want to maximize power, you're going to use a closed bridge, meaning your pointer finger loops around the cue to give you more control during the stroke. (See Chapter 3 for a full discussion of bridges.)

If you're breaking in the middle of the table, where you won't be resting your hand on a rail, you want to employ a bridge just like the one shown in Figure 11-9.

Figure 11-8:
Keep your feet a bit closer together, bend your knees, and give yourself plenty of room to swing the cue.

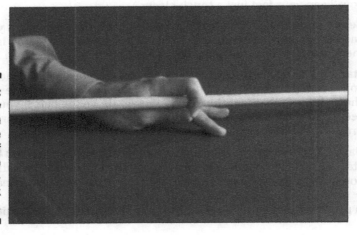

Figure 11-9:
A sturdy bridge is an absolute necessity if you want to build a reliable break stroke.

With your thumb and ring finger below the cue and your pointer finger wrapped around it, you have a strong bridge that should stand up to the pressures of a break stroke.

REMEMBER

With a closed bridge, the three fingers that touch the cue's shaft should be touching one another. The tips of your pointer finger and thumb will be pressed against one another. These two fingers will be pressed against one another and touching the side of your straightened middle finger.

Just as you put a bit of weight on your bridge hand during a normal stroke, increase the pressure on your bridge during the break. By leaning forward a bit more, you'll have more weight keeping your bridge hand glued to the table.

If you're not breaking from the middle of the table, you still want to employ a closed bridge. But now, you'll be using the rail to keep your cue from getting out of line.

Figure 11-10 is a perfect example of a rail bridge when breaking. Notice how the cue is resting on the rail, with the pointer finger still wrapped around the top.

Figure 11-10:
With your cue on the rail, you can still use a closed bridge to control your cue.

With this bridge, it is important to know the three points of contact between your hand and the cue. First, your pointer finger will be resting on the right side of the shaft. Because it's wrapped over the cue, it also acts as a deterrent, keeping the cue down against the rail. On the left side of the cue, the tip of your ring finger and the bottom of your thumb should keep the cue aligned with the intended contact point.

The distance between your bridge and the cue ball often changes with the type of stroke. Chapter 3 discusses how to use a short bridge length for shots that require a high degree of accuracy and a longer bridge for shots that call for more power. To that end, use a longer bridge length for your break. Increase the distance between your bridge hand and the cue ball by two or three inches. (If you have trouble making an accurate hit on the cue ball, however, shorten up a bit.)

While you might have a little weight on your bridge hand, you want to keep your bridge arm relaxed and bent at a slight angle. Locking your elbow not only stiffens your upper body, but it also inhibits the natural movement of your torso and back arm.

Keep your arm steady and relaxed so that it can let the rest of your body do what it's supposed to do.

Easing into the backswing

The proper backswing on the break seems illogical. You want to hit the cue ball really hard, right? So it makes sense to jerk the cue back and then ram it forward. But take it easy.

Your backswing should be slow and relaxed. To start, you may even want to exaggerate your backswing by inching the cue back. By slowing yourself down, the cue has less chance to wander off line.

When you're ready to move from the backswing to your break stroke, concentrate on making a smooth transition in the direction of your stroke. Focus your attention on a constant acceleration of the cue instead of a herky-jerky, out-of-control throwing of the cue.

Following through in a big way

Because you're stroking faster than normal, your follow-through is going to be exaggerated. By allowing the cue to continue on its track into and through the cue ball, you're resisting the temptation to yank the cue to a stop. Yanking the cue to a stop not only decreases power, but it hurts your accuracy as well.

Some pros — namely Johnny Archer, one of the greatest players of all time and the acknowledged player of the decade in the 1990s — have an almost comical follow-through. After the break, Archer throws his cue at the head ball, so his cue is high in the air with the tip floating around the footspot.

This huge follow-through may be a bit too much for you, but it's a sign that you need to let the cue continue after impact.

A big-time follow-through can also give you a hint as to your accuracy. Your cue should head straight toward your aiming point. If it doesn't, you know you're favoring one side or the other. A straight follow-through means you're on your way to a straight stroke.

Throwing your body into your break stroke

You can create only so much power with your back arm. After you can consistently hit the head ball squarely with the cue ball, which then stops near the middle of the table more often than not, you're ready to put your body behind your break.

Start slow. During your final stroke, gently push your weight forward, from your back foot through your front and onto your bridge hand. You should be able to hit the cue ball a little harder than when you just use your back arm.

The minute you lose the ability to control the cue ball, you need to step back. If you can't hit the head ball with the cue ball, you need to scale back the body movement until you're comfortable and accurate.

As you become more and more comfortable with transferring your weight during the break, you should see better results — like more balls being pocketed more often and fewer balls hanging around the footspot.

For most beginning to intermediate players, body movement on the break is fairly limited. You want to remain in control, so throwing your body into the shot like a wild man isn't prudent. Stay focused on accuracy on the break and only incorporate more body movement when you know that you're ready to handle it.

Adding Accuracy to Your Break Stroke's Power

If you've ever played golf, you know that controlling a shot with your putter is easier than controlling one with your driver. Well, think of the break as your drive in golf. You want power, but you can't sacrifice everything to get it. (See the section "Gaining Power on Your Break Stroke," earlier in this chapter.)

Hitting the head ball as full as possible

In almost every situation, you want to hit the rack as hard as possible. To do so, you have to hit the head ball as full as possible. This transfers the most energy from the cue ball to the object balls, which helps you accomplish the goals of a successful break. (For more on these goals, see the section "Defining goals for each break," earlier in this chapter.)

While a few exceptions do exist, I want to stress the importance of making full contact with the head ball. If the cue ball hits the head ball at an angle, it will ricochet off at an angle. You've not only lost control of the cue ball, but you've wasted energy. The cue ball should nearly stop after impact; only then can you be sure that all your power went into the rack.

If you break from the head spot (in the middle of the table along the head-string), you'll have no problem aiming for the head ball. All you have to do is drive the cue ball straight down the table so that the center of the cue ball meets the center of the object ball.

Breaking from a rail, however, requires a slight adjustment. Just like Figure 11-11, you want the cue ball to strike the head ball

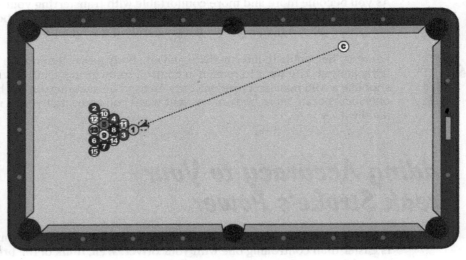

Figure 11-11:
If you break from a rail, be sure to adjust your aim so that you're still striking the head ball as full as possible.

Aiming to hit the top of the head ball could be trouble. In Figure 11-12, the cue ball will bounce to the right, which puts you in danger of scratching in the opposite side pocket.

Figure 11-13 shows a quick way to check your accuracy when you're breaking from the side rail. This simple drill provides immediate feedback. Place a ball on the footspot, exactly where the head ball would be for a rack of 8-ball or 9-ball. Now, try to hit the ball just like you would during your break. You should be able to kill the cue ball in the middle of the table, while the object ball goes flying around the table. You may be surprised what this drill tells you about your break. If you can stop the cue ball, you're doing great. If you can't, spend some time working on this drill. It will definitely pay off.

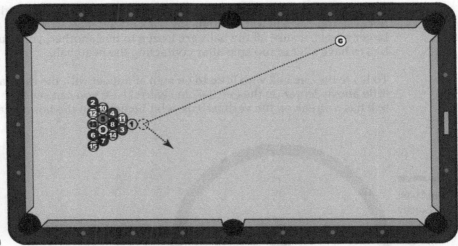

Figure 11-12:
Hitting the
top of the
head ball is
dangerous.

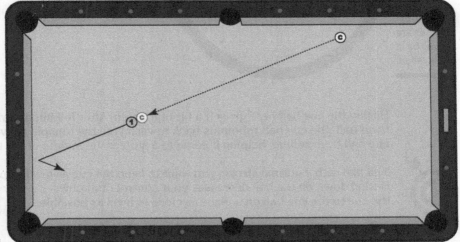

Figure 11-13:
Looks sim-
ple, right? A
controlled
break from
the side rail
isn't as easy
as it looks.

Finding where to cue the cue ball

Just as important as the contact point on the object ball, where you hit the cue ball with your cue determines what kind of control you'll have on the break.

You want the cue ball to stop shortly after it collides with the head ball. Because the cue ball will be bouncing back off the rack, which has a much larger mass because all the balls are frozen to one another, you want the cue ball to have a bit of top spin after contacting the head ball.

To leave the cue ball with little to no spin at impact with the rack, aim just a little above center on the cue ball. In Figure 11-14, you can see that the cue ball has a streak on the vertical axis, a bit higher than the horizontal axis.

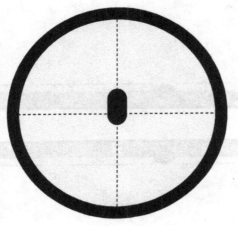

Figure 11-14: Exactly where you hit the cue ball will depend on many factors, but chances are it will be in this range.

Hitting the cue ball here gives it a bit of topspin. After full impact with the head ball, the cue ball rebounds back toward you; the topspin prevents the cue ball from rolling, helping it come to a stop in the middle of the table.

Just like with a normal stroke, you want to keep the cue as level as possible. Hitting down on the ball decreases your control (and power), so try to deliver the cue to the cue ball on a plane as close to level as possible.

Knowing When to Mix It Up

Proof that there are exceptions to every rule, pool has a few specialty breaks that are worth investigating, should you ever need them in the heat of battle.

8 for the game

Some leagues and tournaments have the rule that a player who makes the 8 ball on the break automatically wins that game. (Other rule sets call for the 8 to be spotted in such a case, which means the ball is put on the footspot, or that the balls are reracked and the same player breaks again.)

If you're playing where this rule is in effect, you can take advantage of this rule. Using a specialty break (shown in Figure 11-15), where you aim for a ball in the second row of the rack, you can increase the chances the 8 ball will head toward the opposite side pocket. With the ball on the rail along the headstring, aim to hit the ball in the second row as full as possible. If you hit the cue ball low, you'll send the cue ball off the side rail and back toward the stack of balls.

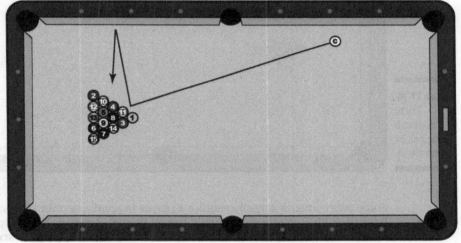

Figure 11-15:
Go for the
win, if you
feel lucky.

The cue ball will hit the stack twice. The initial impact on the second ball (in this case, the 11 ball, which is touching the 8) pushes the 8 ball toward the opposite corner pocket. If the 8 doesn't head toward the side pocket, the cue ball will rebound off the rail and may hit it again. While it may not be your every-game break, this little trick is worth knowing.

Soft break

Controversial among pros, the soft break is a way to manipulate the predictability of the 9-ball rack. In essence, professional players can tinker with speed, spin, cue ball location, and so on to consistently pocket a ball on the break. And, with reduced speed on the break, controlling the cue ball is easier.

By hitting the 9-ball rack at a reduced speed, a player can have greater accuracy. So if she figures out how to make the *wing balls* — the balls on the outer edges of the diamond (in this case, the 2 and 3) — go into the corner pockets, she can consistently pocket balls on the break. Figure 11-16 shows what can happen during a good 9-ball break.

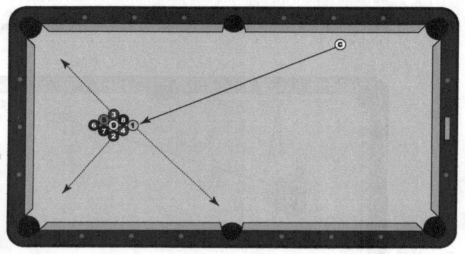

Figure 11-16:
Try to
pocket a
wing ball or
the 1 ball.

Some tournaments actually require a player to send a certain amount of balls back up table, with the hope that it forces them to break as hard as possible. Whether or not it spells the end of 9-ball, the soft break can work, so study up.

Safety breaks

Some games, most notably straight pool and one-pocket, require the breaker to play safe on the game's opening play. Sounds strange, right? Well, these games (see Chapter 20) are for the more advanced pool player, though most any player can benefit from practicing them.

In straight pool, the player with the break is at a disadvantage. The goal is to run as many balls as possible in a row, so setting up a shot on the break is pretty hard, right?

For the break in straight pool, you want to place the cue ball on the right side of the table, a little more than a diamond from the rail, as shown in Figure 11-17. The goal is to clip the back ball with a little high, right English. The cue ball bounces off two rails in that same corner before heading back up table near the short rail.

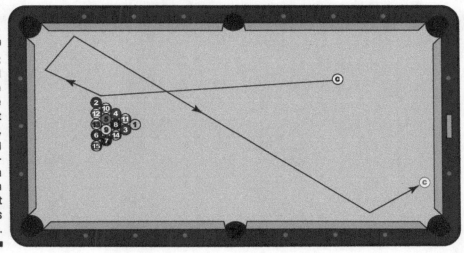

Figure 11-17:
The goal
is to glue
the cue
ball against
the top rail,
keeping
your oppo-
nent from
having an
easy shot
to start his
turn.

Movement among the balls in the rack should be minimal, so you'll be safe from your opponent starting a long run.

Similarly, in one-pocket — where you want to shoot as many balls as possible in one bottom corner pocket, while your opponent wants to shoot them in the other — the break is a safe. But unlike straight pool, the player who breaks in one-pocket should be at an advantage after playing safe on the break (see Figure 11-18).

As you can see, the point of the break is to push balls toward your pocket, while leaving your opponent little to nothing.

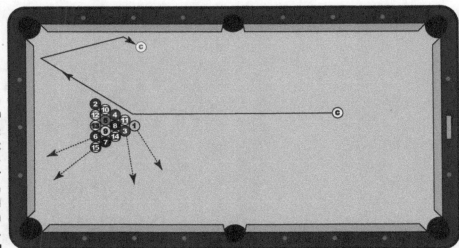

Figure 11-18:
You've got
the bot-
tom corner
pocket, so
you should
be at an
advantage.

Movement around the table is the price that should be paid must, so that the side from your cue ball can't start off a long run.

similarity, in one pocket — where you want to stand is that your cue ball is possible into the bottom corner pocket, while your opponent wants to shoot them in the other — the break is a safe. Technically, the 8-ball pool. Therefore whoever breaks, the pocket should be at an advantage after the dig of the initial break (see Figure 11-17).

As you can see, the point of the break is to push balls toward your own pocket while leaving your opponent little to settle.

Chapter 12

Thinking Ahead: Position and Pattern Play

. . . .

In This Chapter

▶ Planning to make a series of balls

▶ Finding the easiest route from ball to ball

▶ Seeing position zones

. . . .

The very first time you picked up a cue, what was the first thing you wanted to do? Make a ball, I'm guessing. Pocketing a ball is the very basic function of pool, so it's only natural that you wanted to get right to it.

But after a little practice, you'll be able to make various shots with relative ease. When you can make one ball, the key to playing pool becomes the ability to get yourself in position to make another shot. Focusing not on only making a ball, but leaving the cue ball in position to make the *next* ball, is position play. And playing for proper position is vitally important, regardless of whether your goals in the game include holding your own in a local league or becoming the next world champion.

In this chapter, you discover how to plan for more than just making one ball. You begin to see the table as an open canvas for you to draw your route from ball to ball.

After all, once you can see how to play the table, it's just a matter of doing it, right?

Beginning to See Patterns

No matter the game, every rack of pool has an infinite variety of possible layouts. So planning for specific situations is nearly impossible. I can, however, talk about some generalities that pop up from time to time. After you see these common situations, you can simplify the process of planning your route to victory.

Limiting cue ball movement

If you want to find the easiest way to pocket another ball, you're not going to play the cue ball off five rails for position on the next ball. Instead, you want to keep the cue ball's movement to a minimum. Simplify things.

One of the most common exercises in pool is the three-ball drill. This drill is a great way to begin playing position because it simplifies everything to a trio of balls.

Figure 12-1 shows three balls strewn across the table in a random manner. You've got ball in hand — meaning you can put the cue ball anywhere you want. So how are you going to make the 1, 2 and 3 balls?

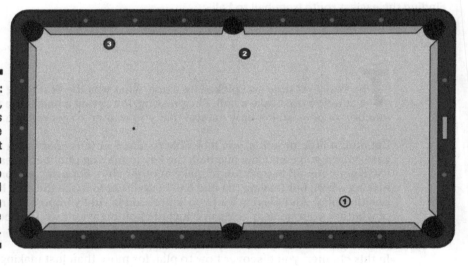

Figure 12-1:
Three balls, many ways to make them all, but try to find a way to keep the cue ball from flying around the table.

The stop shot (see Chapter 7), where you make the cue ball stop at impact with the object ball, is often the easiest way to play position. In the layout shown in Figure 12-1, can you see how you can play position with a pair of stop shots?

You can hit the 1 ball in the corner pocket, stopping the cue ball at impact for the 2 ball in the side pocket, as shown in Figure 12-2. Hit the blue ball in the side, stopping for the 3 ball in the other side. See how you can clear these three balls with the cue ball barely moving after it contacts the object balls?

Obviously, you're not always going to have a chance to play one stop shot to another as you work your way around the table. But minimizing cue ball movement is a good rule to follow and simplifies position play.

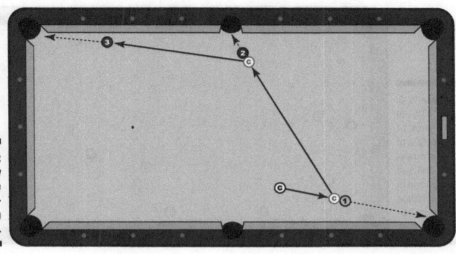

Figure 12-2: Here's how to keep cue ball movement to a minimum.

Playing successive stop shot isn't easy when you're new to the game, so don't get discouraged if you can't clear this layout. Getting out of position, even by an inch or two, can cause a lot of problems. Try to play the three balls just as they're shown in Figure 12-2, but don't beat yourself up if you struggle at first.

The three-ball drill is exactly that — a drill. But the skills learned in this practice method directly translate to real situations. As in a game of 8-ball, if you have two of your balls left and the 8 ball, isn't that just a three-ball drill where you have some obstacles (your opponents balls) on the table?

You're in good position in Figure 12-3. You're playing 8-ball, and you're stripes. It's your shot, and you're close to victory. But how do you formulate a plan to win the game?

Picking out a key ball is one way players choose which order they'll play a series of balls. The *key ball* is usually the last ball before the game winner, which means the last ball of your suit in 8-ball, with the 8 ball being the final ball.

In this situation, the key ball is the 12 ball. It's sitting near the 8 ball on the short rail. Because both balls are close to each other on the same side of the table, you won't have to move the cue ball very far to get position on the game-winning 8.

Luckily, you have an open shot on the 9 ball, which can lead to position on the 12 ball. Because of this setup, your route is pretty much settled for you — going from the 9 to the 12 to the 8 for the win (see Figure 12-4).

You could play the 12 ball first in this series, but look how much more the cue ball will have to travel going from the 12 to the 9 to the 8. Reducing the distance the cue ball travels reduces the chance for misplaying position.

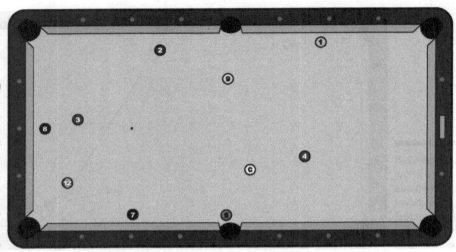

Figure 12-3:
This is another example of the three-ball drill, but placed in the middle of a game of 8-ball.

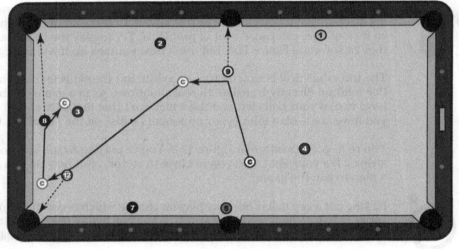

Figure 12-4:
This is the natural route through these three balls.

While you're only dealing with three balls in this example, you should still re-examine your plan after every shot. If you don't get perfect position on the next ball, you should ask yourself whether there's an easier way to pocket the rest of the balls.

Staying in control with pocket speed

It looks cool to slam the ball in the pocket as hard as humanly possible, doesn't it? You can send a message to everyone within earshot: You're here to play! In reality, though, slamming a ball as hard as possible is one way to send the message that you're not skilled in the finer points of the game.

The truth is that if you want to be successful, you're going to limit your speed on a majority of your shots. Often, you hear someone refer to *pocket speed,* which simply means hitting a shot at a speed that will deliver the object ball to the pocket with minimum speed — just enough to allow the object ball to fall into the pocket.

Pocket speed often makes position less risky because you're in greater control of the balls. Limiting your speed helps you keep greater control of the cue ball and object ball. And in a game as precise as pool, control is good.

When you're playing 8-ball, you often want to maneuver your balls so that they block pockets from your opponent. Hitting shots with pocket speed ensures that the object ball, if it doesn't go in, remains in the area of the pocket, which may block your opponent from pocketing a ball in that same pocket.

Soft is not always better. Position play can force you to travel *into* a position zone, rather than across it, which might make a firm hit a better choice in some situations. As a general rule, though, you want to keep as much control over the cue ball as possible, which usually means a softer hit, if all other variables are equal.

Just remember that pocket speed is your best bet if it will accomplish the goals of a certain shot, which usually means simply pocketing one ball and leaving the cue ball in prime shape for your next shot.

Avoiding contact

In the spirit of being in total control, you don't want the cue ball rolling into other balls after it hits a ball into a pocket. This avoidable contact complicates things because planning precisely what the result of a collision will be is nearly impossible. Also, this contact changes the lay of the land, which forces you to re-evaluate your plan for running a series of balls.

If you *must* make contact with another object ball, try to minimize the changes to the layout of the table (with the exception being when you need to break up a cluster of balls, which I cover in the next section). Also, avoid creating clusters of balls that may make your *runout* (clearing the rest of your balls to win the game) trickier than need be.

Position Play: Seeing into the Future

If you could shoot every shot with pocket speed, pool wouldn't be a very exciting game. No, with position play, meaning leaving the cue ball in proper position for the next shot, you often have to hit the cue ball a little harder than necessary to get the object ball into the pocket.

Looking at Figure 12-5, you know you could easily pocket the 1 ball in the corner pocket. If you use pocket speed, the 1 will dribble into the pocket, and the cue ball will gently roll off the side rail.

Figure 12-5:
This is one instance where you need to hit the cue ball firmly to give yourself position on the next shot.

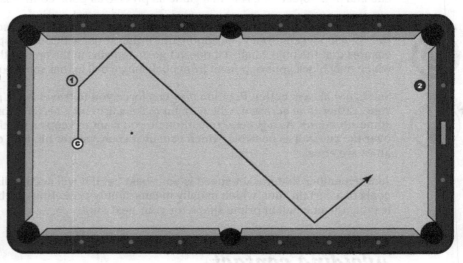

But what if you want to pocket the 2 next? You're going to have to hit the 1 ball a little harder than absolutely necessary to pocket the shot. Here, you have to send the cue ball off at least two rails and clear across the table to get position on the 2 ball.

Playing three balls ahead

In the earlier section "Limiting cue ball movement," I discuss the three-ball drill, where you take ball in hand (putting the cue ball anywhere you'd like on the table). Keeping the cue ball moving as little as possible is also a basis for formulating a strategy to make multiple shots in a row.

Every professional player can look at a table layout and state her next three shots, if not every shot needed to win the game. This process, known as *thinking three balls ahead,* constantly keeps you planning for the future.

Unlike the three-ball drill, this strategy keeps you constantly evaluating the table. After every single shot, you should revisit the table's layout and make sure that you know how you're going to make the next three balls. (And because things rarely work out as planned, this three-ball route can always be adjusted if you don't execute perfectly.)

Figure 12-6 is a normal layout in 9-ball. Because, in 9-ball, you're always aiming at the lowest numbered ball on the table, you need to make sure that you have a way of putting the cue ball in a position where you can shoot at the next ball.

Figure 12-6: In a game of 9-ball, you go from the 1 to the 2 and so on, which means you're depending on luck if you don't plan for the future.

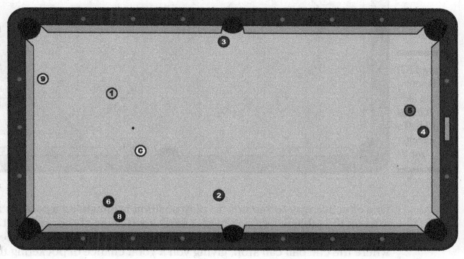

Now you have a shot on the 1 ball, with natural position on the 2. If you make the 1 ball with a simple stun shot, the cue ball will drift into the middle of the table, giving you an angle on the 2 ball.

And because you're looking three balls ahead, you know that you can get position on the 3 ball by making a stop shot on the 2.

You are *always* thinking three balls ahead, so when you make the 1 ball, you need to plan for position on the 4. When you make the 2, you need to plan for position on the 5. Always know the optimal spot for the cue ball.

Positioning your cue ball

Keeping your cue ball in proper position is one part planning and one part execution. First, see where your cue ball needs to be and how it can get there. Then, take care of business and put it there.

In Figure 12-7, you're making the 1 ball in the corner, while the cue ball needs to go across the table for position on the 2.

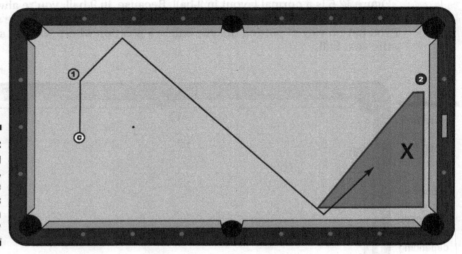

Figure 12-7: Shooting the one ball, can you see the 2 ball's position zone?

One effective way to see how to play position is imagining a *position zone* — an area on the table where you have a fairly good angle at the next shot. In Figure 12-7, the position zone is a triangle behind the 2 ball. This zone is the area where the cue ball can stop, giving you a good chance of pocketing the 2.

While it's good to know the entire area where you can leave the cue ball and have a shot, it's best to think of a precise spot to aim. In Figure 12-7, for example, you might aim for the X, which is in the middle of the position zone.

Aiming at an exact spot forces you to think precisely. If you aim for a general area of the table, you might get mentally lazy, settling for an okay position when you should be aiming for perfect position (while still knowing that it is okay to miss this exact spot if you can keep the cue ball in the position zone).

If you're stuck in a tough spot, the center of the table can act as a safety zone. Begin looking at what possibilities you might have if you send the cue ball to the center of the table because you'll be within a few feet of every ball on the table. While this approach may not solve every problem, it can help as a starting point to find a solution to your position problem.

Playing to a zone, not across it

In the previous section, I talk about limiting cue ball movement as a way of increasing your margin for error. Along the same lines, you should always try to play into a positional zone, instead of across it.

Look at Figure 12-8. You're playing 9-ball, and you're lining up your shot on the 8, just two balls from victory.

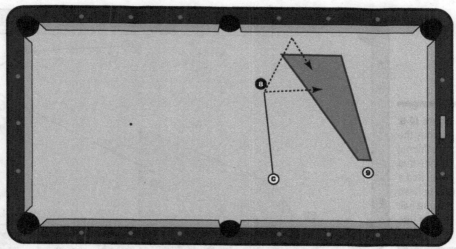

Figure 12-8: Make your position play a little easier by playing *to* a positional zone.

You have a slight angle on the 8 ball for the side pocket. With the 9 sitting by the corner pocket, you have some options on how to get onto the game winner.

First, you could hit a stun shot, where the cue ball deflects at a right angle from the direction of the 8 ball. The cue ball will drift to the right, ideally stopping in perfect line with the 9 ball and the corner pocket.

This option, though, requires a fine touch to leave the cue ball in the position zone. You're sending the cue ball toward the skinny part of the shaded area, meaning you have little room for error should you send the cue ball too long or leave it short.

Look instead at driving the cue ball to the long rail so that it rebounds in line with the 9 ball. Going to the rail changes the angle of the cue ball. Instead of traveling perpendicular to the line from the 9 ball to the side pocket, as you would with a stun shot, the cue ball is coming in at an angle that is nearly in line with the 9 ball to the corner pocket. This angle gives you a bigger cushion should you go too long or leave the cue ball a bit shorter than originally planned.

Being able to identify a feasible way for you to send the cue ball into a positional zone instead of across it will develop with practice. In Figure 12-9, you have to travel to the other corner of the table, but it's not as complicated as you may think. You will roll into the short rail at the right after pocketing the 5 ball, letting the cue ball drift into position for the 8 ball.

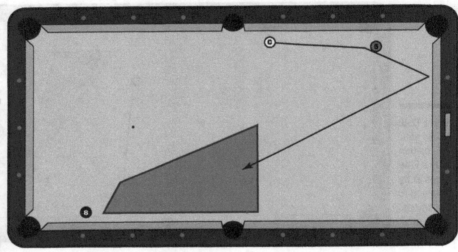

Figure 12-9: Identify the positional zone and then find a way to have the cue ball ease into the space.

Seeing these angles will come with practice, if you're able to identify the positional zone.

Limiting cue ball movement and playing into a positional zone require a balance. Oftentimes, you may be able to improve your angle toward a zone, but it requires sending the cue ball off additional rails. With a little experience, you'll begin to get a grasp of when to limit cue ball movement instead of improving your angle to a position zone and vice versa.

Getting on the right side of a ball

Going from ball to ball is rarely as easy as getting any angle on the ball you want to pocket. Instead, you usually need to get on a specific side of a ball, which allows you to get an angle on the next ball.

Getting on one side of an object ball often creates a natural angle to the next ball. Look at Figure 12-10, where you're on the 5 ball in a game of 9-ball. Notice that after making the relatively simple shot on the 5, you need to get into position to go from the 6 ball in the side pocket to the 7 ball on the other end of the table.

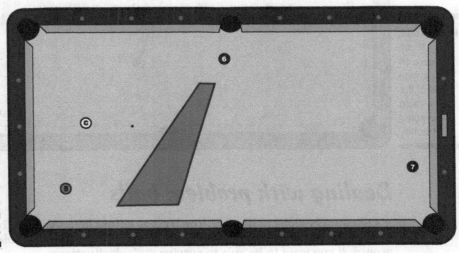

Because the 6 is right by the side pocket, you should be able to make it from almost anywhere on the table. But you need to do more than just make the 6: You need to get down by the 7. Knowing the specific path toward position for the 7, you now need to get on the proper side of the 6 ball.

In this case, you want to leave the cue ball on the left side of the 6 ball, preferably somewhere in the shaded area in Figure 12-10. Being here, the cue ball naturally rolls into position for the 7 ball.

Now, if you fail to get on the left side of the 6 ball, you'll have a much more difficult time getting across the table. Figure 12-11 shows one situation where you pocketed the 5 ball, but the cue ball is on the wrong side of the 6 (to the right).

The cue ball is headed toward the wrong side of the table, so now your position play is much more difficult because the cue ball will be traveling a longer distance off more rails.

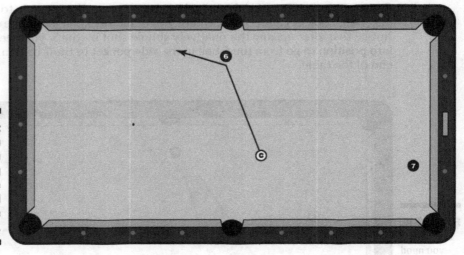

Figure 12-11:
If you were on the wrong side of the ball, you'd be in some trouble.

Dealing with problem balls

It's not always going to be easy. You'll come across layouts where balls are clustered together. You'll need to plan to break up these troublesome groups, if you want to be able to survive difficult situations.

When you first come to the table, you need to identify problems immediately. Whether one ball only goes into one pocket or two balls block each other from a pocket, you must address these problems immediately, if only by formulating a solution for later on.

In Figure 12-12, you're solids in a game of 8-ball. As you can see, the 3 and 4 balls are clumped together along the short rail. This two-ball cluster is a simple example of problem balls, but it will keep you from winning the game unless you deal with the problem.

With the angle you have on the 6 ball, you're in a perfect situation to break out the 3 and 4 balls. By pocketing the 6 ball in the corner, you can send the cue ball toward the 3-4 cluster.

Try to send your cue ball into clusters when you have an *insurance ball* — the 1 ball in Figure 12-12. Having insurance usually means you'll have another ball sitting by a pocket, so you'll be hard-pressed not to have an angle at it. Sending the cue ball into a cluster is rather unpredictable, so you want to be sure that you have a backup plan should your attempt to break up a cluster not work out ideally.

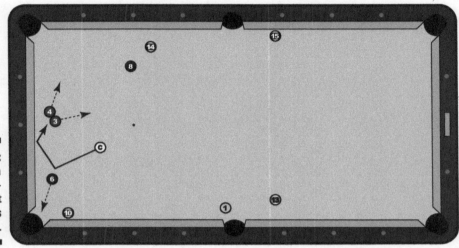

Figure 12-12:
Here's a
simple situ-
ation that
needs
attention.

Chapter 13

Shot-making: Tackling the Most Frequent Situations

In This Chapter

▶ Getting a grasp on some basic guidelines for pocketing balls

▶ Looking at a spectrum of angles, from straight-on to the thinnest of cuts

▶ Understanding the possibilities (and limitations) with a ball hanging in the pocket

▶ Demystifying shots on a ball against a rail

*I*t sounds pretty obvious, really, when you hear a player described as being a "great shot-maker." The ultimate goal in pool is to put the balls in the pockets, right? So it's only natural that a good player is also a good shot-maker.

But in reality, there's something to be said of the skill. I'm guessing by now you've realized that pool is much more complex than simply making shots. To that end, some players are exceptional at playing position, others are defensive masterminds, and some are deadly shot-makers — those gun-slinger-types who can drill the most difficult shots from tough angles (often making it look easy).

Beyond the simplest straight-in shots, there are an infinite variety of angles and distances and situations that will pop up in pool. Because of these variables, being a good shot-maker means you're going to have to familiarize yourself with the shots you're bound to encounter during a game of 8-ball, 9-ball, or whatever.

In this chapter, I cover some basic tenets to developing your shot-making, along with descriptions of the most common shots. The guidelines in this chapter should lead to you pocketing more balls.

Enough Speed's Enough

In Chapter 12, I talk about the need to limit your speed when it comes to play-ing position for your next shot. It turns out that limiting the power of a par-ticular shot also increases the odds you'll make the ball.

The first thing that speed kills is your stroke. You want to remain in total con-trol of your cue as you smoothly accelerate into the cue ball. When you go full throttle into a shot, you're going to sacrifice accuracy for power.

But power also causes problems for the object ball on its way to the pocket. With more speed, the ball is more likely to get stuck up in the pocket. The *jaws* of the pocket — where the rail angles in toward the pocket — can be unforgiving of balls that come screaming toward them.

Imagine that you're faced with the shot in Figure 13-1. You're shooting the 8 ball to win the game, so you don't have to be too worried about position. Now, if you go ahead and try to demolish the 8 ball by hitting this shot as hard as possible, you're running the risk of it getting caught up in the pocket.

Figure 13-1:
The harder you hit this shot, the better the chance you rattle it in the jaws of the pocket.

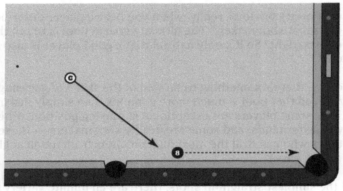

Hit this nice and easy, though, and you have a larger margin for error. If the 8 ball catches any point on the inside of the pocket, it will most likely go in. So, when it comes down to it, play pocket speed — or the slowest speed that still allows you to play position, if need be.

It's not unusual to see a table with pockets that are misshaped so that the pocket jaws appear opened up to the table. When you're playing at an unfamil-iar table, be sure to check the pockets.

Open pockets can cause major problems for balls hit down the rail, like the shot in Figure 13-1. Looking at the pocket on the right in Figure 13-2, you can see how the angle of the jaws will naturally lead to balls bouncing in and out of the pocket.

Figure 13-2:
Always
check the
angle of the
pocket jaws.

Keep Your Shot Process Simple

It should be slightly encouraging, in a backward sort of way, to know that the best players in the world have repeatedly made the same mistakes you make from time to time. You missed a straight-in shot that was begging to go in? So has every single person who's ever picked up a cue.

But before you accept your fate as an imperfect pool player, know that the best way to avoid errors is to simplify the process of making a shot. With all the little things that go into pocketing a ball, you don't need to incorporate more than is necessary.

When you don't have to use English, don't. When you can just as easily send the cue ball off one rail for position instead of two, err for the simpler solution.

In Chapter 12, I talk about a rule of position play that says you should play *to* a position zone instead of *across* it. Often, playing into a position zone means taking a longer route to your next shot. While it's a good guideline to limit cue-ball movement, know that it's not an unbreakable rule. As you gain experience with the cue ball's movements, always ask yourself whether there's an easier way to get on the next ball.

Looking at a Spectrum of Angles

Every once in awhile, the cue ball will come to a rest in perfect line with the next object ball and the pocket. This type of shot is a *straight-in shot,* a shot with no angle, a shot that is on a single plane from the cue ball through the object ball to the pocket.

The large majority of the time, however, you'll be faced with a *cut* — meaning you have to hit the object ball at an angle to the right or the left so that it will go into the pocket. Cut shots can range from just a millimeter off of straight-in to the extreme of hitting the object ball at a right angle. *Thin cuts* — shots where you're going to have to send the object ball in a direction close to 90 degrees to the right or left from the direction of the cue ball — can be among the most intimidating shots for beginners.

Getting used to cuts

Chapter 4 discusses how you aim any shot at any angle using the Ghost Ball System. But simply knowing how to shoot these types of shots is one thing. Executing them is another.

To become familiar with shot-making means bridging the gap between knowledge and execution. So the following sections give you ways to develop a feel for certain shots.

Making the spot shot

To begin your exploration of the nearly infinite varieties of cut shots, start with a setup nearly halfway between straight-in and super thin: the *spot shot*.

Technically, the spot shot refers to a ball on the footspot where you have ball in hand behind the headstring. But for this conversation, I want to simplify the process of making this shot. Forcing you to stay behind the headstring only increases the difficulty of pocketing this shot, without giving you a way to focus on the feel of aiming.

Put the cue ball anywhere in the gray area in Figure 13-3. You're still faced with a healthy cut, while the cue ball is only a diamond or two away, instead of four. First, aim to pocket the object ball by cutting it to the right. Don't worry about scratching at first. You want to focus totally on where the object ball goes (for now, at least).

To make this shot, follow the normal routine of lining up a shot. Find where the ghost ball (the dotted-line ball in Figure 13-4) must be in order to pocket the object ball and then replace the ghost ball with the cue ball (see Chapter 4).

With pocket speed (just enough to get the object ball to and in the pocket), attempt this shot ten times. Take a break for a few minutes and try it another ten times. With a bit of practice, you should be on your way to gaining at least a sense of the angle this shot requires.

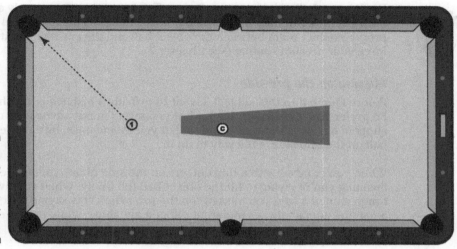

Figure 13-3:
The spot shot can be a reference point for cut shots.

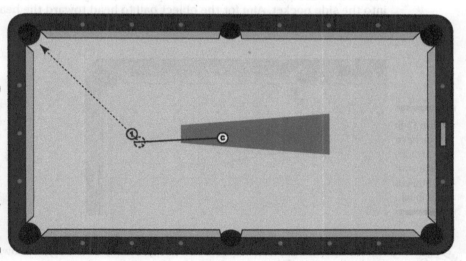

Figure 13-4:
Put the cue ball where the dotted-line ball is, and you should be on your way to making this shot.

To ensure that you can place the balls in exactly the same positions, use tiny marks of chalk on the cloth as place holders. If you're exceptionally handy, you can also use paper reinforcements (little rings that are sticky on one side), which you can stick directly on the table.

As you become more familiar with this shot, take note of where the object ball is headed on each attempt. If you're overcutting the ball, you know you have to hit it farther to the left. If you're undercutting it, you need to hit it farther to the right.

Don't just mindlessly repeat each shot. Take your time to properly aim with each attempt. Not only will consistent focus help you develop a feel for the proper contact point between the object ball and the cue ball, but it will reinforce your preshot routine (see Chapter 2).

Missing on the pro side

Before I jump into this subject, I want to provide a disclaimer for this section: I'd prefer you make every single shot you take. I'm not advocating missed shots in any way. But that being said, if you *should* miss, hitting the object ball on the thin side is the way to do it.

When you're faced with a thin cut, err on the side of *overcutting* the ball — meaning you're trying to hit the object ball too thinly. When you overcut a tough shot, it's said you missed "on the pro side." This saying is because amateurs almost always undercut difficult cut shots, while pros aren't afraid to live on the thin side of a cut shot.

Take a look at Figure 13-5. The shot requires a pretty thin cut on the 4 ball into the side pocket. Aim for the object ball to head toward the nearer point of the pocket so that you're erring on the pro side.

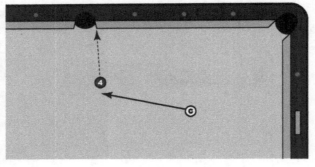

Figure 13-5:
If you have to miss, make sure that you cut it enough.

Throw is when the cue ball throws the object ball a few degrees toward the cue ball's original direction due to friction at the moment of impact. Aiming on the pro side is one way to negate this effect because you're consciously trying to overcut the ball, which will compensate for the small effect of throw.

After impact: Feeling angles and distances

Cue-ball control is a pretty important part of the game, which is why I dedicate all of Part II to this subject. So if you're going to get used to cutting balls at any and every point from 0 to 90 degrees, you have to learn how to control the cue ball after impact.

To pocket the object ball, you've got a specific angle in mind — the one that sends the ball straight into the pocket. But what does this angle do to the cue ball? To play effective pool, you need to know how shots at different speeds and angles will change the path of the cue ball.

If you hit an object ball as fully as possible, nearly all the cue ball's energy will be transferred to the object ball. The white ball will drop dead at the moment of impact, while the colored ball goes racing around the table at nearly the same speed of the cue ball in the millisecond before impact.

Follow (topspin) and draw (backspin) will change how balls react after impact (see Chapters 8 and 9). Initially, I am speaking about shots involving stun, where the cue ball hits the object ball with no spin. A stun shot is the simplest example of the transfer of speed between the cue ball and the object ball following a collision. And, as you might guess, the transfer of speed is directly related to the angle of the cut.

Two rather extreme examples can go a long way toward helping you visualize the transfer of speed (or energy) from the cue ball to the object ball. The shot shown in the top of Figure 13-6 is a relatively straight shot on the 6 ball. If you would hit this shot with a stun shot (where the cue ball has no spin at impact) at pocket speed, the cue ball would stumble only a few inches to the right before coming to a stop. Most of the cue ball's energy was transferred to the 6 at impact, so the 6 travels much farther — almost five diamonds farther — than the cue ball.

Conversely, when you thinly cut a ball into a pocket, you're transferring much less speed because the angle dictates the cue ball contact the object ball near the outer edge, transferring less speed to the object ball. In this case, in the bottom of Figure 13-6, assuming that you hit the 7 with a stun shot, the 7 would travel just a diamond or so, while the cue ball's path would be much longer.

When you're dealing with a naturally rolling cue ball at the point of impact, the object ball and the cue ball will travel roughly the same distance for a half-ball hit (when the center of the cue ball is lined up with the outer edge of the object ball at impact). As a result, both balls will deflect at an angle around 30 degrees at the same speed.

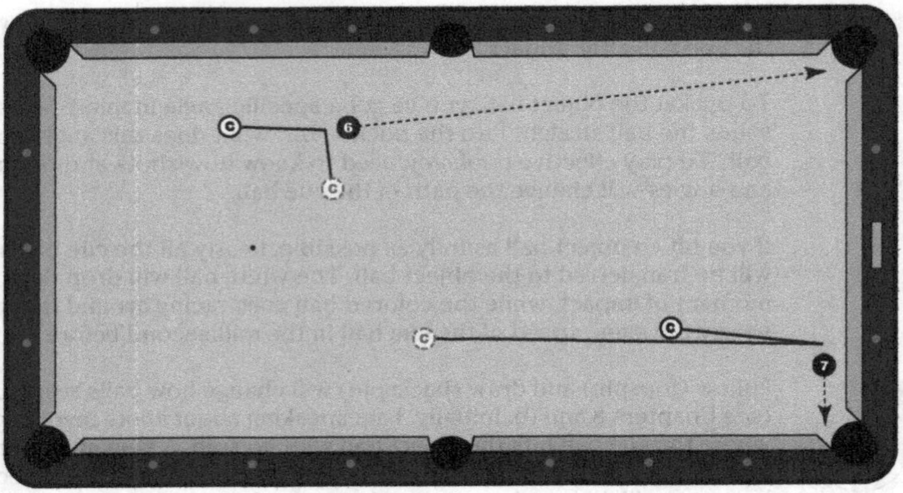

Figure 13-6:
See how the
distances
traveled by
the cue ball
are quite
different?

Dealing with Hangers

A *hanger* is exactly what it sounds like — a ball just sitting in a pocket, barely hanging on, just waiting for you to tip it over the edge. And while such a shot won't be keeping you up at night with its overwhelming difficulty, a hanger is often more complicated than just tapping it into the pocket.

One reason hangers can be the downfall of your run to victory (and accompanying glory, of course) is a lack of planning. After all, a hanger is going to go in the pocket, barring some drastic error, so it's just a matter of hitting the ball, right?

Wrong. Chapter 12 goes into massive detail about the importance of playing for your *next* shot. This requirement doesn't stop just because you have an easy shot on a ball hanging in a pocket (unless of course, it's to win a game, but even then you should be taking the necessary precautions to avoid scratching).

As an example, you're on the 8 ball in a game of 9-ball in Figure 13-7. You won't have much difficulty pocketing the 8, but what's your plan for the 9? You have to go across the table to pocket the game winner, so you better have a plan that will give you an angle on the 9 without scratching into a corner pocket.

If you cut the 8 ball to the right, the cue ball will deflect to the left. If you hit the cue ball at the correct angle, the cue ball will bounce off three rails on its way into position for the 9 in the upper-left corner. Getting the right angle, though, is extremely important. If you're off by just a quarter inch, the cue ball can head in a very different direction.

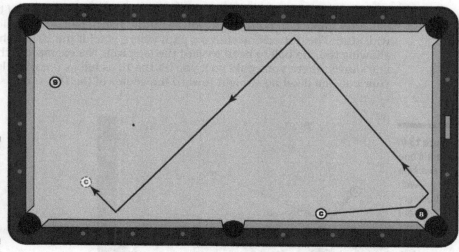

Figure 13-7:
Plan for the cue ball's long route across the table.

You can play the shot in Figure 13-7 in a number of ways, but some options can be very difficult. You can draw the cue ball straight back off of the 8, but losing control of the speed is easy to do. You can also thinly cut the 8 ball so that the cue ball touches only the head rail, but again, any error in the contact point on the 8 may lead to an awkward angle on the 9.

In this case, you may find this shot easier if you use a bit of left English (running English) on the cue ball. (Chapter 10 talks about English.) English isn't necessary to get position on the 9, but it just may make it easier for you. If you can make the 8 ball and get shape on the 9 with a center-ball hit, experiment with a little bit of left English.

Cheating the pocket

With a ball hanging in a pocket, you have a large margin of error. Hit almost any point on the edge of the object ball that's farthest from the pocket, and you're going to make the shot.

The object ball being so close to the pocket not only makes the shot easier, it also opens up more options for you to play position. After all, hitting an object ball thinly will send the cue ball in a different direction than if you were to hit it on the thick side.

Taking advantage of this situation is called *cheating the pocket*. Normal pockets are at least two-balls wide. Because of this width, you're able to aim to make the ball on one side of the pocket or the other, which will change the path of the cue ball after impact. This flexibility lets you create a number of different paths for the cue ball on the same shot.

In Figure 13-8, you can see how you can greatly change the path of the cue ball after impact. In both shots, you're hitting the 10 ball into the side pocket with stun. The dotted line shows a path where you hit the 10 ball thinly, allowing the cue ball to head toward the long rail. The example with the black line shows where you could go if you hit the 10 as full as possible, leaving your cue ball heading straight toward the center of the short rail.

Figure 13-8:
Here's one example with two very different routes off the same shot.

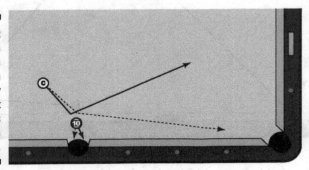

You may have only one option when you're playing a hanger, but you should at least know to look to cheat the pocket. It'll make position play easier.

Rail-first possibilities

Another option that can open possibilities for position is hitting the cue ball off of the rail *before* contacting the object ball. This little trick is especially useful when you're nearly straight in on the object ball, which normally limits the options you have for position.

Look at Figure 13-9. You've got to get on the 8 ball with the 11 ball tucked in the corner. This shot is pretty hard to miss, although it's certainly possible, if you get careless. If you can bounce the cue ball off the rail and then into the 11, you will have a much better angle to get position on the 8 ball.

To aim shots like the one shown in Figure 13-9, use the Ghost Ball System, just as you would for any normal shot. Picture where the ghost ball must be to pocket the 11 ball. Knowing that you have to go off the rail first, find the point on the rail where you can hit the cue ball to send it toward the ghost ball.

You can see in Figure 13-10 that the cue ball must contact the rail just to the left of the first diamond from the corner pocket. If you can send the cue ball off the rail at the point shown by the white arrow, you'll pocket the 11 ball.

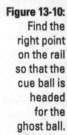

Figure 13-9:
Go rail first
on the 11
for perfect
position on
the 8 in
the side.

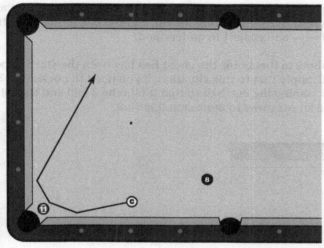

Figure 13-10:
Find the
right point
on the rail
so that the
cue ball is
headed
for the
ghost ball.

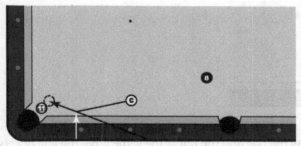

The farther the object ball is from the rail, the harder it is to go rail first. Ideally, you'd like to limit these shots to cases where the object ball is just a few inches from the pocket and the rail. Otherwise, you risk missing the shot, so whatever position you may get will be useless.

Making a Shot Along the Rail

When an object ball is frozen to the rail — meaning it's resting against the lip of the rail — some players, even some rather experienced shooters, get a little nervous.

The situation may seem daunting, but the phobia of shots along the rail may just be a result of confusion. You can approach the same shot in a couple of ways. Where should you aim? To hit the rail first? The ball first? Somewhere in between?

While there is no consensus among professionals and instructors as to what approach is best, I believe hitting the rail and the ball at the same time is the most effective — and easiest to understand.

For all the shots in this book, the ghost ball has been the starting point for aiming. Well, apply that to this situation. If you need to pocket the 3 ball in Figure 13-11, aiming the cue ball so that it hits the 3 ball and the rail at the same time is an easy way to approach this shot.

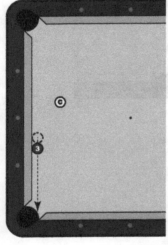

Figure 13-11: The ghost ball is touching both the 3 ball and the rail.

If the cue ball hits the ball and the rail at the same time, the line of centers will aim directly toward the pocket. For many shots, aiming the cue ball to hit the rail and ball will work. But because of *throw* — friction between the cue ball and object ball — the ball-and-rail method isn't ideal. In some cases, the cue ball will throw the object ball into the rail, and it will then bounce away from the pocket.

Ideally, you want the cue ball to hit the rail just before it hits the object ball. The cue ball will push into the rail while still moving toward the object ball. If you hit the rail at just the right spot, you'll send the object ball directly along the rail and into the pocket.

I've told you time and time again to slow down; don't kill the cue ball. Well, again, here's another situation where you want to hit this shot as soft as possible. A firmly struck object ball may rattle in the jaws of the pocket, while one with pocket speed may just find its way into the hole.

While I may recommend hitting the ball and rail simultaneously, you can pocket this shot in various ways. If you couldn't, I might question why people claim rail-first or ball-first is the best method for this situation.

But both are viable options, so they're both worth a look. That being said, hitting either the ball or the rail before the other is a tiny adjustment from simultaneous ball-rail contact. You still want to aim the shot in the same way — these approaches are just slight alterations.

Both of the following options are just a tad more advanced than hitting the rail and the ball simultaneously. If you're not able to pocket this shot regularly, incorporating ball-first and rail-first methods will just complicate matters.

- **Ball first:** Hitting the ball first will leave you with similar results to the ball-and-rail approach. In this scenario, shown by the dotted line in Figure 13-12, a rolling cue ball will push the object ball toward the pocket before hitting the rail. Hitting the object ball first will slightly change the cue ball's rebound angle off the short rail, but only by a few degrees.

- **Rail first:** This option is the more extreme of the two alternatives to the original solution. When you hit the rail first with stun (no spin), the cue ball will deflect off the object ball at a 90-degree angle, right along the tangent line. Because the cue ball is heading toward the middle of the table directly after contact with the object ball, it will travel at a right angle from the direction of the 3 ball. (You can also hit this shot against the rail with follow, which would cause the cue ball to travel along a line similar to the earlier ball-first example.)

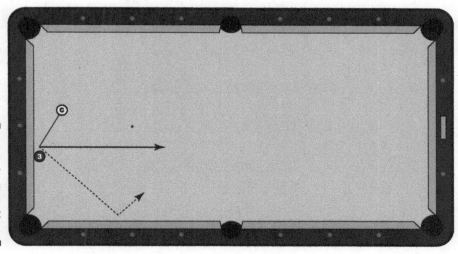

Figure 13-12:
Here are two other options with a ball against the rail.

Chapter 14

Eying Combinations: Making Shots with Multiple Balls

In This Chapter

▶ Figuring out why combinations are often very difficult

▶ Avoiding impossible combinations

▶ Discovering how to aim basic combination shots

Combinations look so cool, don't they? The cue ball setting two or more object balls in motion, leading to one falling into a pocket. It's almost like magic when you set in motion a chain reaction that involves multiple object balls.

But while combination shots may be the siren song of the beginner, they're usually very difficult, if not spilling over into the territory of impossible. However, some combinations are very useful.

After all, in a game like 9-ball, a combination can directly result in victory, if you can find a way to knock the 9 ball with a legal hit. With combinations, though, discretion is the better part of valor.

In this chapter, I explain why these shots may look rather simple, but prove to be pretty darn difficult. I also outline some makable shots that you can use in a variety of games.

Understanding the Difficulties

A *combination*, as the name suggests, involves an object ball being struck by the cue ball before hitting another object ball into a pocket. If you had never read this book, I still think you'd learn that combinations are much more difficult than you originally thought. But you are reading this book, so the following sections show you *why* these shots are so tricky.

Removing your wiggle room

Say you find yourself in the situation shown in Figure 14-1. You're stripes in a game of 8-ball. Both your balls are lined up with the corner pocket, so how are you going to solve this problem?

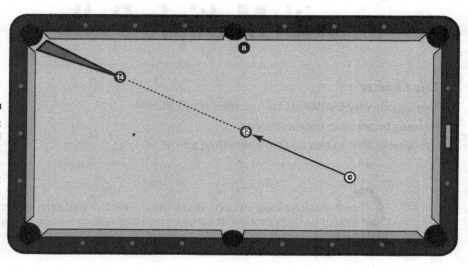

If you try to hit the 12 into the 14 into the corner pocket, you're dead wrong. With all three balls in a perfect line, it may seem like a simple shot, but you have very little chance of pulling off this combination.

The primary reason why combinations have an increased level of difficulty is that your margin for error is greatly reduced. In a normal shot, as long as you send the object ball into the pocket, it's usually considered a success. With a combination, you need to send the first object ball to a very small contact point on the second object ball that will send the second ball into the pocket.

Most pockets are around 4.5 or 5 inches wide. That's a much bigger area than an exact spot on the second ball in which to aim the first ball.

For another example, take a look at the shot in Figure 14-2. It's a straight-in shot on the 1. You have a little wiggle room with this shot, shown by the gray area. You can hit it a bit to the left or right of center and still make it without worry.

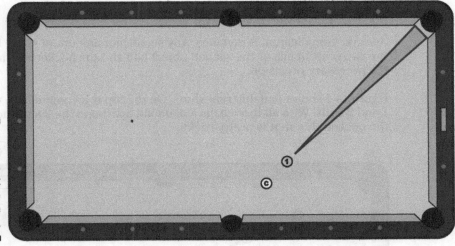

Figure 14-2:
The 1 ball
will go in
if it's sent
anywhere
within the
gray area.

Now look at Figure 14-3, which has the 2 ball added to make it a combination. Look at how the gray area — where the 1 ball can go and still result in a made shot — has shrunk to an even smaller sliver than in Figure 14-2. Basically, if you attempt this combination, you're doing so with absolutely no room for error.

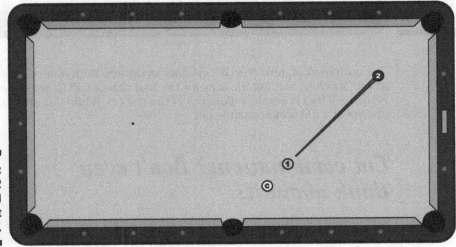

Figure 14-3:
Add the 2
ball, and
things get
sticky.

Distance dooms

Another complication is distance. Any significant amount of space between the two object balls or the second object ball and the pocket will maximize the necessary precision.

Figure 14-4 shows two different shots. On the top is a combination with the 1 and 2 balls. With all three balls a diamond apart and the 2 a diamond from the pocket, this shot is pretty tricky.

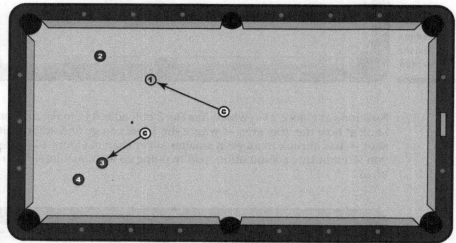

Figure 14-4:
See how distance complicates things?

The bottom shot, however, is certainly an option. Both object balls are close to one another, limiting the area for the first object ball to get out of line. Also, the 4 ball is within a diamond of the pocket. While this shot isn't a no-brainer, it's not an impossible bet.

Cut combinations? Don't even think about it!

In the earlier sections of this chapter, I cover only shots where the balls are close to being in a perfect line with the pocket because of the difficulty associated with cutting a ball along a specific line. As a general rule, you want to avoid combination shots that involve some sort of cut, either the cue ball cutting the first object ball or the first object ball cutting the second.

In Figure 14-5, cutting the 6 ball into the 5 into the corner pocket is simply too much. Because both balls have to be cut at rather exact angles, you'll be lucky to get the 5 ball anywhere near the pocket.

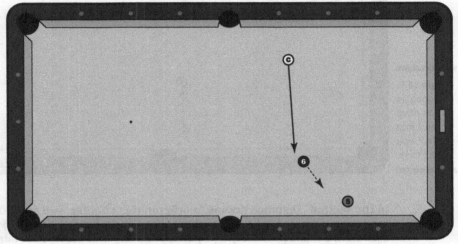

Figure 14-5:
You'll be well off avoiding cutting balls like this one.

Finding Makable Combinations

While combination shots require an exponentially increased level of accuracy, you should be able to identify some makable shots.

Only when you can see the difference between the plausible and impossible will you be ready to make the most of combinations.

Hangers

A ball that is hanging in a pocket is easier to make than one in the middle of the table, right? A shorter distance between the ball to be made and the pocket also helps when it comes to combinations because the second ball has a larger area where it can be struck and still fall in the pocket.

Figure 14-6 shows the 2 ball hanging in the side pocket. With the ball so close to falling in the pocket, you'd be hard-pressed to hit the 2 ball and *not* pocket it.

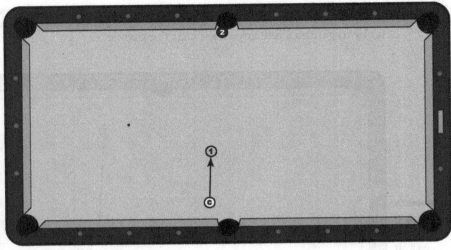

Figure 14-6:
As long as
you drive
the 1 into
the 2, you
can't miss.

In the section "Distance dooms," earlier in this chapter, you saw how distance can kill potential combinations shots. Well, here you have the opposite situation; a ball's proximity to a pocket actually makes the shot fairly simple. As long as you hit the second object ball in the general direction of the pocket, you should successfully pocket the ball.

Also, the distance between the first object ball and the hanging second object ball is of little concern, as long as you can hit the first ball so that it makes contact with the second.

If a second object ball is hanging in the pocket, you may be able to hit it anywhere, but you should aim for an exact spot. Aiming for a precise spot will keep you in focus, and you'll be less likely to get lazy with any part of the shot.

Regardless of what game you're playing, you need to be mindful of *insurance balls.* When a ball is hanging in a pocket, you can easily make the shot from nearly anywhere on the table. Because you can make the ball without a problem, you shouldn't pocket it right away, instead holding onto your insurance ball for when you find yourself in trouble. Remember that you can pocket an insurance ball with a combination if need be. The ball in the pocket can also prevent your opponent from hitting her ball in that pocket, unless she uses one of her balls to knock your ball in. Either way, you're at a tactical advantage with a ball sitting in the jaws of a pocket.

Dead combinations

A ball closer to the pocket is more likely to go in. Similarly, you're more likely to be successful with a combination where both object balls are in close proximity to one another.

If distance is the enemy, two balls within an inch or two of each other should be considered friendly. For example, Figure 14-7 shows the 3 and 4 balls within one ball's width of one another. And, lucky for you, they're lined up perfectly with the corner pocket.

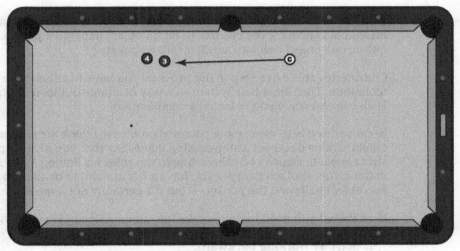

Figure 14-7: Because the 3 ball hardly has time to veer off course, this combination shot is worth considering.

When two balls are touching one another while lined up with a pocket, they are considered *dead* — meaning the ball closest to the pocket is all but dead because it *has* to go in. Look for these situations; they'll make your life much easier if you're lucky enough to come across them.

The example in Figure 14-7, meanwhile, is almost dead. Believe me, you can misplay this shot, but the balls are lined up in a way where it's not as difficult as other combinations.

Aiming for Multiple Balls

Combinations are a little different than a regular cue-ball-into-object-ball-into-pocket shot. With the addition of another object ball, you're dealing with a more complex equation. But don't stress. You can compartmentalize aiming combinations so that you aren't facing information overload when you're about to stroke a shot.

Finding the contact points

When you line up any shot in pool, you should have a very definite line on which you want the object ball to travel. For simple one-ball shots, this line means hitting the object ball so that it takes off in a direction for a pocket.

Well, combinations are just one step removed from a one-object ball shot. Instead of aiming for the cue ball to hit an object ball into a pocket, you're hitting one object ball into another into a pocket.

Considering this extra step in the process, you have to adjust your aiming technique. The Ghost Ball System — a way of aiming outlined in Chapter 4 — is also useful when you're facing a combination.

Because more balls mean more potential problems, I think the process of aiming combinations deserves a step-by-step guide. Say that you need to pocket the shot shown in Figure 14-8. According to the rules for finding makable combinations, this shot isn't easy— you have a fair amount of distance between the two object balls and the pocket — but it's certainly not impossible.

Here's what you need to do to make the combination in Figure 14-8:

1. **Start by working backward.**

   Your final goal is to pocket the 5 ball. Draw a line from the center of the pocket through the center of the 5. According to the Ghost Ball System (see Chapter 4), if the center of the 4 ball is on this line at the moment of impact (shown by the dotted-line ball in Figure 14-9), the 5 ball should go straight into the corner pocket.

2. **After you figure out where the 4 ball must hit the 5, aim just like it's any other shot.**

   You need to hit the 4 ball so that it travels along the dotted line. Again using the Ghost Ball System, shown in Figure 14-10, you now know where you have to send the cue ball. The center of the cue ball and the center of the 4 ball should form a line pointing directly to the ghost ball that will pocket the 5 ball.

3. **Hit the cue ball so that it will replace the dotted-line ball shown in Figure 14-11.**

   If you can accurately strike the cue ball, you should have this problem solved!

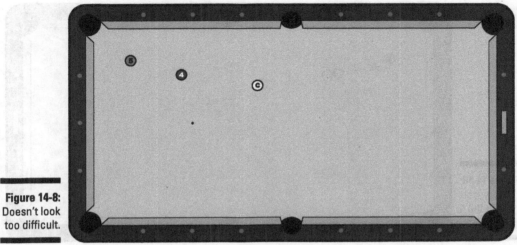

Figure 14-8:
Doesn't look
too difficult.

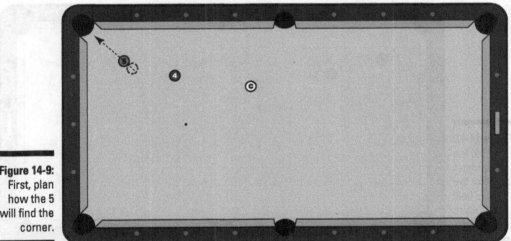

Figure 14-9:
First, plan
how the 5
will find the
corner.

As you can see in Figure 14-12, this combo shot has a lot going on. Adding up all three parts to aiming and executing this shot, you can see how easily things can go wrong with a combination. But, knowing when and how to approach combinations is a great start.

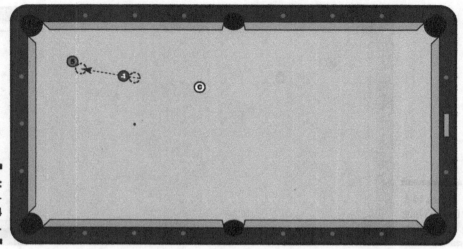

Figure 14-10:
Now, calculate the 4 ball's line.

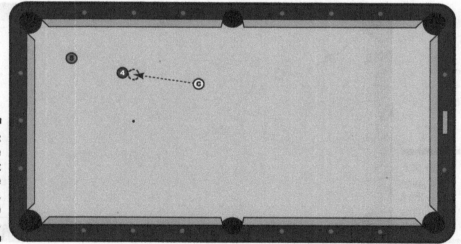

Figure 14-11:
Find the contact point for the cue ball, and you're ready to go.

If you really want to become more comfortable with combinations, you're going to have to practice. The following drill helps you get a feel for all kinds of combinations:

1. **Spread all 15 balls out on the table, making sure that no balls are bunching up into clusters.**

2. **With ball in hand, attempt any two-ball combination.**

    It's in your best interest to try the easiest one you can find.

3. **Regardless if you make or miss the shot, take ball in hand and continue working your way through the rack.**

   As the balls become fewer, you'll quickly see an increase in difficulty.

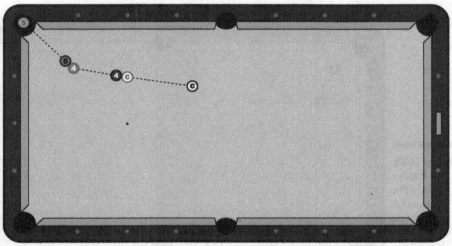

Figure 14-12:
Putting all
the pieces
together,
you can
see what
goes into a
successful
combination.

Focusing on one aiming point

While it may take a few steps to figure out where each ball has to go in order to pull off a combination, you simply can't think about every facet of the shot when you get down to attempting it.

I talk about the mental aspect of pool in Chapter 22. One of the keys to keeping your head in line is keeping your thoughts focused on specific things at specific times. When you're standing up and walking around the table, it's time to develop your strategy. In this case, you need to figure out the contact points for the different balls (see the preceding section). You're looking at the whole picture so that you can be confident in your plan.

After you find the aiming point for the cue ball, though, you're ready to narrow your focus. When you get down on your shot, you need to focus on where you have to send the cue ball into the first object ball.

One way to *normalize* combinations — that is, to make them more like your run-of-the-mill shots that deal with just one object ball — is to pretend you're trying to drive the first object ball to a point on the rail.

In the shot shown in Figure 14-13, you need to hit the 7 ball along the dotted line to pocket the 8. By extending this line to the rail, you give yourself a definitive point on the rail to aim the first object ball. Picturing the ghost ball snuggling up with the 8 ball may be a bit tough because it's in the middle of the table and at an angle from where you're aiming to hit the 7.

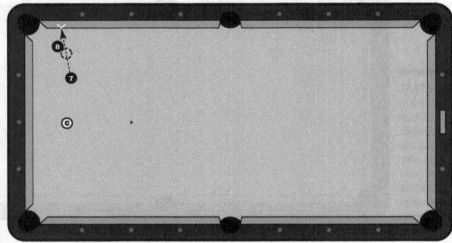

Figure 14-13: Picture where the 7 would hit the rail, if the 8 wasn't in the way.

The point on the rail keeps your focus on the 7 ball. It should also provide some comfort because most shots involve aiming an object ball for a rail or a pocket.

Simplifying the Execution

The first part of this chapter dealt with the difficulties involved in combination shots. So, knowing these are shots not to be taken lightly, you need to reduce the number of variables you introduce into the execution part of a combination.

Never stray from center ball

English (see Chapter 11) ratchets up the complexity of a shot. So, when you're lining up a combination, try to minimize the spin you put on the cue ball. By hitting the center of the cue ball (see Figure 14-14), you're avoiding things like deflection, throw, and other complications that come with English.

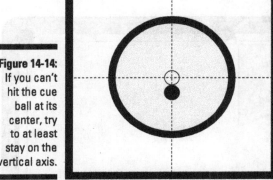

Figure 14-14:
If you can't hit the cue ball at its center, try to at least stay on the vertical axis.

Using draw and follow (see Chapters 9 and 10) — which mean hitting above and below the exact center of the cue ball are not as problematic as right and left English. That being said, try to stay as close to center as you can.

Playing position

Positioning the cue ball for your next shot is usually very important. With most combinations, though, you have to focus almost exclusively on pocketing the intended object ball — to the detriment of your next shot.

When you're playing a combination, you want a general idea where the cue ball will come to a stop, but you're usually going to be restricted from playing for anything more than basic position on your next shot.

When you're faced with a difficult shot, you must make sure that you're going to successfully complete the shot at hand. Looking ahead to the next few balls does you no good when you must execute a tough shot to stay at the table.

Position zones are often rather large areas where you can stop the cue ball and still have an angle on your next shot. (For details, see Chapter 13.) When you're attempting anything but the easiest combinations, you may want to have such a zone in mind.

One instance where you can — and often need to — play position is when you're playing a combination on a hanger. Imagine if you were playing 8-ball, and you had two solids left before the 8 ball (see Figure 14-15). If one ball was hanging in a pocket and you had to play a combination, you'd need to pocket the first object ball in the next shot.

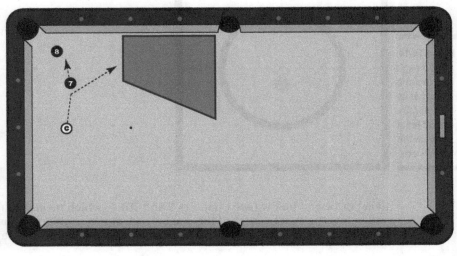

Figure 14-15:
Concentrate on making the 8 ball, with the idea that the cue ball will end up in the shaded region.

When you're experimenting with combinations involving hangers, try to see how the first object reacts when you hit both sides of the second object ball. In Figures 14-16 and 14-17, you can see how a slight tweak in how you hit the 1 ball will result in two very different paths for the 1 ball (should you hit it with a little too much speed).

If you want to control the first object ball in a combination, you must limit the speed of the shot. I've said it over and over again, but it's absolutely vital that you hit combinations with as little power as necessary to pocket the second ball. This will limit the speed of the first object ball after impact with the second object ball.

Also, you'll keep the first object ball under control if you aim to hit the second ball as fully as possible. For example, if you hit the 1 so that it hit the 5 fully, it would simply roll a few inches toward the pocket, instead of moving from side to side.

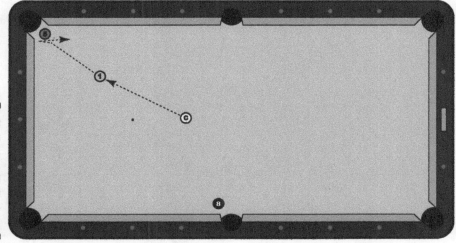

Figures 14-16: Hit the 5 on the left side, and the 1 ball will rebound off the short rail.

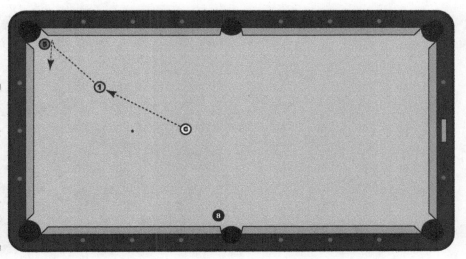

Figure 14-17: Hit the 5 on the right side, and the 1 ball will rebound off the long rail in a very different direction.

Chapter 15

Billiards and Caroms: Finding New Ways to Pocket Balls

In This Chapter

▶ Seeing opportunities to play billiards

▶ Looking for caroms

▶ Understanding when it's not all that risky to play billiards or caroms

▶ Jumping a cue ball over an obstacle

In any sport, a difference exists between what one athlete knows and what that same person can execute. In pool, this disparity can be maddening. You can be one of the most well-read and intelligent players in the whole room, but if you can't make the balls behave as they should, you're in for a frustrating night.

This chapter focuses on billiards, caroms, and jumps — three types of advanced shots. But, in reality, you can incorporate them into your game, if you can see when the opportunities present themselves.

This chapter is an introductory lesson to billiards and caroms — one that will leave you with some tangible information that you can actually use when you're at the table.

Billiard Shots: Using the Cue Ball After Impact

The *billiard* (or billiard shot) is a way to use the cue ball after it hits one object ball to pocket a second. (The name *billiard* is a reference to the game of three-cushion billiards, which involves sending a cue ball off of one ball and three rails before hitting a second ball. For more information on three-cushion, see Chapter 20.)

Understanding how the cue ball behaves after it hits an object ball is a pretty important part of pool. Usually, you use this knowledge to set up your next shot. But with a billiard, the cue ball's path is utilized to pocket another ball (or, in some cases, to play a defensive safe shot).

Throughout this book, I beat the drum about simplifying your game, whether it be in moving the cue ball or in position play. Well, playing a billiard shot certainly complicates the shot, but oftentimes, you don't have a choice. Other times, the reward is well worth the risk.

Run through this list to see whether your billiard is a possibility or whether you're grasping at straws:

- **Think about the distance from the pocket.** The distance between the second ball and the pocket can ratchet up the level of difficulty. Keep your focus on balls that are within 3 or 4 inches of the pocket.

- **Watch the distance between balls.** The distance between the two object balls will make certain shots harder, but you can be successful even if the cue ball has to travel a significant distance between the first and second object balls.

- **Ease up.** Use only the speed necessary to successfully complete the shot. Adding power to a shot when you aren't confident in its outcome is an easy mistake to make. But this tendency can lead to many unnecessary misses. A gently rolling cue ball is much better than one that's rocketing around the table.

- **Be conscious of the first object ball.** When you're planning a billiard, think about where the first object ball will go after you hit it. You don't want it mucking up the cue ball's path to pocketing the second ball.

Knowing when to use a billiard

When the cue ball doesn't behave exactly as it should, you often find yourself in trouble on your next shot. Sometimes, you may not have a clear shot. And sometimes, a billiard shot can do a lot to help you out in a tough spot.

In Figure 15-1, you're playing a game of 9-ball, in which you have to hit the lowest numbered ball on the table first. You don't really have a feasible way of pocketing the 7, so what do you do?

Well, judging by Figure 15-1 and this chapter's title, you may want to consider a billiard. In this example, the 8 ball is hanging in the corner pocket, while the 7 ball is just a few inches away. If you have a working understanding of how your cue ball will bounce off the 7, you can send it into the 8 so that you can stay at the table.

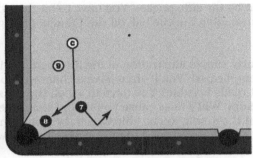

Figure 15-1:
No clear
shot? Not
unless you
see the
billiard.

Hangers — balls sitting right in a pocket — are great targets for billiards. Because they're so close to the pocket, you don't have to be perfect with your contact point.

Another important factor is the distance between the two object balls. Just like combinations (see Chapter 14), the degree of difficulty increases with the distance between the object balls. Also, you don't want to try to pocket balls that are more than a few inches from the pocket. The precision needed to pull off a mid-table billiard is something that can challenge the world's best players.

Another time to go for a billiard shot is when the reward is well worth the risks of complicating the shot. One perfect example of such a situation is in a game of 9-ball. Because you win if you sink the 9, it's imperative that you keep your eyes open for situations like the one shown in Figure 15-2.

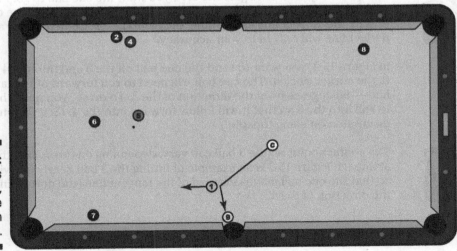

Figure 15-2:
The 9 is
right there,
ready to be
knocked in
the side.

The 9 ball is sitting right by the side pocket. You have to hit the 1 ball first, so what's to stop you from sending the cue ball off the 1 and knocking the 9 into the side for the win?

While Figure 15-2 is a fairly simple illustration of the idea behind billiards, things are often a bit complicated. You'll often have a chance of going for a shot on the 9, but is it really feasible? You have to weigh the risks and rewards of such an attempt. Will a miss cause you to lose the game? If you opt against taking aim at the 9, will you be able to run the remaining balls? This decision is a tough one, but you need to mix aggressive play with what gives you the best chance to win.

After you have an idea of *when* you can try a billiard, you're ready to concentrate on the *how* of billiards.

Finding an aiming line

Billiards, unlike a large majority of normal shots, force you to concentrate almost exclusively on the direction the cue ball takes. You aren't so worried about where the first object ball goes — as long as it stays out of the way of the cue ball and the second ball — so it's a bit of a different aiming process.

When you see a billiard shot that you can make, you want to imagine the exact line the cue ball will take from the first object ball to the second. When you picture the shot in your head, you'll have an idea of the cue ball's angle off the first object ball, which is hugely important.

Plan precisely. Don't imagine the area you want the cue ball to go. Planning for generalities will decrease your accuracy. Even if you can't send the cue ball in exactly the correct line all the time, the mental exercise of thinking about the perfect line will only help your accuracy.

In Figure 15-3, you want to send the cue ball off the 3 and into the 4 hanging in the corner pocket. The cue ball will need to roll forward of the tangent line — 90 degrees from the direction of the 3. To do so, you need the cue ball to roll into the 3 so that it will follow forward into the 4. (See Chapter 8 for a discussion on using topspin.)

The contact point on the 3 ball can vary, depending on the spin of the cue ball at impact. Figure 15-3 is an example of hitting the 3 ball nearly full with follow so that the cue ball moves forward of the tangent line (the dotted line) and in the direction of the 4.

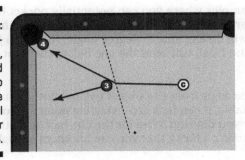

Figure 15-3:
With a rolling cue ball, you should be able to send the cue ball right for the 4.

But you can approach this same shot in another way, shown in Figure 15-4. (A 3–4 combination is a possibility, but focus on the billiard shot for now. Combinations are covered in Chapter 14.) If you clip the right side of the 3 ball, you'll just barely redirect the cue ball — hopefully toward the 4 ball.

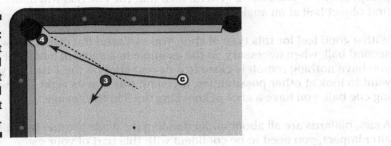

Figure 15-4:
A thin cut on the 3 ball can also put the cue ball on the right path.

By thinly cutting the 3 ball on the right side, the cue ball will still be on course to pocket the 4 ball. Simply put, because the first object ball's path means little to the success of the shot, you have options on how to approach billiards. The key is finding a line for the cue ball that you can comfortably execute.

While you often have different paths to the same object ball, not all routes are created equal. Using certain angles from the first ball to the second will make billiards easier for you.

Stunned cue ball: 90 degrees

In Chapters 7–9, I talk about how to angle the cue ball off of an object ball. The 90-degree rule — a cue ball with no spin at impact deflects at a right angle off the object ball — is a great way to eye billiards. Also, half-ball hits and other common angles should give you a feel for where the cue ball's headed.

Figure 15-5 shows two examples where you can potentially pocket the game-winning 9 ball with a billiard shot. If you can hit the 1 ball so that the cue ball has no spin, you know it will deflect at a 90 degree angle. Now, you just have to aim so that the hit on the 1 ball will send the cue ball in the right direction to pocket the 9 ball.

While the perfect 90-degree angle from one object ball to another may not happen every turn at the table, it can be a great starting point for your understanding of billiards. After you develop a feel for the cue ball deflecting at 90 degrees, you can start to tinker a bit so that you can try shots at slightly different angles.

Rolling cue ball: 30 degrees

The naturally rolling cue ball is one of the cornerstones to understanding cue-ball control. (In Chapter 8, you can find out about topspin and its effects on the cue ball.) For shots that are in the general area of a half-ball hit — so half the cue ball overlaps with the object ball at impact (from the shooter's perspective) — you have a general idea that the cue ball will deflect off the first object ball at an angle between 30 and 35 degrees.

With a good feel for this type of shot, you can send the cue ball toward the second ball, when necessary. In the example in a game of 9-ball in Figure 15-6, you have nothing remotely close to a decent shot on the 1 ball, so you may want to look at other possibilities. If you hit the 1 on its right side with a rolling cue ball, you have a shot of knocking the 9 in the corner.

Again, billiards are all about understanding the angle the cue ball will take after impact, you need to be confident with this part of your game.

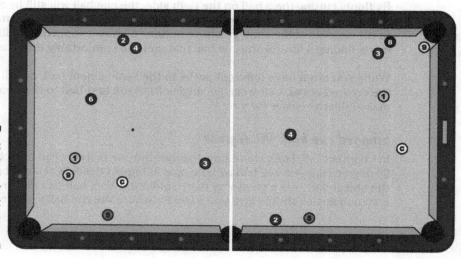

Figure 15-5: Here are two opportunities for stun-shot billiards in 9-ball.

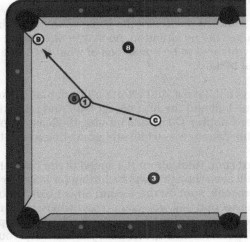

Figure 15-6:
Using a naturally rolling cue ball is another way to get a feel for billiards.

Straight (or nearly straight) draw

The final reference points for billiard shots are situations where you can hit the first ball nearly full with draw to leave the cue ball headed for the second object ball.

As you can see in the shot on the 2 ball in Figure 15-7, you can plan for the cue ball to come directly back to you with a full hit on the object ball and a fair amount of draw. This shot is by no means simple, but it demonstrates an important aspect when dealing with billiards.

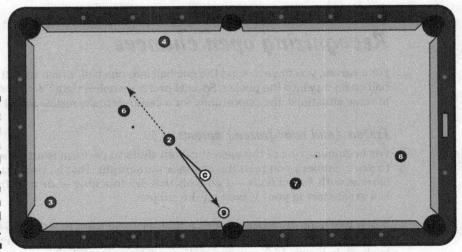

Figure 15-7:
Billiard shots with draw and follow may be more common than you'd guess.

For the game winner?

While billiard shots are useful in pocketing the game-winning ball in 9-ball, they can oftentimes be used in any situation, no matter what game you're playing. In these cases, you need to be conscious of what the table will look like after your successful billiard.

In order to be sure that you'll have a shot after a billiard, plan accordingly — in regards to both the cue ball and the first object ball. And most times, proper position play (see Chapter 12) means moving the least amount of balls the shortest possible distance — while still pocketing a ball, that is.

So when you see a billiard shot, think about the speed of the cue ball. You want to keep control of the ball, even though it will be hitting (at least) two other balls. Also, plan to hit a specific spot on the second object ball. By knowing where you want to hit the second ball, you can predict where the cue ball will head after impact. With proper planning — in regards to both speed and angle — you can leave the cue ball in a spot where you can keep your run alive.

Caroms: Sending an Object Ball Off Another

A *carom shot* is one where you send the cue ball into an object ball with the intent of sending that object ball off another ball. In the simplest terms, a carom shot is similar to a billiard, only instead of the cue ball hitting the second object ball into the pocket, the first object ball ricochets off a second object ball on its way into the pocket.

Recognizing open chances

For a carom, you have to send the cue ball into one ball, which will hit another ball on its way into the pocket. Sounds pretty complex, right? Well, it can be, but in some situations, the opportunity for a carom actually makes a shot *easier*.

Frozen (and near-frozen) caroms

For beginners, one of the easiest carom shots to perform is also the hardest to see . . . unless you read the next few paragraphs, that is. Understanding caroms with *frozen balls* — two balls that are touching — or near-frozen balls is a great start in your lesson on the subject.

When two balls are frozen (for example, as 7 and 8 are in Figure 15-8), you can hit the first ball anywhere on its right side and make the shot in the corner. In short, in Figure 15-8, you can make the 7 because of the 90-degree rule of deflection. This rule says that a ball that hits another ball with stun will deflect at a right angle. In this case, the line of centers between the object balls is perpendicular to the pocket, and the 7 ball will head straight for the hole.

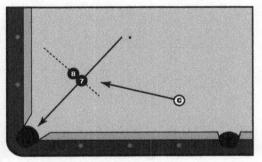

Figure 15-8:
Lucky you: The 7 and 8 are lined up perpendicular to the pocket.

Now you may think that the setup in Figure 15-8 is pretty unlikely, but you'd be surprised how many times these frozen balls line up with a pocket. And it should be noted that balls in close proximity to each other are definitely pocketable in the same fashion, though with a slight uptick in difficulty.

When two balls are close to frozen, you can still count on the same type of action from the first ball (the one the cue ball contacts). An example is shown in Figure 15-9. If you can send the 13 straight into the 15 so that the line of centers is perpendicular to the corner pocket, you'll make the 13. Also, the farther the ball to be pocketed travels, the more speed you'll need to use.

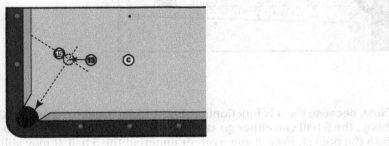

Figure 15-9:
If the balls aren't frozen, hit the 13 at a point perpendicular to the 15 and corner pocket.

Backboard caroms

Sometimes you can use other object balls as bumpers for an object ball. Figure 15-10 shows a pretty standard carom in a game of 8-ball. You're solids, and it's not like you've got plenty of options. The 13 ball blocks a straight shot at the 4 ball and a bank attempt on the 5. Your opponent's balls are out in the open, so a safety isn't really a viable option.

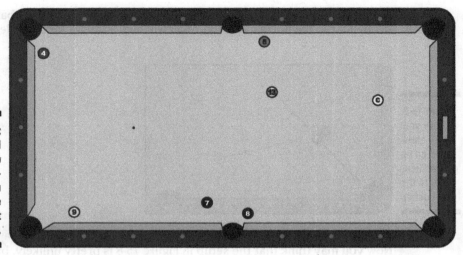

Figure 15-10:
The 4 ball can help ease the difficulty of an otherwise difficult shot on the 5 ball.

You have an angle on the 5 into the top-left corner, though it's a shot that is far from a gimme. But notice how the 4 ball is sitting just to the left of the pocket. With a ball sitting like so, you have a wider margin for error if you go for the 5. If you send the cue ball off the long rail, it can still bounce off the 4 ball and into the corner pocket (see Figure 15-11).

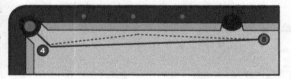

Figure 15-11:
The 4 directs a slightly offline 5 ball right into the pocket.

Now, because the 4 is functioning almost like a backboard on a basketball hoop, the 5 ball can either go straight into the pocket or off the 4 ball and into the pocket. Now, if you over- or undercut the 5 ball, it may still drop because of the 4 ball.

Aiming aids

Aiming a carom is a bit more complex than a regular old shot where the cue ball hits an object ball into a pocket. After all, you're introducing another step into the equation by sending the object ball off another ball. But worry not; some tips can keep you playing makable caroms.

When it comes down to it, all that matters is delivering the first object ball to the correct point on the second ball. It doesn't matter how you get it there, just as long as the object ball is in the right spot at impact.

Aiming caroms is a lot like aiming combinations (see Chapter 14). You want to plan out the entire shot, visualizing how all the balls will interact to give you the result you're looking for. However, after you've made this plan in your mind, you want to focus *only* on where you're going to hit the first object ball. If you're taking your final stroke and still thinking about the second ball or if your angle to the pocket is correct, you aren't focused.

So to aim the carom in Figures 15-12 to 15-14, follow these steps, and you should see how these tricky little shots can really help you out when you're in a jam.

1. **Establish the point where the 1 ball must hit the 2.**

   For the 1 to hit the 2 in the proper spot, the line from the center of the 1 ball at impact to the pocket should be perpendicular to the line of centers (the solid line in Figure 15-12) between the 1 and 2. The dotted line in Figure 15-12 shows the right line of centers for the 1 ball after contact with the 2.

Figure 15-12: Determine where the 1 ball needs to hit the 2 ball so that it heads toward the corner pocket.

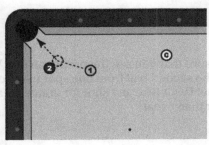

2. **Now that you know where the 1 ball must go, aim your shot on the 1 ball just as you would any other shot, but, like with a combination shot, find an aiming point on the rail by extending the aiming line through to the rail.**

   See the dotted line in Figure 15-13.

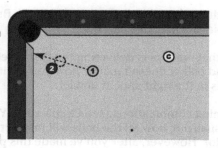

Figure 15-13:
Find a definite point on the rail to aim the 1 ball.

3. **After you know what line the 1 ball must take to hit the 2 at the correct spot, aim the 1 like you would a normal shot.**

   Picture where the cue ball must be at impact and make it happen. Put all the pieces together, and you can see in Figure 15-14 how you can make a carom shot from start to finish.

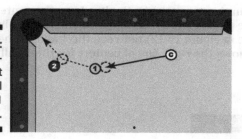

Figure 15-14:
Find a definite point on the rail to aim the 1 ball.

Walk around the balls to make sure that you see the proper angles. What looks like the right contact point on the second ball from one spot may not be the right point after you get up close. Don't take any shot for granted, especially one that's a little more complex than usual.

Jumping to a Conclusion with Jump Shots

The idea of jumping the cue ball over an obstruction to pocket a ball sounds pretty cool. While the jump has become an integral part of the game, it wasn't always so. In fact, jump shots have gained acceptance among many pool players only in the last 25 years.

In fact, for years, jump shots were often regarded as trickery, brushed aside by "real" pool players as great for artistic shots but not a part of the game. Those opposed to jump shots argued that it takes less skill to jump the cue ball over another than to go around the obstacle by hitting the cue ball off a rail before hitting the intended object ball.

Knowing the rules

Keep in mind this important distinction between legal and illegal jump shots. Oftentimes, recreational players hit a jump shot by scooping the cue ball into the air. By hitting the cue ball and the table at the same time, the cue will push under the cue ball, pushing it into the air. But scooping is illegal. It can damage the table (jabbing a cue along the cloth isn't exactly good for the cloth's longevity) and may be a mis-hit.

Properly jumping a cue ball involves a stroke that's very different from that which you use on almost every other kind of shot. To legally execute a jump, you need to raise the back end of your cue and strike down on the cue ball from a steep angle. The force of such a downward stroke forces the cue ball to compress against the cloth and pop up (and hopefully over the obstructing ball).

You can find out how to achieve such liftoff later in the "And stroke!" section of this chapter, but knowing what you can and can't do when lifting the ball off the table is a good start.

Using jump cues

Part of the reason why players are opting more and more to jump the cue ball over a blocking ball (instead of going around the obstacle) is the development of the jump cue, which is a shorter version of the normal cue and has an ultra-hard tip to help pop the cue ball off the bed of the table (see Figure 15-15).

Figure 15-15: A jump cue makes the task of getting the cue ball airborne much easier.

In most cases, such cues are legal, unless expressly outlawed by the pool-room, league, or tournament you play in. And while you can lift the cue ball into the air with your full cue, a jump cue makes the job much easier, especially for developing players.

Setting up to jump

Before you get to the table to try to make your cue ball hop around, I want to flesh out a few important points you need to know so that you can effectively jump the cue ball.

First, if you hit in the middle of the cue ball, it should continue in the straight line from the direction of your cue. Don't try to hit the cue ball anywhere but on its vertical axis. Incorporating English into a jump shot is nearly impossible when you're just starting out.

Second, you need to hit down on the cue ball at a pretty steep angle. While you want to keep your cue level on most shots, you need to pull up the back end of your cue so that you're hitting down into the cue ball.

One safe bet is that the cue ball will jump off the table at an angle about equal to the elevation of your cue. However, the cue ball won't continue to rise on a straight line. Gravity has a way of pulling the ball back down to earth.

As you can see in Figure 15-16, hitting down on the cue ball at an angle of 40 to 45 degrees should be a good starting point. You want the cue tip to hit straight toward the center of the cue ball (or a bit below center), so you'll need to sight your cue to the center of the cue ball from your perspective looking down.

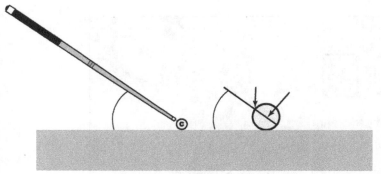

Figure 15-16:
Hit down at about 40 degrees to get good air under the cue ball.

Building a stance

Because the back of the cue has to raise up 45 degrees from parallel with the table, getting stuck in an uncomfortable stance that will limit your movement is easy. However, the stance for the jump stroke has some very similar characteristics to the stance for a regular shot.

Keep the following points in mind as you build your stance:

✔ Because you're leaning forward (see Figure 15-17), you'll have an easier time stroking the jump shot if you move your back hand up on the cue, closer to your bridge hand. This positioning allows your elbow to be somewhere near a 90-degree angle, which is the same as a normal shot.

✔ The bridge itself is a modified open bridge, similar to the one used when you have to get over a blocking ball (see Chapter 3). Groove the cue between your thumb and the first knuckle on your index finger, making sure that you hit down on the cue ball. With some of your weight pressing your bridge hand down, spread the pressure evenly between the two or three fingers that are resting on the table.

Figure 15-17:
Tilt your upper body forward and keep your elbow in line with the shot.

✔ Shift a majority of your weight forward. You want your front leg supporting most of your weight, with some pressure on your bridge hand (to help keep it solidly planted on the table).

✔ Staying in line is another important aspect to a jump shot. You want to normalize the shot by keeping yourself on a similar line to that of any ordinary shot. You want your cue, eyes, back arm, and grip hand all on the shot line. Staying in line is crucial in controlling the cue ball after it clears the obstructing ball on the way to its target.

And stroke!

When you're planted in your stance with an eye on the cue ball, it's time to deliver the cue to the contact point. For almost all shots in pool, you want the cue ball to gradually accelerate into the object ball and push through in a controlled follow-through. Well, forget that. The jump stroke is a short punchy stroke that involves a sort of snap of the wrist. After all, you have only about an inch and a half to follow through, so you need to hit the ball hard. Ideally, the cue will bounce up after contact so that you don't have to worry about jerking it to a stop.

One common mistake that keeps players from getting the cue ball in the air is a perfectly natural fear of slamming the cue into the table. Worrying about hitting the table can cause you to hit away from your intended contact point or to ease up right before impact and leave your cue ball squirting along the cloth. It may take some practice, but you need to learn how to punch the cue tip into the cue ball as hard as possible at the intended point of contact. Only when you're able to hit the cue ball firmly will you be able to send balls flying.

Another common problem with the jump stroke is the grip. You may think that you need to squeeze the cue firmly because you're striking down at the cue ball. But actually, a firm grip can kill any hope of getting a ball airborne. You want to keep your grip hand loose while you're stroking so that the cue will accurately strike the cue ball with a little power.

Because your stroke is a bit more compact, use a brief backstroke of 8 or 10 inches. You don't want to have a long, loopy stroke when you're trying to punch the cue ball.

Extra movements are never good. During a jump shot, remain perfectly still, except for your back arm. Keep your head centered and focused on your contact point. Keep your bridge hand absolutely still and don't let your body sway back and forth.

The strategy of jumping

Now you may be having a ball (bad pun) with your newly acquired jump skills, but don't go wild. You need to follow some important rules to effectively use the jump shot.

✔ **Avoiding blockers:** First, you can't be jumping over balls that are four or five diamonds away. Usually, you want to keep your jumps to a short distance, such as when the obstacle is about a diamond away from the cue ball.

✔ **Seeing a full target:** It's not a likely bet that you'll be precise enough to cut an object ball after sending the cue ball into the air, so keep your jump attempts to situations where you can aim to fully hit the intended target.

✔ **Looking for options:** Often, you can *kick* — sending the cue ball to a rail then to the ball — at a ball that's behind a blocker. This approach is a much better bet, if you have a clean shot at the ball.

✔ **Knowing the necessary height:** If the blocking ball is directly on the shot line, you'll have to jump the cue ball higher than an obstacle that's only partially in the way. Don't try to be a hero by jumping over a full ball when you don't have to.

Chapter 16

Banks and Kicks: Making the Most of the Rails

A t one time or another, you'll find yourself in a position where you won't have a clear line from the cue ball to the object ball to the pocket. Sometimes an obstruction (another object ball) will find its way between the cue ball and the object ball. In those cases, you may have to hit the cue ball off a rail and into the desired ball, in what's known as a kick shot. Being able to deal with this minor detour can help immensely, especially when your opponent leaves you in such a position in an effort to force you to foul.

And still other times, you may find an obstacle between your desired ball and its nearest pocket. In those cases, you may have an opportunity to bank the ball — meaning you shoot the object ball off a rail and into another pocket. Again, the ability to bank a ball is a great way to shoot yourself out of a tough spot.

In this chapter, I detail the whys, whens, and hows of kicking and banking. Although using the rails to your advantage can be a bit tricky at first, with a basic understanding of each type of shot and a little practice, you can develop a feel for banks and kicks.

When you can effectively employ each shot during the course of a game, you are at a point where your game will become well-rounded . . . not to mention that a successful kick or bank looks really darn cool.

Rail First: Banking an Object Ball off the Rail

I'm not trying to scare you, but a *bank shot* (hitting an object ball off of a rail before it goes into a pocket) is rarely simple. A bank shot incorporates a rail into the object ball's path from where it sits to where it will drop into a pocket. Although a bank shot adds some complexity to a shot, sometimes you just have to go for a bank. And when you're lining up a bank shot, you're playing an aggressively offensive shot that can start or save your game-winning run.

Of course, no knowledgeable pool player necessarily chooses to bank a ball because a bank shot is often a result of a lack of an alternative. So you need to know when the time is right to try to bounce a ball off a rail and into a pocket.

Making the decision

Don't make the mistake of thinking a bank shot is easy to make. Many players underestimate the difficulty of a bank shot because it looks easy. In reality, though, a bank shot isn't easy. Here's why:

- ✓ **Rails are unpredictable.** You're sending an object ball into a rail, which is just a stiff piece of semi-flexible material affixed atop the table bed. Not all rails are equal, so you're not always going to get the same reaction on every table.

- ✓ **Spin kills.** The cue ball will often transfer sidespin to an object ball at impact. This spin usually has a minimal effect on a shot because the object ball is headed for a pocket. But when the object ball hits off a rail, this spin comes into play — and can create chaos for your banking angles.

- ✓ **Visualizing a bank isn't easy.** Picturing the exact path an object ball will take from the point where it's hit by the cue ball to the rail and to the intended pocket isn't exactly the easiest thing to do. A bank shot isn't a straight line, so the difficulty of planning the object ball's route is jacked up a bit.

- ✓ **Banks require the perfect mix of speed, direction, and spin.** Successfully shooting a bank is often an inexact science that requires you to use a certain amount of speed to an exact point on the rail, all the while knowing what's happening with the sidespin on both balls.

But ditching all the doom and gloom, you can make banks. (Otherwise, why would I write a whole chapter on them?) So when should you step up and try a bank?

- **Your pockets are blocked.** The most common banking situation is when the preferred pocket is blocked, either by your opponents ball in 8-ball or by another ball in 9-ball. When your pocket is blocked, you have to ditch the ideal and make the best with what's available. Figure 16-1 shows a situation in 8-ball where you have the option to bank the 11 ball in the corner because your opponent's ball is blocking the easy option.

- **You have no safe option.** If you can play a safety that is relatively doable, go for it. But when you don't have that option, you'll need to be aggressive and go for the win. In end-game situations, you'll be more likely to bank a ball because fewer balls are on the table, which means fewer balls to hide the cue ball behind.

- **You want to avoid a scratch.** Another common situation that will force you to opt for a bank is when your cue ball and object ball line up in such a way that you'll definitely scratch. In Figure 16-2, you have to bank the 8 ball into the opposite corner pocket (called a *cross-corner bank*) because you'll scratch in the side if you try to cut it.

Figure 16-1:
Your opponent's ball blocks the corner pocket, so you'll have to bank it across to the other corner.

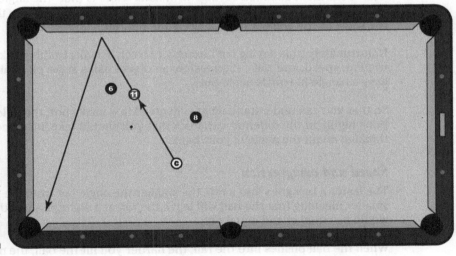

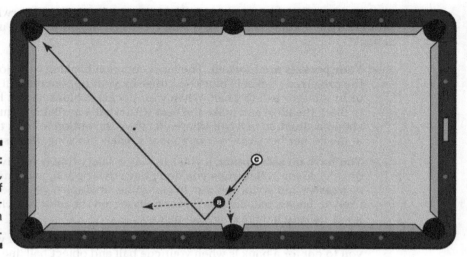

Figure 16-2:
Hit the 8 full,
instead of
the sure-to-
scratch
cut shot.

Altering angles

One of the most common sayings with bank shots is that "the angle in equals the angle out" — meaning that the angle the object ball takes into the rail is the same as the angle it takes away from that rail.

Unfortunately, this saying isn't exactly correct. Thanks to things like spin, friction, speed, and rail compression, an object ball's angle off a rail isn't as easy as angle-in-equals-angle-out.

So that you can understand what's involved in a bank shot, the following sections highlight the different variables that you should take into account when thinking about the angle of your bank.

Speed and compression

The faster a ball goes into a rail, the smaller the angle out from the rail — smaller meaning that the ball will leave the rail at a sharper angle than what would be equal in and equal out.

When the ball pushes into the rail, the harder you hit the ball, the more the ball will compress the rubber in the rail. This interaction, which takes all of a few milliseconds, can greatly affect the angle of the ball (see Figure 16-3).

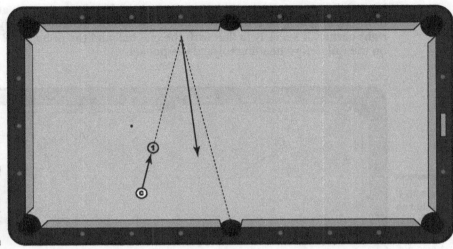

Figure 16-3:
Speed leads
to smaller
angles.

Many great bankers prefer to use some speed on bank shots to limit the amount of roll the object ball develops on the way to the rail. A speeding object ball won't pick up roll and then hit the rail with less spin. You can have greater control over an object ball with no spin (or very little spin). Hitting the object ball with speed reduces the variable of object-ball spin.

Spin into the rail

You can use English — or sidespin on the cue ball — to change the course of the cue ball when it hits a rail (see Chapter 10). In that same arena, an object ball with spin will react differently than one without sidespin when it hits a rail.

Generally speaking, avoid putting spin on an object ball that is bound to hit a rail before heading toward a pocket. Using English greatly increases the difficulty of a shot because an object ball with sidespin is much harder to judge off the rails from shot to shot.

One way to avoid putting unnecessary spin on a banking ball is to try to keep your banks in the area of straight-on. When you cut an object ball, the cue ball imparts a bit of spin on that ball. So, when you cut a ball during a bank shot, the object ball is much harder to control.

Figure 16-4 shows a pair of bank shots (assuming that you can't pocket them without sending the object balls off a rail first). The shot on the 1 into the lower-left corner is one you'd do well to avoid. You have to cut it at an angle to the right. The 2 ball, though, is in a good spot to be banked in the lower-right corner. It's nearly in line with the cue ball and the point the 2 must hit on the rail before heading toward the pocket.

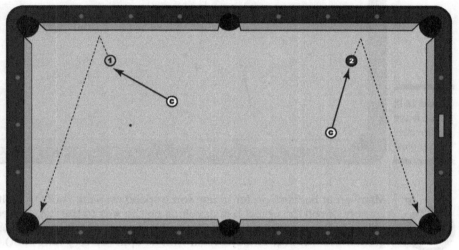

Figure 16-4:
The shot on the 1 ball is a bit of an extreme cut, while the 2 ball is in line with the cue ball.

Aiming banks

If you can determine what can change the angle of a bank, you know what you need to avoid to get the truest angle on your shot. But how do you determine where exactly to aim? You can always guess where the ball needs to hit the rail, but a few systems can help you get a better feel for bank shots.

Intersecting lines

One of the more geometrically dependent aiming systems for bank shots relies on drawing three lines to give you the point on the rail where you need to aim.

Here's a step-by-step run-through of how to get an aiming point for just about any bank shot you may encounter.

1. **Using your cue tip as guidance, find the nearest point to the object ball on the rail where you'll be banking the ball.**

2. **Draw a line from this point to the pocket where you'll be pocketing the ball (see Figure 16-5).**

3. **Draw a line from the object ball to the opposite pocket (the upper side pocket, in this case), as shown in Figure 16-6.**

   The point where these two lines intersect in Figure 16-7 will be directly across from the point on the rail where you need to aim this shot.

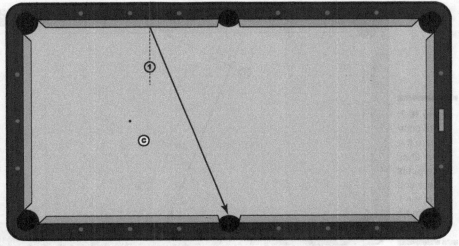

Figure 16-5:
Find the point straight to the long rail and draw a line to the pocket you're aiming for.

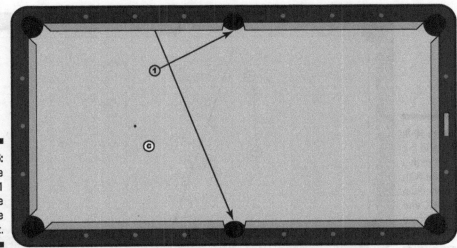

Figure 16-6:
Draw a line from the 1 ball to the top side pocket.

4. **Hit the 1 ball so that it hits the rail where the lines in Step 3 intersect (with medium speed).**

   If you can send the ball to the proper point, shown in Figure 16-8, your shot should be money in the bank.

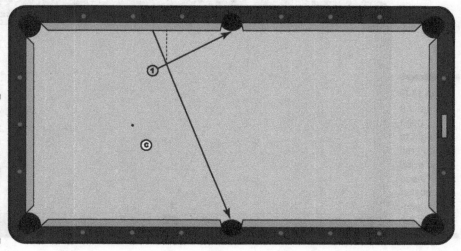

Figure 16-7: The point where the two lines intersect is where you want the 1 ball to hit the rail.

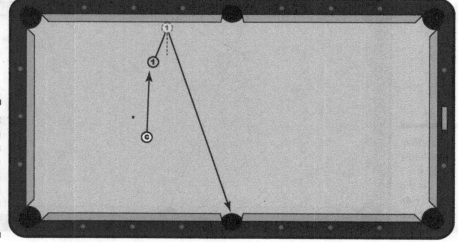

Figure 16-8: Send the 1 to this point with medium speed, and you should be good!

Ghost-table aiming

Just like the ghost-ball aiming, you can use *ghost-table aiming* for bank shots —
both across the table's width and length. The idea here is similar to the ghost
ball (see Chapter 4).

Here's what you need to do:

1. **Picture an entire table overlapping the actual table so that the pockets
   overlap, as shown in Figure 16-9.**

   The shot is on the 2 ball into the corner pocket.

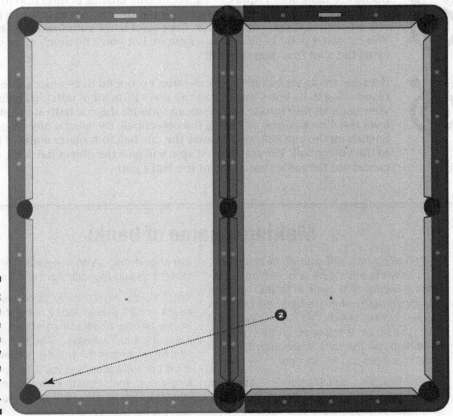

Figure 16-9:
If you can
pocket the
ball on the
imaginary
table, you're
on your
way.

2. **With the ghost-table system, you want to picture where you need to hit the 2 ball so that it would travel across the entire ghost table and into the corner pocket.**

   After you can imagine where you'd need to hit the 2 ball, you have the contact point on the rail, shown in Figure 16-10. The contact point is the point where the imaginary line to the imaginary pocket crosses the real rail.

3. **Hit a ball along the line running to the imaginary pocket.**

   If you've properly visualized the ghost table, you should be making the bank shot in no time.

Because a bank shot requires a rather drastic change of direction for the object ball, get the big picture. Walk around the rail you're going to bank the ball off of so that you can visualize the object ball's path from start to pocket. You can get a point of aim using a system, but you'll be much more confident eying the shot from start to end!

Because an object ball hit into a rail won't rebound in an angle perfectly corresponding to its entry angle, you can use a little bit of outside English in your bank shots. *Outside English* means you hit the cue ball on the side away from the direction you're hitting the object ball. By using a tiny bit of outside English on the cue ball, you'll cause the cue ball to transfer some of that spin to the object ball. The transferred spin will give the object ball a bit of spin to cancel out the rail's shortening of the ball's path.

Making a game of banks

If you really want to drill yourself on bank shots, head down to your local pool hall and challenge a regular to a game of banks. The idea is fairly simple: You have to bank every shot (as you may have guessed). You can play with a full rack (15 balls) or 9-ball banks. After you make more than half the balls in any rack (8 for full rack, 5 for 9-ball banks), you win!

Oh, and this game isn't about luck — you have to call every ball into the pocket. While this game will definitely work your banking skills,

you should also try to keep your eye out for safeties so that your opponent won't run wild.

While not the most popular tournament game, banks is still played today, most commonly in the middle Appalachian states, such as Kentucky and Tennessee. The biggest bank-pool tournament in the world is held every year in the Louisville area, and you'd be a smart rail-bird (a pool spectator) to put your money on a local boy. The local crop of players can shoot with the best players in the world.

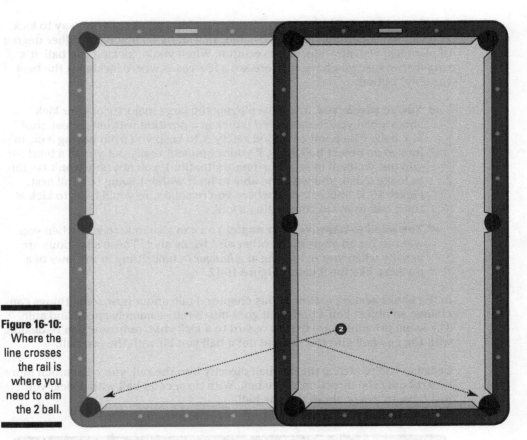

Figure 16-10:
Where the line crosses the rail is where you need to aim the 2 ball.

Rail First: Sending the Cue Ball off a Rail

A *kick shot* is just like the bank shot, where the object ball goes off a rail before heading toward a pocket. The difference? A kick shot is where you send the *cue ball* off a rail before it makes contact with an object ball, while the bank shot involves the object ball going off the rail. Whether you're escaping your opponent's devious safety or playing a tricky shot of your own, the opportunity to kick will come up. And you'd be best served having a good idea how to send the cue ball off a rail.

Just like with bank shots, you probably shouldn't go out of your way to kick at balls. While certainly not impossible, kick shots do involve a higher degree of planning, visualization, and execution. When you're kicking at a ball, it's usually because you have to. Here are a few cases where kicking is the best (or only) option:

✔ **You're snookered.** You'll be playing the large majority of your kick shots when you're *snookered* (stuck in a position without a clear shot at a ball). The point of a good safety is to keep you from having a clean look at an object ball. Now, if your opponent really put you in a bind (or you put yourself in an unfortunate situation), you not only won't be able to make a ball, you won't be able to hit it without going to a rail first. Figure 16-11 shows a case where you're solids, so you'll have to kick at the 5 ball to avoid committing a foul.

✔ **You need to improve your angle.** You can also look to kick when you want to get an angle on an otherwise tricky shot. These situations are usually when you're looking at a *hanger* (a ball sitting in the jaws of a pocket), like the 9 ball in Figure 16-12.

In the banks section earlier in this chapter, I talk about how some things can change an object ball's path as it goes into a rail — namely speed and spin. The same principles are true in regard to a kick shot, only now you're dealing with the cue ball into the rail and not a ball you hit with the cue ball.

Because you're hitting the cue ball directly into the rail, you have much more control over the direction of the ball. With no second ball with a kick, you just have to worry about the cue ball.

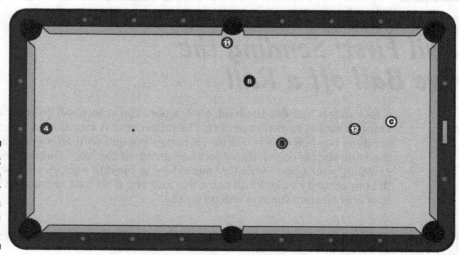

Figure 16-11:
You're behind your opponent's ball, so you have to kick.

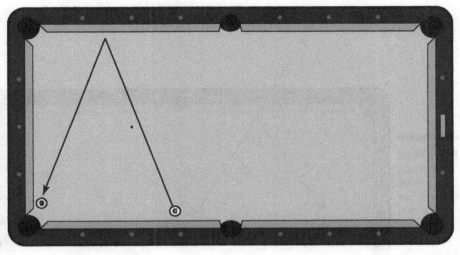

Figure 16-12:
The 9 ball is sitting by the corner pocket, and you're out of safety options.

Aiming for the cue ball off a rail

In the "Aiming banks" section, I discuss the ghost-table aiming system, which involves imagining an entire table behind the rail off which you want to bank the ball. We can use that same principle for kick shots, but with some slight modifications because we'll be sending the cue ball to a particular ball that isn't necessarily hiding near a pocket.

So how do you find the magical point where the imaginary 7 ball in Figure 16-13 is floating out in space? Well, the answer isn't that magical. When you're lining up a kick shot, run through these simple steps to find a contact point:

1. **Measure the distance from the 7 ball to the rail where you're going to send the cue ball.**

   You can do so by putting the tip of your cue at the edge of the 7 (without touching it!) and marking the point on your shaft that crosses the edge of the rail, marked with an X in Figure 16-14.

2. **Now put the tip of your cue on the edge of the rail (see Figure 16-15).**

   The point X is at a distance from the rail equal to the 7 ball. This spot will be your aiming point.

3. **Find the point on this aiming line that crosses the rail.**

   The floating X will be the point on the rail where you'll aim to successfully kick at the 7 ball.

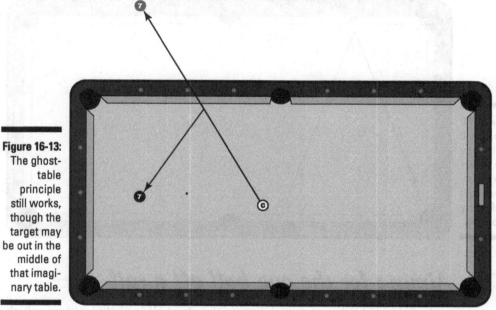

Figure 16-13:
The ghost-table principle still works, though the target may be out in the middle of that imaginary table.

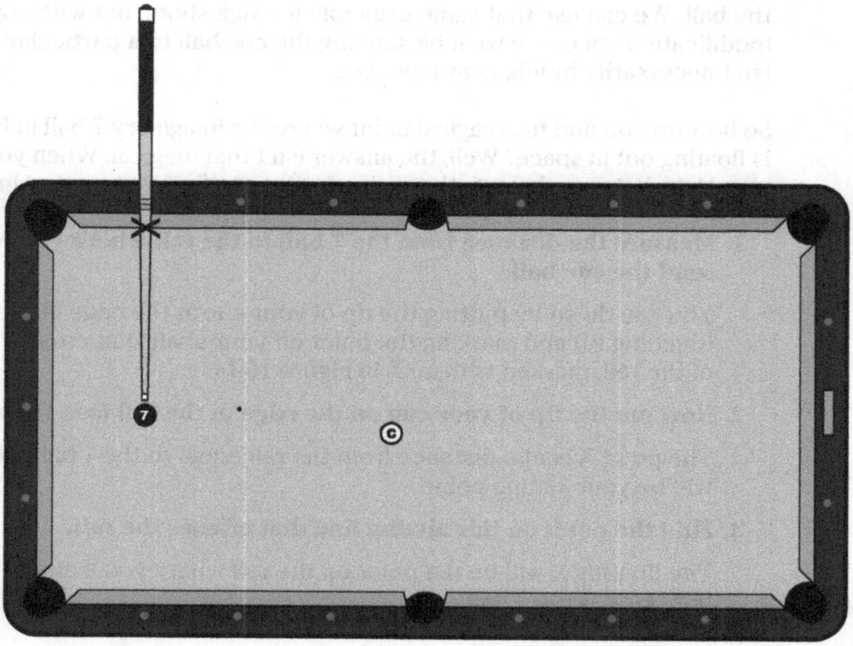

Figure 16-14:
Tip to the ball, find where your shaft crosses the rail.

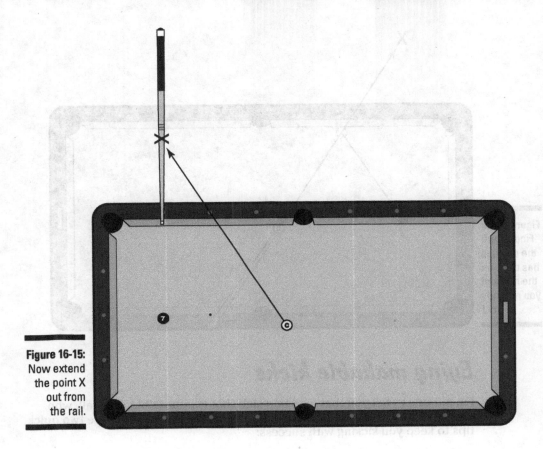

Figure 16-15:
Now extend
the point X
out from
the rail.

The contact point and aiming point aren't the same thing. You can see in Figure 16-16 that the cue ball will make contact with the rail at a point a little higher than the aiming line. If you cause the cue ball to make contact on the rail at the aiming point, you might miss the shot.

Just like your bank shots, you can put a bit of *running English* on the ball to get a nice, even reaction from the rail. Running English means hitting the cue ball to the side it will be deflecting to. So in Figure 16-16, you'd hit the cue ball on its left side to give it running English as it heads toward the 7 ball.

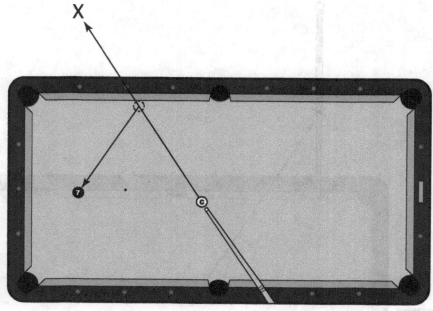

Figure 16-16:
Find where
the cue ball
has to be on
the rail, and
you're ready
to kick!

Eying makable kicks

I'm not one to tell you that a certain kick shot is impossible. After all, who am I to say what you can and can't do? In general, though, here are two quick tips to keep you kicking with success:

✔ **Finding big balls:** Sophomoric jokes aside, a key to kicking is finding the biggest balls — the balls that give you the biggest cushion for error. In an example in 8-ball, where you have to hit any ball of your suit — stripes or solids — big balls can be a group of balls in one corner of the table. You also have a large margin for error with a ball next to a rail, because you can either hit the ball directly or bounce off another rail before making contact.

In Figure 16-17, you're stripes, so you're hooked behind the 7 ball. You'll have to kick at a stripe ball — luckily, you've got a few options. If you kick at the 14 ball, you have the bottom rail to help you. Should your kick go long (to the right side of the 14), the cue ball can ricochet off the bottom rail and hit the 14 to the left long rail. Your target area is larger than a ball sitting in the middle of the table. (You might even get lucky and knock the 14 into the corner pocket.)

Also notice the 10 and 15 balls. You're more likely to make a successful hit aiming at these balls because you can hit either one. You have a target zone more than twice the size of a kick on a ball by itself.

✔ **Picking a side:** When you develop a feel for kicks, you can start to pick a side of the object ball to aim for. This will give you a better idea where the cue ball and object ball will be headed after impact. (It's also a more precise way of aiming, and precision when aiming is always a good thing.)

Figure 16-17:
See the kicking options?

In Figure 16-18, you can see one example where knowing which side of the ball to aim for is helpful. You're playing 9-ball, which means you have to hit the 5 ball first. If you hit the bottom side of the ball, you can send the 5 up table, while the cue ball heads down table to hide behind one of four blocking balls. You're playing for a bit of luck, but your opponent will be hard-pressed to find a good shot if you put the 5 ball a table's length from the cue ball.

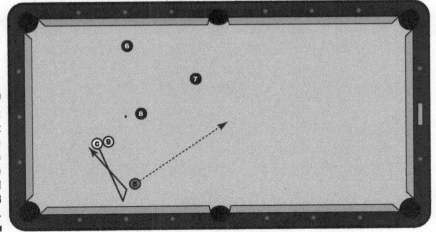

Figure 16-18:
Aim to hit the bottom side of the 5 and hide the cue ball behind the 8 and 9 balls.

- **Picking a side:** When you develop a feel for kicks, you can start to pick a safe at the object ball to aim for. This will give you a better idea where the cue ball and object ball will be headed after impact. (It's also a more precise way of aiming, and precision when aiming is always a good thing.)

Chapter 17

Thinking Defensively: Playing Safe

Maybe the biggest distinction between the just-out-for-a-few-laughs *game* of pool and the competitive version of the *sport* is the incorporation of defense. No doubt, there is a stigma among many casual players against *playing safe,* meaning you aim to leave your opponent in a bad position instead of trying to pocket a ball yourself. Some consider playing safe to be unsportsmanlike; some may even tag it as cowardly.

But the defensive side of the game is a vital part of developing into a winning player. You're not always going to have a clear path to shoot yourself to a win, so learning proper defensive strategy (see Chapters 18 for 8-ball and 19 for 9-ball) allows you to make the most of certain situations.

In this chapter, I discuss when you should play safe. After you understand the when, I give you some clues as to the how. You can use some basic tenets of defense when you need to leave your opponent in a tough spot.

What to Achieve: Setting Goals for Defensive Play

When you don't have an opportunity to make a ball, you need to do what you can to make sure that you'll have an improved position the next time you come to the table. So, you need to first understand what you want to achieve with a defensive shot — only then can you truly focus on the strategy and execution of safeties.

First and foremost, the ultimate goal of a defensive shot is to make your opponent foul (see Chapters 18 and 19 for common fouls), which will give you *ball in hand* (meaning you can put the cue ball wherever you please before your next shot). However, provoking a foul isn't the only goal. If you can't induce your opponent into a foul, then you can at least make it quite difficult for him to pocket a ball or play a return safe.

Sometimes you can win a game by *not* pocketing a ball. While literally, you can't end the game with a safety, you can alter the landscape of the table to a point where you gain an advantage. A properly played safety can lead to a chance for you to run to victory, so take note of how to leave your opponent in dire straits.

Finding blockers

One of the most effective ways to keep your opponent in a poor situation is by using blocker balls. This method of playing safe means putting your opponent in a spot where he is unable to shoot directly at his object ball(s).

In Figure 17-1, you're playing a game of 9-ball (meaning the cue ball has to hit the lowest number ball remaining on the table first). In this case, you have to hit the 3 ball, but you can't easily pocket it. So how can you hit the 3 so that a few blocker balls are between the cue ball and the 3?

One easy way would be to hit the cue ball using a stop shot (see Chapter 7), which would send the 3 ball down table to hide behind the 4, 5 and 6 balls, while the cue ball stopped in place at impact. Now, you have left your opponent in a very tough spot because he has no direct route to contact the 3.

Figure 17-1:
In this layout, you can see a natural line of blocker balls to keep your opponent from a good shot.

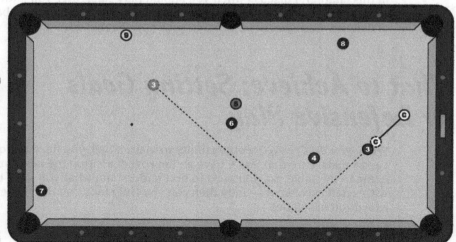

When you've left your opponent without a straight shot at his ball, you've *hooked* him. Being without a direct path to the object ball is a common occurrence in many games of pool, even to the point where you can hook yourself by making a shot but leaving no clear angle on a ball.

The closer the cue ball is to blockers, the more effective the safety. Looking back at Figure 17-1, imagine if the cue ball was up against the 4 ball. Putting the cue ball directly behind blocker balls limits the angles your opponent can shoot the cue ball.

That being said, if you can really hide the object ball close to one or more blockers, you've increased the probability of your opponent making a *bad hit* — meaning he hits another ball besides the lowest numbered ball in 9-ball, or he hits the 8 ball or one of your balls in 8-ball.

In pretty much every set of rules for every game, it's mandatory that, after the cue ball contacts an object ball, a ball must hit a rail for the shot to be considered legal. So when you're playing safe, you must plan for either the cue ball or an object ball to hit a rail after initial contact.

Creating distance

When you first started playing pool, I bet it didn't take long for you to realize that long shots are more difficult than short ones. Well, you can use this knowledge to your advantage when you're trying to play a safety.

While leaving distance between the cue ball and one or more object balls can be a safety technique that may be available at any time, players most commonly use it at the end of a game, when fewer balls are on the table to act as blockers.

The example in Figure 17-2 shows an end-of-game situation in 9-ball. Only the 8 and 9 are left on the table. It's your turn, and you don't really have much chance to pocket the 8 and 9 to win the game, so it's time to play defensively.

With only one other ball on the table (the 9), you can't really use it as a blocker. You can, however, leave the cue ball on the right side of the table, sending the 8 ball to the other end. The ideal shot would leave both balls up against the rails (see next section) and a full table-length apart. From this spot, your opponent would be hard-pressed to leave you without an angle on a pocket for the 8.

These methods of playing safe are meant to be mixed and matched. While some situations will leave you with only one option, say to use blockers, you want to incorporate as many elements as possible to make things hard for your opponent.

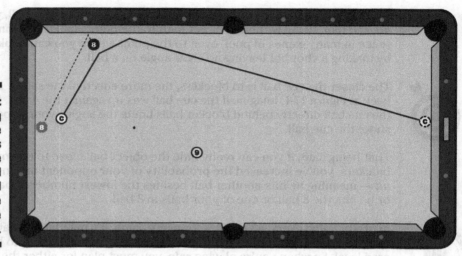

Freezing the cue ball

A third principle, which is best used as more of a complementary feature to a safety, is leaving the cue ball on a rail or up against another ball.
Professionals often try to leave the cue ball *frozen* to either a rail or another
ball. Freezing the cue ball means that it comes to a stop while in contact with
a rail or ball.

A ball that is frozen to another ball is a very difficult proposition for the
incoming player. In most cases where you're frozen to another ball, you're
limited to hitting the cue ball at an angle that will not result in moving the
ball it is frozen to. As you can see in Figure 17-3, you must cue over the 5 ball
and send the cue ball to the short rail so that you can make a legal hit.

Similarly, leaving the cue ball up against a rail complicates your opponent's
next shot. When it's frozen to a rail, the cue ball is mostly hidden underneath
the lip of the rail, leaving only the top sliver available to hit with your cue.
Not only does this shot require extra care to make a clean hit, it also severely
limits your options for position.

In Figure 17-4, you're faced with a shot where the cue ball is glued to the rail.
Because you have to strike the cue ball above its center axis, you have to
use follow (see Chapter 8), which limits your control of the cue ball. On your
shot in Figure 17-4, it will be nearly impossible to get a good angle on your
next shot.

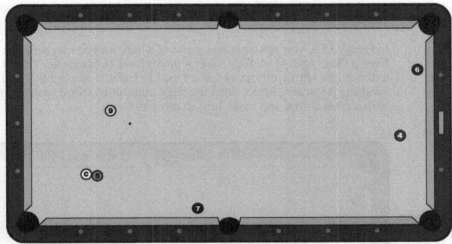

Figure 17-3: A cue ball frozen to an object ball isn't what you want to see when you come to the table.

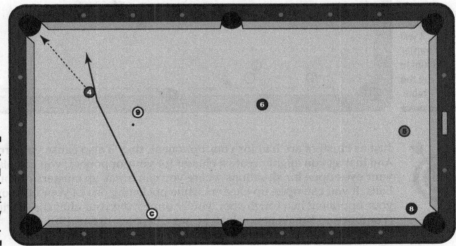

Figure 17-4: Getting position for your next shot is very difficult.

Bunching it up

A fourth aspect to defensive strategy involves creating *clusters* — or groups of balls that aren't easily pocketed in succession. This method of safety play is especially effective while playing 8-ball (see Chapter 18). Creating clusters for your opponent is a valuable safety tool because you're shooting at a different set of balls from your opponent, whereas in 9-ball you're both shooting at the same nine balls.

In Figure 17-5, you're solids in a game of 8-ball. As you can see, you don't have a clear path to victory, so you might have to play safe. Your 4 ball is in a direct line with your opponent's 9 and 12 balls. If you lightly hit the 4, it will send the 9 toward the 12. With the right amount of speed, you'll leave him with a cluster that will make his job more difficult.

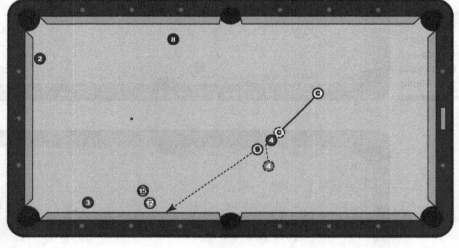

Figure 17-5: If you can create a cluster for your opponent, it will be harder for him to run the table.

Just as clusters are bad for your opponent, they'll also cause you problems. And just as you might create a cluster for your opponent, you can also keep your eyes open for situations where you can break up clusters of your own balls. If you can open up clusters while pocketing one of your balls or leaving your opponent in a tough spot, you're improving your chances of winning. (For more on breaking up clusters, see Chapters 18 and 19.)

Percentage Play: Knowing When to Play Safe

At almost any time in any game of pool, you could probably come up with a way to play safe. But when is it in your best interest to do so? Finding that perfect balance between offense and defense — the right mix of the go-for-broke gunslinger and duck-and-cover scaredy cat — is important to finding your own identity as a pool player.

Defense is a vital part of the game, but there is an inherent problem with it. You're giving your opponent a chance at the table. Granted, if you're a superb defensive player, he won't have much of a chance. But still, you can't win the game with a safety.

So how do you know when your playing style has become too aggressive or too meek? Try to think of the odds of each possible shot. For every situation on a pool table, you should be able to guess how often you can successfully complete a given shot. Whether it be pocketing a table-length bank or executing a safety, you need to put a percentage on your success rate.

If you can pocket a specific shot only 10 percent of the time, then you know it's time to look at playing safe because you're basically praying that the ball goes in. Similarly, if you can successfully play a safety 80 percent of the time, you know that's the direction you should go.

But things get complicated when the numbers start to creep closer to one another. A safe bet is that if you can make a ball two-thirds of the time, you should probably go for it. There is always a chance of misplaying a safety, which can leave your opponent in great shape, so you need to know when the odds tell you to go for it.

That being said, if, during this same shot, there is a killer safety that you can hit perfectly 99 percent of the time, then you may have to re-evaluate. The point is that there is a balance between offense and defense, and top players know when to play aggressively and when to hold back.

Check out Figure 17-6, which shows a moderately difficult shot that offers possibilities for both offense and defense. If you feel confident with this shot, then go for it. If you know you're not likely to make it, play safe in the hope of improving your position.

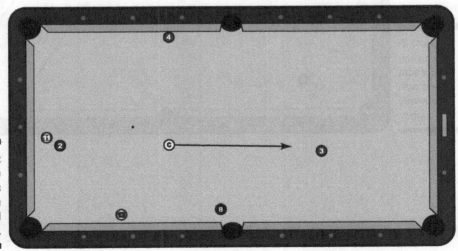

Figure 17-6:
Weigh the options between offense and defense.

The Two-Way Shot: Taking Out Insurance

Playing the percentages (see preceding section) of offense and defense can lead to some tough decisions. But if you keep your eyes open to the possibility of a two-way shot, you can relieve some of the stress of in-game decisions.

A two-way shot means that you're mixing both offense and defense into the same attempt. Looking at Figure 17-7, you're stripes in a game of 8-ball. You have a long shot on the 11 ball, which is not exactly a gimme. So what do you do?

Play a two-way shot. It's not the easiest angle, but aim for the 11 in the upper-right corner pocket. If you make the shot, you'll have a natural angle for the cue ball to hit two rails and roll out toward the middle of the table for the 13.

But what if you miss? Well, if you play this right, your opponent will have little to no chance of pocketing the 4 ball. Plan to leave the cue ball on the other side of the table. If you make the 11, you have a shot on the 13 and natural position on the 8 ball. If you miss, your opponent is a table's length away from the 4 ball with a near-impossible angle.

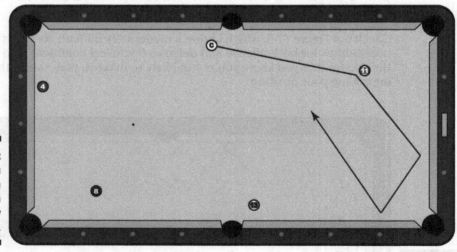

Figure 17-7: You can have it both ways with a two-way shot.

The One to Know: Getting to Know Stop-Shot Safeties

For those who are unfamiliar with the idea of playing safe, it can be bit of an adjustment. For starters, when you play a defensive shot, you need to plan for the final resting spot for the object ball — something you don't worry about when you pocket it because speed means nothing as long as it goes in the hole.

Cue-ball control (see Chapter 7) is a vital part of the game, and this is especially true when playing safe. If you're hiding the cue ball behind a blocker, you need to be as precise as can be to ensure that you have properly hooked your opponent. If you're leaving the cue ball on a rail, you have to be confident in controlling the speed of the cue ball.

So, toward that end, here is one common method of playing safe. While the number of possible safeties are literally infinite, the stop-shot safety is a good start.

The stop shot, where the cue ball stops at impact with an object ball (see Chapter 7), is an amazingly simple and effective way to play safe. Because the cue ball dies at the spot it hits the object ball, you're in complete control of it. When you're looking for a way to play safe, determine whether you can use a stop shot to hide the cue ball behind a blocker. This approach is especially effective in 8-ball, as shown in Figure 17-8, because you have multiple balls you can aim for.

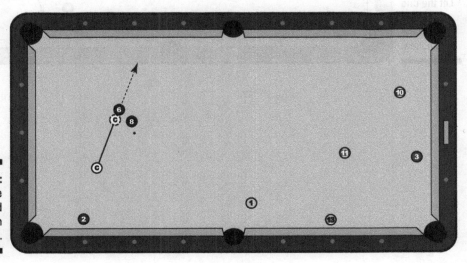

Figure 17-8:
Stop the cue ball, and you're in great shape.

You don't have an easy way to pocket a ball, but you're in great shape to drop the cue ball behind the 8 ball. Playing a nice, easy stop shot on the 6 ball, you can leave your opponent in a tough spot.

Similarly, if you use a stun shot (see Chapter 7) — a stop shot that isn't straight-on — the cue ball deflects from the object ball's path at a 90-degree angle. Knowing this information, you can easily predict where the cue ball will go after impact.

In Figure 17-9, you're solids in a game of 8-ball. Knowing you can hit the 2 ball with a stun shot, the cue ball will drift right behind the 4 and 8 balls, leaving your opponent in need of a miracle to make contact with his ball.

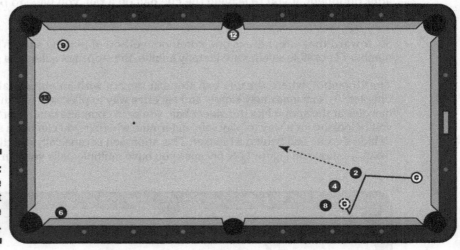

Figure 17-9:
Let the cue
ball drift
behind the
blockers.

Part IV
The Games You'll Play

In this part . . .

While pool is undoubtedly a sport, you can play many different games on a pool table. In this section, I pack your brain with the necessary rules, strategy, and tips to play great 8-ball, 9-ball, straight pool, and any other discipline that involves a slate table and a cue.

Chapter 18

The Magic of 8-Ball

It's no secret that 8-ball is the most recognized pool game. Also known as Stripes and Solids, 8-ball often serves as a gateway of sorts for those who are just starting to play pool. The biggest reason why 8-ball trumps all other games in popular support? People of all skill levels, from absolute newbie to seasoned professional, can play the game. Certainly the world's best players operate on a higher level of execution and strategy, but two newcomers to pool can battle over a game of 8-ball, while enjoying the thrill of pocketing a few balls (and, eventually, the game-winning 8 ball).

Globally, pool leagues attract players of all skill levels to pool halls and bars. And more often than not, the game is 8-ball. Unlike 9-ball (which I cover in Chapter 19) where you have to hit the balls in numerical order, 8-ball allows for some wiggle room. You can make one shot and still have any one of your balls (stripes or solids) to shoot at. In 8-ball, you have options, so you don't have to play pinpoint position on every shot (though playing position can help a bit!).

In this chapter, I run through the rules of the game and talk about strategy, which can get pretty cerebral at times. I also run through some house rules. While the general idea of 8-ball remains the same no matter where it's played, some rules change from location to location — and sometimes from table to table within the same pool hall!

Getting Started in 8-Ball

Before you can win a game of 8-ball, you should know how to win, right? The goal of 8-ball is to clear all the balls of your group (either stripes or solids) and pocket the 8 ball with a legal shot. But before you run through all your balls, you need to know the basics behind the game of 8-ball.

The following sections take a look at what it takes to start a game.

Producing a playable rack

The game of 8-ball begins by racking all 15 balls in a triangle formation with the top ball on the footspot (usually marked with a black sticker or mark), as shown in Figure 18-1.

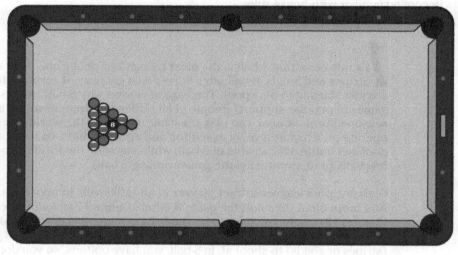

Figure 18-1:
The head ball is on the footspot, and the cue ball's behind the headstring.

While you can arrange most of the balls randomly, two stipulations must be met for a rack to be deemed playable:

- ✔ **8 in the center:** The black ball always goes in the center of the rack — in other words, the middle ball of the third row.

- ✔ **Alternate in the back corners:** Most league and tournament rules call for the back two corners to be from opposite groups (so one solid and one stripe).

While some people believe the 1 ball must be up front, most rulebooks don't call for a specific ball to be on top of the rack. As long as the balls are randomly placed (except for the 8 and both back corner balls), it really doesn't matter how the other 12 balls are arranged.

Randomly arranging balls doesn't mean you (or your opponent) can purposely place the balls in a specific order. In most cases, rules are in place against racking in a predetermined order.

After you get the placement down, try to leave all the balls touching one another. When the balls are *frozen* — touching — they're more likely to scatter around the table during a nice, firm break. So first, you want to push the full rack in place, with the triangle squared up to the table and the head ball over the footspot.

The most effective way to keep all (or at least most of) the balls in contact is to push the back row of balls up toward the top of the triangle. To do so, put your thumbs in the middle of the back of the rack, between the triangle and the balls, with your pinkies out near the corner of the triangle, again between the rack and balls. Use your other fingers to push the balls, using your thumbs and pinkies to hold the rack in place.

When you think you've got a tight rack, lift your hands off the balls and slide the triangle up, no more than half an inch or so. Ideally, the balls won't move at all. If they don't move, you've got a tight rack. If they do move, put the rack back down on the table and repeat the process.

Making a "break" for it

To ramp up the power behind your break, check out the detailed look at the break stroke in Chapter 11. In this section, I want to describe some things that are unique to the break in 8-ball.

When you're getting ready to crack open the rack of balls, you need to decide where to place the cue ball. Because you want to hit the stack with as much power as possible, put the cue ball just behind the headstring. Placing the cue ball here will put you as close to the head ball as possible.

You have options for where to place the cue ball along the headstring. I recommend that you start out directly in front of the head ball. This way, you're staring directly at the top ball, which you want to hit as fully as possible.

With some time, though, a rail break is another option for the placement of the cue ball, shown by the dotted-line ball in Figure 18-2. When you break from the side, you change the cue ball's angle of impact, which changes the way the balls break apart.

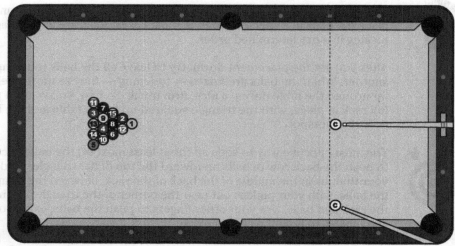

If you should make the 8 ball on the break, a few different sets of rules cover this situation. In many leagues, if you make the 8 on the break, you win the game. Other rules, though, give the break a choice if the 8 is pocketed on the break. She can call for the 8 to be *spotted,* which means that the ball is put back on the table on the head spot (or as close to the head spot as possible, if a ball is blocking it). If a spotted 8 isn't much help to the breaker, she can then decide that the balls be reracked so that she can break again.

Choosing stripes or solids

After the balls are broken up (and hopefully spread out across the whole table), you and your opponent must first decide which player will be shooting at which group of balls — either solids, balls 1 through 7, or stripes, balls 9 through 15.

You can determine who will be shooting at what in a number of ways. One universally accepted way of doing this doesn't exist, so here are a few of the most common methods of choosing side:

✔ **Open after the break:** This approach to break means that the table is open, no matter what was made on the break. The point of keeping the table open is to leave it to the breaker to decide, instead of a group being assigned to her by virtue of balls in on the break. The open-after-the-break approach is the most common rule and also the fairest (because the player then has the option to decide which group to play).

✔ **Balls on the break:** What (if anything) was made on the break is one way to determine groups. In this version, if you broke the balls open and made the 5 ball (a solid), you're solids. If you made only the 9, you're stripes. If you made one of each, the table remains *open* — meaning players haven't chosen groups — until you or your opponent legally pockets a ball, at which time the player who made the shot will be shooting at that group. And if you made two stripes and one solid, you're stripes.

✔ **No balls or a foul:** If nothing was made on the break or the breaker scratched, the table is considered open for the incoming player.

Most rule systems allow for a bit of a quirk while the table is open. With an open table, you can use any ball on the table to pocket the first object ball. You then assume the group of the first pocketed ball. For example, if you hit the 11 ball (a stripe) into the 4 ball (a solid) and the 4 is pocketed, you're solids.

Hitting a ball other than one in your group is normally a foul, but that rule doesn't apply because the players have yet to decide who is what.

You can — and should — take a strategic approach to choosing whether you're stripes or solids. This decision may just be the most important one you make during a game. For more on the strategy behind this decision, see the section "Choosing your group," later in this chapter.

Winning the game

Winning a game of 8-ball is pretty straightforward: You have to clear all the balls in your group and then pocket the 8 with a legal stroke (without fouling or scratching) in the pocket you called before the shot.

In some leagues, if you scratch while shooting the 8 ball, you lose. In other leagues, you lose only if you scratch and pocket the 8. Also, if you pocket the 8 ball by mistake, before you clear your other balls, or if you pocket the 8 in a pocket other than the one you intended, you lose.

Fouling: Common No-Nos

With 15 balls on the table and two players looking to navigate their way to the 8 ball, a near infinite amount of situations can arise. But for every shot imaginable, some things you just can't do. Scratching is the most known way of committing a foul. Simply put, a *scratch* means the cue ball was pocketed during a shot. In this case, the incoming player gets *ball in hand,* meaning that she can place the cue ball anywhere on the table to begin her turn. Contrary to many bar-room rules, where the incoming player has to put the cue ball behind the headstring, most leagues and tournaments allow you to have ball in hand so that you can put the ball anywhere.

You can also foul by hitting a ball so hard that it jumps off the table. This rule is especially important on the break, when the cue ball can hit the rack of balls and hop up and off the table.

But scratching isn't the only major foul or illegal shot. The following sections look at other common fouls.

No hit or illegal hit

The variations of the no-hit or illegal-hit rule are many, but in most cases, it's a foul if a player doesn't hit one of his balls with the cue ball. If you hit the cue ball and it doesn't hit a ball in your group first (or the 8 ball, if you've cleared your balls), it's a foul.

The two most common scenarios related to this type of foul are

- ✔ **No hit:** If you hit the cue ball and it doesn't make contact with any other ball on the table, it's a foul. In some versions of 8-ball, usually played in bars, you don't scratch if the cue ball hits three rails. But just know that in almost every official rulebook, a shot where the cue ball contacts no other balls is considered to be a foul.

- ✔ **Illegal hits:** If you hit one of your opponent's balls first (stripes if you're solids, for example), it's considered a foul. Once you or your competitor determine groups, you must hit a ball in your group first.

No rail

To avoid endless safety battles where players just tap the cue ball off one of their balls, if a ball isn't pocketed, a ball must hit a rail *after* the cue ball makes a legal hit on a ball.

This rule sounds pretty simple, but it's not widely understood outside of league and tournament players that a shot that doesn't send a ball to a rail after cue-ball impact is a foul.

As an example, look at shot shown in Figure 18-3. You're stripes, and your opponent is on the 8 ball. If you hit the cue ball off the short rail and into the 11, is it a foul? The shot is, in fact, a foul, because a ball didn't hit a rail *after* contact between the 11 ball and the cue ball. The cue ball hit the short rail, but that is of no consequence because no rail was hit after impact.

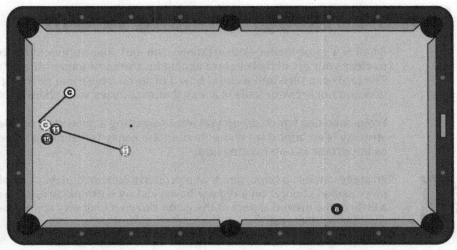

Figure 18-3:
The cue ball
hit a rail,
but not after
the cue
ball struck
another ball.

Other common fouls

A few more fouls are helpful to know, though they're not as common as the ones I list in the previous sections.

- ✔ **One foot on the ground:** You can put yourself in some interesting positions to get set for a shot. No matter if you're stretching across the table or sitting on an edge to get a better angle, you need to keep one foot on the ground during your shot.

- ✔ **Double hits:** If the cue ball is close to another ball (but not touching it), you run the risk of a *double hit* if you stroke toward the object ball. A double hit is just what it sounds like — the cue tip hits the cue ball twice.

- ✔ **Unintentionally moving an object ball:** Most leagues and tournaments adhere to the principle of *cue ball fouls only*. This rule means that any inadvertent action that moves an object ball isn't a foul. Rather, if you should move an object ball by mistake, your opponent can choose to leave the ball where it is or move it back to its original position. The other option is *all ball fouls*, which means that any contact with an object ball is a foul, whether the ball moved or not.

- ✔ **Unintentionally moving the cue ball:** If you hit the cue ball during a practice stroke, it's a foul, unless the unintentional stroke resulted in a legal hit.

8-Ball Strategy: Thinking to Win

8-ball is a game loaded with strategy. You and your opponent are both trying to clear your set of balls before aiming for the same game-winner (the 8 ball). The table can turn into a chess board of sorts, where you're trying to position and pocket your balls in a way that maximizes your chances of winning.

From choosing which group you want to getting a good shot on the 8 ball, strategy is an important component of the game. Outthinking someone is just as important as outshooting him.

Strategy can be so important that a properly educated player can often beat a more skilled shooter on a regular basis, just by outthinking him. So studying a little of the mental aspect of the game can go a long way toward becoming a winning 8-ball player.

Choosing your group

The most important decision of the game is choosing which group of balls to play. If you're in a position to make the decision, meaning that it's your turn and the table is considered open, you need to consider several things to ensure that you make the correct decision.

The first thing you want to do is look for clusters of balls that may present problems when you're clearing your balls on the way to the 8 ball. A *cluster* is any group of two or more balls that may restrict your options when you need to pocket one or more ball in the cluster.

If three solid balls are all grouped along a rail, this clustering will be an obstacle should you choose solids. While you need to consider other factors, clusters can make one group of balls look much less desirable than the other group.

The typical layout in Figure 18-4 is a great example of how clusters can cause some problems for one group. If you had the option for stripes or solids, you'd be in much better shape if you looked to pocket a striped ball. While you have an easy shot on the 6 ball to begin your turn, look at the three solids clustered in the top-left corner. As these balls sit, you can't pocket any of them without some trickery.

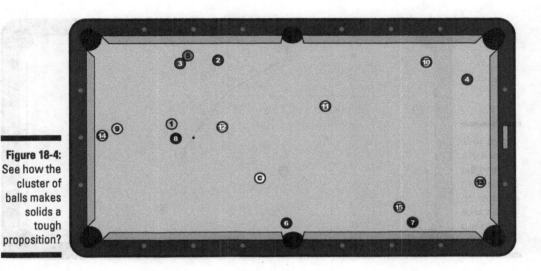

Figure 18-4:
See how the cluster of balls makes solids a tough proposition?

The stripes, meanwhile, are open for you to string a few shots together. The 9 and 14 balls are almost clustered together on the short rail, but you could pocket both balls in both corner pockets, so you don't really have to worry about that group.

If a cluster has both stripes and solids in it, however, things can get a little more complicated. In this case, you may have to find a ball that will let you *break out* your ball(s) from the cluster. Breaking out means pocketing one ball and sending the cue ball into the cluster, knocking your ball out into an open space on the table.

Breaking a ball out of a cluster can be tricky business, but you can make things easier on yourself if you have an *insurance ball*. An insurance ball is one that you can pocket from just about anywhere on the table. When you send the cue ball into a group of balls, you know you'll have the insurance ball to shoot at after breaking open the cluster.

In Figure 18-5, you're solids. You have a great chance to pocket the 1 ball and send the ball into the cluster of the 2 and 3 balls. Even better, the 7 ball makes for a perfect insurance ball. You'll be hard-pressed to predict exactly what will happen when you hit the 2 and 3 balls. But having the 7 sitting in the corner, you'll most likely have a shot.

Figure 18-5:
When you
send the
cue ball into
a cluster, an
insurance
ball is a
great help.

Identify problem balls

Just as clusters can muck up your plans for victory, balls sitting all by themselves may present problems should you choose that group of balls. These problem balls should be identified so that you can take them into account when you're choosing sides.

In most cases, problem balls are deemed trouble because they don't have a natural line to a pocket. Sometimes, balls in the opposite group block them; sometimes balls in their same group block them. No matter the case, you need to be aware of any potential difficulties with a given group.

Look at the example shown in Figure 18-6. You can see a majority of balls on one side of the table, which makes things a little crowded. But the 7 ball is the biggest problem. It's up against the long rail, which wouldn't be all that bad if striped balls weren't blocking it from going to either corner pocket. The 2 and 3 balls are also problematic, but the 7 ball certainly isn't helping either.

Conversely, some of the stripes are grouped around the footspot (the black dot where the balls are racked to start the game). But you can shoot the 9, 13, and 12 balls in multiple pockets. And the 11 ball on the other side of the table can't go in the top-left pocket, but it can go in the other corner pocket and either side pocket.

You want to give yourself as many options as you can. A ball that is married to one pocket will force you to play perfect position, a luxury you may not have when you want to shoot that ball.

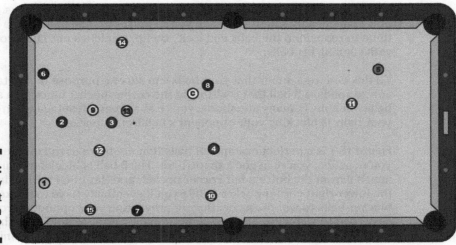

Figure 18-6:
See any
balls that
might be a
pain?

Taking action

Planning is an important part of 8-ball. But after you've chosen the more desirable group, you're ready to take your opening shot. In the next section of this chapter, I go into detail about *pattern play* — formulating a route through all your balls and the 8. In this section, I offer tips to help you choose the right first shot.

First and foremost, no rule says that you *must* shoot the easiest shot on the table. Because choosing groups is so darn important, you need to choose a shot that will help you get the group you want. Oftentimes, the easiest shot on the table isn't going to help you here.

What you want to do is pocket a ball in your desired group, if possible. If it isn't possible, or maybe plausible is more accurate, you may have to play a safety that will prevent your opponent from making a ball. (See Chapter 17 for a full description of safeties.)

Using your balls

8-ball is a bit funny because every player's natural inclination is to pocket as many balls as possible in the hopes of getting to the 8 ball. But this approach is one of the biggest mistakes that you can make.

If you run through all seven of your balls but have no prayer of making the 8, you've just made life easier for your opponent. Now, he has no obstacles (except for the 8 ball) on the table; he's got a wide open table if he wants to start pocketing his balls. Or, if your opponent is especially devious, he can play some deadly safeties, forcing you to foul. With ball in hand, he can continue to reposition the balls and lock you up in safeties until he's comfortable with running his balls.

To this end, remember that your balls can serve a purpose on the table. If you're solids, a 3 ball that is sitting in the corner pocket blocking a stripe can be invaluable. In many situations, you're at a great advantage when one of your balls is blocking your opponent's ball from a pocket.

Figure 18-7 is a perfect example of balls that are more useful on the table. If you're solids, you're in good shape here. The 5 ball is blocking your opponent's 9 from the bottom-left corner pocket, and the 1 ball is blocking it from the lower-right corner pocket. While you'll eventually have to pocket these blocker balls to win the game, they're preventing your opponent from an easy road to victory. If at all possible, you may want to hold onto those balls for last — or at least until you're confident that you'll soon be winning the game.

If you're not confident that you can run the table for the win, ask yourself, "Would my opponent be in better shape if I pocket this ball?" If you get rid of a ball that blocks a pocket, your opponent may be thankful that you made a shot.

Just because you don't think you can run out from a certain position doesn't mean that you should play safeties all day (and night) long. Try to pocket balls that are out in the open, while saving those that are causing problems for your opponent. And if you have to miss, try to do so by leaving your opponent in a tough spot. (You can find more on this topic in the "Playing Defensive 8-Ball" section of this chapter.)

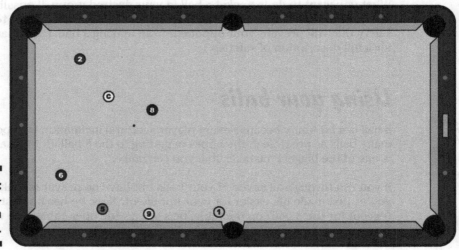

Figure 18-7:
If you're solids, you're in good shape.

Planning your way out

After you know your group, you need to plan how you're going to pocket all your balls and the 8 to win the game. What you want to develop is a pattern that will lead you from one ball to the next. And because you can have as many as seven balls to shoot at, you've got some possibilities.

While every table's layout is different, some general guidelines can help you find a route that connects all your balls to the 8.

These guidelines for pattern play are exactly that — guidelines. You won't be able to fulfill all these points on every shot. You'll be best served, though, by keeping them in mind when you're eying your run. These guidelines may not always apply, but they'll be helpful when they do.

Minimize cue-ball movement

Keep things as simple as possible when you move the cue ball in position for your next shot. A major way of making things easy on yourself is to limit the distance you move the cue ball. Even for the best players in the world, the more the cue ball moves, the more chance for error.

You want to keep the cue ball under your complete control. This approach is easier when you're moving short distances from one shot to another, instead of going from one side of the table to the other and back. *Stop shots,* where the cue ball stops at the point of impact, are especially valuable because the cue ball doesn't move at all.

When you have to move the cue ball, don't try to kill yourself getting within a foot of the next ball. Having the right angle on the next object ball is much more important than being close to it. You'll be in good shape if you're always shooting shots at slight angles (because straight-in shots limit your opportunities to play position).

Playing position for your next ball is just as important as making the shot in front of you. But don't let one area dominate your thoughts when you're preparing to shoot. Think how you're going to make the shot at hand and how it will lead to another shot. Focusing too much on one of these areas often leads to failing in the other.

Going from one side to the other

Because a primary goal of planning your route to victory is to minimize cue-ball movement, you should look for balls that are grouped on one side of the table. Identifying balls that you can make in succession can help you devise a plan from the first ball to the 8 ball.

Imagine you've got ball in hand on the table shown in Figure 18-8. First, if you need to choose which group to shoot for, you can see that solids would present two problems. The 7 and 3 balls would be difficult to pocket because they're both on the rail, with a striped ball in close proximity. The stripes, though, are pretty open, with no solids causing any major obstacles.

To minimize the distance the cue ball travels, look to work from one side of the table to the other. Because the 8 ball is on the left side, near the footspot, you may want to start with the balls on the other side of the table. You can pocket the three balls on the right side first — the 10 and 13 in the upper-right corner and the 15 in the lower-right corner. Luckily, you have the 14 ball near the side pocket. The 14 can be a sort of transitional ball as you move the cue ball from the right to the left. If you can stop the cue ball somewhere near the 14, you can then shoot the 12 in the upper left, the 11 in the lower-left corner, and the 9 back in the upper-left corner. Now all that is left is the 8 ball, which can go in both side pockets and the near corner pockets.

Obviously, clearing all the balls is a lot easier said than done. Even though no clusters or solids are blocking your way, trouble is never far from the table. You shouldn't expect to clear this layout the first time you try. What this example can do, however, is help you see how to break your balls into smaller, more manageable tasks. You have the 10, 13, and 15 to pocket. Then you can move to the 14 and the balls on the other side of the table.

Developing a pattern to play a group of balls isn't an exact science. Get the ten best 8-ball players in the world to look at the same table, and I guarantee they would have more than one "right" answer. But start with these principles of planning your pattern and work with your strengths. Over time, you'll get an understanding of what patterns work best for you.

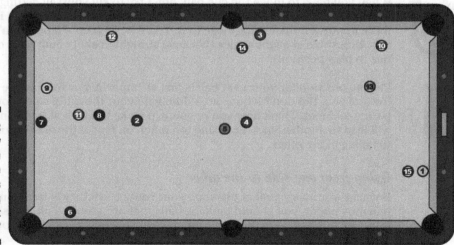

Figure 18-8:
See how you can clear the stripes starting on the left side?

Don't ignore problems

It won't be long before you're faced with a layout that has a number of problem balls from both solids and stripes. In this case, you're going to have to deal with them — and sooner is better than later.

Your balls can be obstacles for your opponent. If you clear all the easy shots and leave a few balls that are tied up, you've just made life much easier for your opponent.

You're better off dealing with problem balls as soon as possible. Whether you plan on playing a nasty safety on your opponent to get ball in hand or you want to pocket a ball and send the cue ball into your problem ball's cluster, don't let your difficult balls sit around for too long.

Imagine that you're solids in Figure 18-9. The 1 and 2 balls are bunched up near the short rail. You need to get the 1 and 2 separated to win the game, right? Try to pocket the 4 or 5 so that the cue ball will hit the cluster and break the balls apart. If you sink the 4 and 5 without addressing the problem, you only set yourself up for disaster when you're left without a shot.

"As soon as possible" doesn't necessarily mean "on your next shot." Work yourself into a good spot to address your problem balls. Even if it takes a shot or two, at least you're consciously trying to deal with your most difficult ball(s).

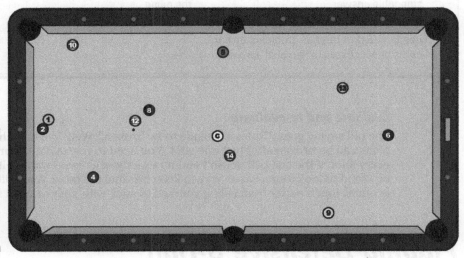

Figure 18-9:
Deal with the 1 and 2 balls early so that you won't reach a dead end.

Finding a good 8-ball coach

Whether you're in a nationwide league system or you rarely venture out of your basement to play, finding a good coach can be a tremendous help for your improvement. Regardless of whether this coach is someone you take paid lessons from or just another player who you look to for advice, there are a few things you need to look for in a pool coach:

✔ **Is she knowledgeable?** This trait may seem like a no-brainer, but you'd be surprised how many "coaches" don't know too much about the game. While your coach doesn't necessarily need to play at a professional level, you want someone who is a player first and a coach second. A good player doesn't always make for a great coach, but it's a start!

✔ **Is she approachable?** You want a coach to be someone you can ask anything, no matter how basic or trivial the question may seem. Look for someone who understands your questions and always has an understandable answer.

✔ **Can she empathize with you?** A coach needs to listen to your problems or concerns or successes (about pool, anyway).

✔ **Can she make things make sense?** You'll be at a different level of play, so you need someone who can explain things to you in a way that is informative and complete, without being demeaning.

✔ **Do you get along?** It's a simple thing, but compatibility can be very important. You have to have a good rapport with your coach. You don't have to be best buddies, but an open line of communication between the two of you will help immensely when someone gets frustrated or fed up.

You can find professional instructors just about any place there's a pool table, so you shouldn't have a problem finding a coach if you want to pay for lessons. Top instructors charge anywhere from $30 to $100 an hour. But you may also come across a knowledgeable player who'll give you free advice at your local pool hall. Be polite and approach someone with a question; pool players love talking about the game.

Evaluate and re-evaluate

The old saying goes, "Rules are made to be broken." Well, in 8-ball, the best laid plans can be broken after just one shot. You need to re-evaluate your plan after every shot. If the cue ball doesn't end up exactly where you wanted it to, don't be afraid to look for an easier way to keep clearing the table. A modified plan of action is much better than killing yourself to stick with your original script.

Playing Defensive 8-Ball

While you're not always going to have a way to run out and win the game, you can stay in control of the table by keeping your opponent tied up. While

Chapter 17 details defensive strategy, some tactics are especially important in 8-ball.

- ✔ **Balls as pocket blockers:** You can play defense by placing your balls between your opponent's pockets. Unlike 9-ball, where you and your opponent are shooting at the same ball, 8-ball offers you a chance to reposition your group of balls during a shot so that your opponent's balls are tied up.

- ✔ **Balls as cue-ball blockers:** One of the most effective ways to play safe in 8-ball is to hide the cue ball behind one of your balls so that your opponent can't see any of his balls. The more balls you have on the table, the more opportunities you have to hide the cue ball behind one or more of them.

Imagine that you're stripes in Figure 18-10 — you don't have much of an offensive opportunity. But if you play one successful safety, you can have a shot of clearing the final three balls and the 8. Just lightly tap the 13 so that it barely hits the rail, blocking the cue ball from the 6. Your opponent will be in a rough spot.

Chapter 17 talks about the importance of the stop-shot safety. This shot is especially valuable in 8-ball because you know exactly where the cue ball will come to a rest (right at the point of contact, where it stops). Look at Figure 18-11, which is the same layout as Figure 18-10, just with a different spot for the cue ball. Again, you don't have much of an opportunity to run out. But if you can hit the 10 ball against the long rail and kill the cue ball behind the 8, your opponent will be struggling to hit his ball legally. With ball in hand, you'll have a chance to win.

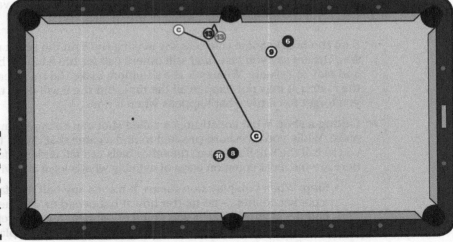

Figure 18-10: Use the 13 as a blocker, and you're relatively safe.

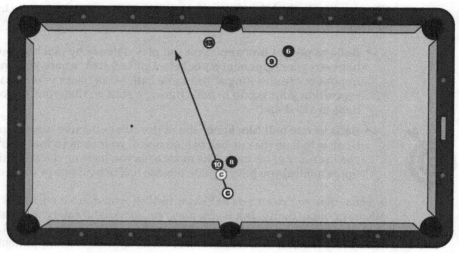

Figure 18-11:
In this situ-
ation, hide
the cue ball
behind the 8
ball.

Exploring House Rules

8-ball comes in a variety of shapes and sizes, with enough different rules that I could write another book on that subject alone. But if you cover these varia- tions, you should be ready to handle most versions of the *house rules,* which are variations of the common rules of the game.

Here are some common interpretations to the basic rules of 8-ball. You should always agree to the general rules of a game before you break the balls. And to help you prepare for common questions with rules, these variations may pop up in the pregame discussion of the details.

- ✔ **8 on the break:** Some rule sets say making the 8 on the break means you win. Others say you lose, and still others call for the 8 ball to be spotted and play to resume. Whatever the situation, make the rule clear before the match. It may not happen all the time, but the 8 will drop the minute you forget to clarify what happens when it does.

- ✔ **Calling a shot:** What constitutes a called shot can change from place to place. While you'd be hard-pressed to find a game that doesn't require you to call the 8 ball's pocket, the other balls can fall under different rules. Here are the most common ways of defining what's legal and what isn't.

  - • **Slop:** When you play *slop counts,* it means any ball that falls into a pocket counts — no matter how it happened or whether you had the slightest clue it was going to happen. A rather relaxed way to play, slop is often favored by less experienced players who benefit from the addition of the luck factor of a ball dropping without planning.

- **Ball and pocket:** This method of determining legal shots is the most commonly used among amateur leagues and tournaments (or at least some system very close to this basic idea). Like it says, you must call which ball is going into which pocket. That's it. If the ball you call hits off every ball and rail on the table and goes in the pocket you called, it counts.

- **Call everything:** A super-strict version of call-shot 8-ball requires you to call absolutely everything that happens on a shot, including kisses of other balls, object balls that may clip a rail on the way into a pocket, and any other contact between balls and rails. This approach isn't very popular because of the unnecessary attention to minute details. It also opens the door to plenty of did-it-or-didn't-it arguments.

✔ **Team 8-ball:** If you want to include more than two players into a standard 8-ball game, it's easy. Just form two teams. Each person can play an entire inning (meaning until he misses, fouls, or wins the game).

✔ **Last pocket 8-ball:** One of the most popular variations on the plain, old game of 8-ball is called *Last Pocket* or *Last Pocket 8-Ball.* This game means you have to make the 8 ball in the same pocket that you made your last object ball.

This take on the old rules is a way of upping the strategy involved in the game because you have to plan to make the 8 ball in a pocket that isn't specified until the shot before it. As a general rule, avoid playing this version of the game unless you're a rather advanced player.

Using Handicaps to Level the Playing Field

8-ball is a rather difficult game to *handicap* — to even the playing field between two players of different skill levels. Because having fewer object balls isn't necessarily an advantage, you can't just say that the weaker player has to make four balls while the other player has to make all seven.

The most common way to make a match competitive between players of differing skill is by adjusting the games needed to win the match. (A player who needs to win three fewer games is said to have *three games on the wire.*) If your friend is just a little better player than you, you could say he needs to win five games while you only need to win four. Or if he's much better than you, it could be a race to seven for him and a race to three for you. It's a flexible system that lets both players negotiate the number of games depending on skill levels.

You can handicap individual games in many ways, some of which can be pretty creative. You can say that one player gets the first shot on the break, regardless of balls pocketed. Or you can say one player has to play Last Pocket (see preceding section). While giving games on the wire is the easiest and most quantifiable way of handicapping 8-ball, feel free to play around with some crazy spots if you're just out there to have fun.

Chapter 19

9-Ball: The Hustler's Game

While 8-ball is the most commonly played game by amateurs (see Chapter 18), 9-ball has been the most popular game among professionals for the past three decades. It's considered a fast game, a game that is decidedly more offensive-minded than other popular games.

9-ball grew in popularity because of its roots with the hustlers of yesteryear. Years ago, back in the '60s, 14.1 straight pool was considered the professional game. Straight pool was the ultimate test of all-around skill, but it wasn't the easiest discipline to play for money. Enter 9-ball.

You can play a game of 9-ball in five minutes, while a straight-pool match can last for hours. Plus, 9-ball is a fairly easy game to handicap, so players of different skill levels can match up and play for a little money (or pride!).

And while some consider the game of 9-ball to be reserved for intermediate or advanced players, everyone, regardless of skill level, can play it. Not only that, but any player can learn something from playing 9-ball.

Winning a Game of 9-Ball

9-ball is a fairly straightforward game: The first player to pocket the 9 ball legally wins the game. But you can pocket the 9 ball in a number of different ways, so winning isn't all that easy:

✔ The most common way to win the game is by clearing the balls in numerical order — pocketing the 1, then the 2, and so on, until you can finish the game by making the 9.

✔ You can also win the game by making the 9 ball on the break (in most sets of rules, anyway) — called making the 9 *on the snap*.

✔ You can knock the 9 in after hitting the lowest numbered ball on the table. You can pocket the 9 with a combination shot, carom, kiss, or any combination of these shots . . . just as long as you hit the lowest ball first.

The common fouls in 9-ball are almost identical to 8-ball. The biggest difference is that you have only one ball you can shoot at in 9-ball, while you may have as many as seven balls at your disposal in 8-ball. For the basic no-nos related to 9-ball, see Chapter 18.

Racking for 9-Ball

While 8-ball uses all 15 balls, 9-ball uses just nine balls. (Amazing, I know!) To rack for 9-ball, you need to arrange balls 1 through 9 in a diamond formation, as shown in Figure 19-1.

Figure 19-1:
The diamond shape is arranged with the 1 ball on the footspot and the 9 ball in the center.

Under most tournament and league rules, you can arrange the nine balls in any order, with two exceptions:

✔ **The head ball:** The 1 ball needs to be racked on top of the diamond. The 1 ball is known as the *head ball*, and you place it directly on top of the footspot.

✔ **The 9 ball:** The 9 ball is the game-winner, so you place it in the middle of the diamond-shaped rack.

Outside of these two requirements, you can arrange the other seven balls in random order behind the 1 and surrounding the 9. As with most every racking situation, you want the balls to be touching one another. This setup is especially important in 9-ball because the *wing balls,* those on the left and right corners of the diamond, are more likely to go into a pocket if the rack is tight.

Using a normal triangle-shaped rack in 9-ball is perfectly acceptable (and often preferred). Just as you would push the back line of balls up toward the front of the table in a full 15-ball rack to ensure that all the balls are touching, you should keep your fingers on the back three balls. Pushing them into the other five balls should help get a nice, tight rack where all balls are frozen to one another.

After you think all the balls are tight, carefully remove the rack. Make sure that the top three balls are touching one another. Having the top three balls all in contact is a good indicator of whether the rack is acceptable or not. If you see any gaps, rerack and try again!

Sometimes, usually due to some problems with the table's cloth, you may not be able to get a completely tight rack. If you can't get an acceptable rack, you may want to talk to your opponent about possible solutions, including tapping the balls (see Chapter 11) and/or trying to flatten the footspot by rubbing it with your palm.

Taking the Break

Breaking the balls in 9-ball is almost always an advantage. You are in control of the table, and, if you can pocket a ball, you'll have first shot at the open table.

If you're just getting started with 9-ball, the power break is by and large the best approach to take. The harder you hit the head ball in the rack, the more action you'll get from the balls. The more action you get from the balls, the more likely it is that one or more will fall into a pocket — meaning that you're still at the table and you get first shot.

To break the balls in 9-ball:

1. **Place the cue ball for the break.**

   You have some options as far as placement, but the cue ball has to be behind the headstring. The most popular spot to place the cue ball is to one side, just a few inches out from the rail, as shown in Figure 19-2.

   If you're having trouble with any part of the break, whether it's making balls or controlling the cue ball or just feeling comfortable during the shot, don't be afraid to switch the starting spot for the cue ball. You can break from straight-on or from a spot between the rail and straight-on. The side rail position is just the most common, but by no means is it the only correct spot!

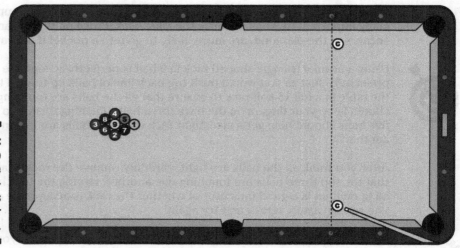

Figure 19-2:
These two spots are good starting points for your 9-ball break.

2. **Rest your cue so that it's sliding comfortably on the rail, with your hand over it in the rail bridge, as described in Chapter 3.**

   You want to line up so that you drive the cue ball fully into the 1 ball.

3. **Hit the cue ball in its center with as firm a stroke as you can (while still controlling the cue ball, of course!).**

   The cue ball should smash into the rack, hitting the 1 ball as full as possible, and come to a stop in the center of the table.

While most of the balls will randomly sprint around the table, a few common patterns will emerge. Knowing a few of these keys can help you pocket balls with more regularity.

For starters, the wing balls might start rolling toward the nearest corner pockets (see Figure 19-3). These are the balls that professionals first examine to see whether they can find a way to consistently pocket them. The head ball, always the 1, also has a tendency to drift in the direction of the side pocket on the side opposite from your break.

Obviously, any one of these balls isn't guaranteed to go on the break. They're just the most likely to go into a pocket.

If you're playing on a table other than your own, look for signs of wear along the headstring. If the cloth looks extra worn in a certain spot, it may be because the regulars have found it's the best place to break.

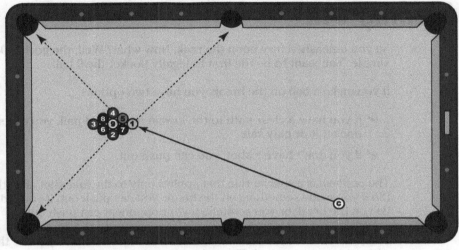

Figure 19-3:
Look where the wing and head balls go during your break.

The soft break

One of the recent trends in 9-ball is the development of the *soft break*. This approach to the game's first shot is just what it sounds like: The player hits the break softer than usual, with the hope of pocketing a ball and leaving himself a shot on the lowest ball. Another benefit of the soft break is that the object balls largely stay on one side of the table, so picking each ball off on the way to the 9 ball can be easier.

Corey Deuel, one of the best American players of the last decade, is largely credited with popularizing the soft break. He is one of the most creative players around, and he figured that he could pocket balls on the break with impressive regularity by hitting the 1 ball a bit off center with a medium stroke.

Deuel is certainly not the only player to use such a break, but he's often at the heart of the hard-versus-soft-break debate. Some players (call 'em old-schoolers, if you want) think that the power break is a part of the game. It's an exciting

shot that requires an impressive amount of hand-eye coordination and athletic ability. Other players think the soft break is a natural evolution of the game. If you can consistently pocket a ball and get a shot on the lowest ball, why should you kill yourself trying to smash the rack?

Well, some tournament directors and promoters are trying to guard against the soft break by instituting certain rules to force players to crank up the power. One way to keep players from breaking softly is by saying three balls must be pocketed or pass the headstring — something that you can't do with the soft break. Other events operate on a more subjective, no-soft-break rule, without stipulating what, in fact, constitutes a soft break.

Whatever the rules may be, the average amateur shooter is best served by developing a powerful and controlled break. The soft break takes a tremendous amount of understanding of the rack and different break strokes and spins. So, if you're thinking of laying off a bit, let 'er rip!

Pushing Out

So you unleashed fury upon the rack. Now what? Well, the goal of 9-ball is simple: You want to be the first to legally pocket the 9 ball.

If you make a ball on the break, you have two options:

- ✔ If you have a clear path to the lowest numbered ball, you can shoot to pocket it or play safe.
- ✔ If you don't have a shot, you can push out.

The *push-out* is a special rule that applies only to the first shot after the break. (So if you made something on the break, you can push out. If you didn't make a ball on the break or you scratched, your opponent can push out.)

The push-out rule allows the shooter to hit the cue ball any place they want without incurring a foul. This rule means that you don't have to hit a rail, and you don't have to hit the lowest numbered ball first. The catch? The other player then gets to choose if he will play the table as it is, or pass on it, which means you'll have to play the first shot.

This rule was put in place to protect the player at the table after the break. Imagine if you hit a perfect break shot, dropping a few balls in the pockets, only to see the cue ball snuggle up to the 9 (see Figure 19-4). Chances are, you'd be blocked from any clear shot on the lowest numbered ball, so the push-out is a way to even the playing field.

Similarly, if your opponent didn't make a ball and left the cue ball glued to the 9, you'd be penalized for his good luck. Appropriately, a push-out is allowed on the first shot after the break, no matter whose turn it is.

In the case of Figure 19-4, you'll definitely want to push out. So where should you think about leaving the cue ball? Well, because your opponent can choose to shoot, you don't want to leave an offensive option. Leaving a makable shot will only give your opponent a chance to fire away and win the game.

But you don't want to leave the cue ball in such dire straits that it will take a miracle to make a legal hit on the next shot. Your opponent can pass the shot back to you, which means you'll be the one in need of a miracle.

The push-out in Figure 19-5 is a standard play. You tapped the cue ball into the upper-left corner of the table. The cue ball has a direct path to the 1 ball, but you have no chance of cutting it into the corner pocket. Also, the two balls have an entire table between them, so you'll have to play any defensive shot with pinpoint accuracy and speed.

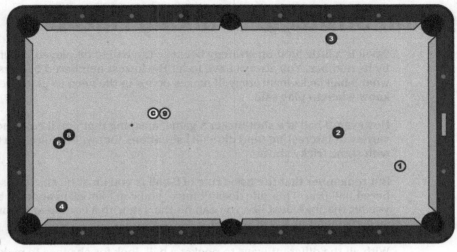

Figure 19-4:
You don't
have to play
the 1 ball if
you decide
to push out.

The push-out is a thinking player's shot. If you know you do one thing better than your opponent — say, banking balls — play the push-out to leave a chance for a bank. Play to your strengths and your opponent's weaknesses.

For more on strategic thinking ,see the upcoming section "9-Ball Strategy: Thinking Ahead."

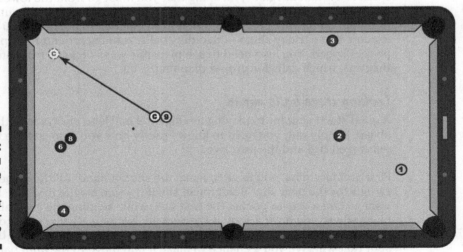

Figure 19-5:
Would you
rather have
this shot or
give it
to your
opponent?

9-Ball Strategy: Thinking Ahead

9-ball is a little light on strategy because the ball to be played is determined by its number. You always have to hit the lowest numbered ball first. But what 9-ball lacks in strategy, it makes up for in the need to plan ahead and to know when to play safe.

However, 9-ball is a shot-maker's game, meaning that you'll come across a variety of interesting (and difficult) situations that will require you to come with some tricky shots.

But remember that the basic rule of 9-ball is you must hit the lowest numbered ball first. This rule doesn't mean you can't knock in another ball after you hit that ball. Just like you can hit the 9 in with a combo or carom or kiss, so can you hit in any other ball.

With all the different ways to pocket a ball, look for chances to make balls in unconventional ways. 9-ball can be a spectacularly thrilling game, with all the interesting shots that come up, so don't be afraid to look for a shot that may not jump out at you right away.

Playing position

9-ball is a *rotational game,* meaning that you must go from the lowest numbered ball to the next lowest numbered ball. Accordingly, 9-ball puts a premium on playing precise position from one ball to the next. You have to execute some tricky shots — avoiding balls, running around rails, playing perfect speed. You also need to see plausible ways of going from one ball to the next, which calls for proper planning.

Looking three balls ahead

A good starting point to playing intelligent 9-ball is to always look three balls ahead. Simply put, you need to know exactly how you'll pocket the lowest numbered ball and the next two.

First and foremost, you have to make the shot at hand. All the diligent preparations for the next shot don't mean squat if you miss the first ball. So, you want to find a way to pocket the first ball, while sending the cue ball to a place where you have a shot at the second. Not only do you want to play proper position on the second ball, you also want to leave the cue ball in a spot that will give you a chance to make it and move to the *third* ball.

Figure 19-6 shows one way to look three balls ahead. First, the 1 ball can go into the near corner pocket. When you're planning on what to do with the 2 ball, though, you have a little more to think about. You want to have a makable shot that also gives you a chance at the 3 ball. In this case, if you plan to make the 2 ball in the side pocket, you'll have a shot on the 3 if you leave the cue ball anywhere in the area of the 2.

What's important here, though, is that you leave the cue ball on the *right side of the 2 ball*. If the cue ball is to the right of the line drawn from the side pocket through the middle of the 2 ball, you know the cue ball will want to drift to the left after contact. In this case, you want the cue ball to stop near the center of the table, in perfect shape for the 3 in the other side pocket.

After every shot, you have to plan for the next three balls. So if all nine balls are on the table, when you make the 1 ball, you have to adjust your plan so that you're thinking how you'll make the 2, 3, and 4. Make the 2, and you have to plan for the 3, 4, and 5.

In 8-ball, you want to re-evaluate your plan after every shot. Well, it's the same in 9-ball. You should plan three balls ahead, but you're not legally bound to follow that original plan. Always, always, always rethink your plan. If your plan has to change, no problem. If it doesn't, great!

Figure 19-6:
Always look
three balls
ahead.

Simplifying position play

Because position is so important in 9-ball, you need to formulate a workable plan. In addition to the position guidelines in 8-ball (see Chapter 18), identifying position zones is a big part of 9-ball.

When you're figuring out where to send the cue ball for your next shot, try to imagine a *position zone* — an area where the cue ball can stop that will give you a shot on the next ball. Now, try to find a way to send the cue ball *into* this zone instead of going *across* the zone.

The shot in Figure 19-7 is the first shot from the previous example. You want to leave the cue ball on the right side of the 2 ball and the top side pocket. If you leave the cue ball anywhere in the shaded zone, you should be in good shape.

To have a better shot of leaving the cue ball here, you want to send the cue ball off the rail and into the zone. If you try to hit the 1 ball with a stun shot, you'll be sending the cue ball across the position zone, which means your speed must be exactly right.

Although this section deals with general areas instead of a single spot, you should always aim for an exact point within the position zone. Aiming for a single spot forces you to aim precisely and focus on hitting the ideal spot, instead of settling for anywhere that's acceptable.

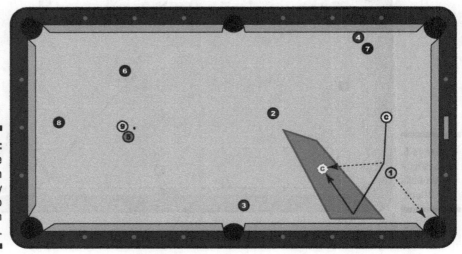

Figure 19-7:
Increase your margin for error by playing into a position zone.

Breaking up clusters

Just like in 8-ball, groups of balls all clumped together usually spell trouble. Often, you'll face two or more balls in a cluster, which can prevent you from easily clearing the table on the way to the 9 ball.

And just like in 8-ball, you want to deal with clustering problems early. The 1, 2, and 3 balls may be out in the open, but if the 4 is tied up with the 8 ball, you're going to run into trouble eventually. If you don't address the problematic 4 ball early, it will only trip you up later.

As you would with a cluster in 8-ball, try to find a ball that you can pocket while sending the cue ball into the cluster. If you can free up the 4 ball, you'll be able to continue your run.

Playing safe

Though 9-ball is considered a high-octane, offensive game, defense is a vital aspect of 9-ball strategy. You have just one ball on the table that you can hit first, so you need options when you don't have a viable way to pocket that ball.

The most effective way to play defense is to hide the object ball, the cue ball, or both balls behind blockers. Hiding balls is considerably easier in 9-ball than in 8-ball, where your opponent may have multiple balls he can legally hit.

When you're trying to find a way to play safe, think of safety zones. Identify spots on the table where you could leave the cue ball that would leave your opponent in a tough spot.

Say you misplayed your position to pocket the 4 ball, so you're in the position shown in Figure 19-8. You can try to bank the 4 ball in the lower side pocket, but that's pretty risky. (Even if you did make it, where would you make the 5?) With the cue ball in this position, you're probably best served playing safe in this situation. Notice that the 5 and 9 balls are clumped together in the middle of the table. This cluster is a good start for your safety; it can provide nice cover if you can could leave the cue ball on one side and the object ball on the other.

Getting the cue ball as close to a blocking ball as possible is always a good idea. This positioning limits your opponent's options, which include jumping over the blockers, if possible. But in a situation like Figure 19-8, you should be relatively safe if you leave the 5 and 9 cluster between the cue ball and the 4.

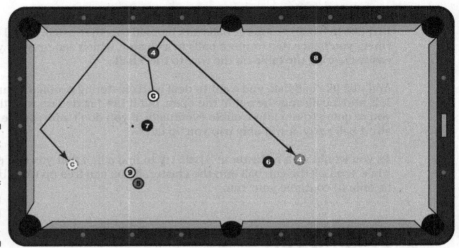

Some safeties can be much trickier than they appear. The simple reason is that you have to control *both* balls. Usually, you just plan for an object ball to go into a pocket and disappear. But with a safety, both balls will still be in play, so you have to take into account speed, spin, and angle with both the object ball and the cue ball.

Forcing three fouls

A common rule that is a part of 9-ball is known as the *three-foul rule,* which is a way of saying, "If you commit fouls on three consecutive shots, you lose the game."

While this situation doesn't sound like it would pop up very often, the three-foul rule is a great weapon if used properly. Oftentimes, you may not have an easy way to go from ball to ball on your way to the 9. In such a case, you can continually lock up your opponent with tough safeties. Do it three times in a row, and you win the game.

The three-foul rule *can* be a great weapon, but don't get too enamored with it. You have to play three pretty tricky safeties to force your opponent to foul his way to a loss of game. Also, if you misplay one safety, know that you may just leave your opponent in a superior position.

Weighing your options

When you're playing 9-ball, it won't be long before you're faced with a tough decision: Go for the offensive shot or duck it and play safe? Answering this question correctly is an important step toward becoming a smart 9-ball player, so it's worth spending some time figuring out how to make the right decision.

One of the easiest ways to think of a shot is in terms of percentages. If you can make one shot 80 percent of the time, you're likely to go ahead and try to make the ball. But if you can only make the shot 30 percent of the time, it may be a good spot to play safe.

The key is knowing your own game. Be honest with yourself. If you're scared of a shot, whether it's a thin cut or a long shot along the rail, you're probably going to miss. So when you're without a high-percentage shot, try to come up with a defensive shot that may lead to you getting ball in hand.

Just as you can make offensive shots a percentage of the time, you can also handicap your defensive game. If you can force your opponent into a foul, say, 80 percent of the time, while you can make your offensive option only 20 percent of the time, you know what you should do. *(Hint:* Play safe!)

It's when the odds get closer together that things get tricky. If you can make one shot 60 percent of the time but you can play a deadly safety 70 percent of the time, what do you do? Well, sorry to say, I can't give you a golden rule. What I can say is that, if you work on reading the percentages, you'll at least have a way of quantifying each option and then you can compare the two.

If players are ever in doubt about what they should do, most players will go for it. This simple fact is hard to forget: You can't win unless you're at the table. So if you're unsure whether you should try to make a ball or play safe, choose the offensive option.

Eying two-way shots

In Chapter 17, I detail the two-way shot, which is a way of combining both offense and defense in the same attempt. Simply put, the two-way shot is a way to shoot at a ball with the intent of making it, while still having a backup plan should you miss.

In 9-ball, the two-way shot is a great way to approach certain shots that you may not be all that confident that you're going to make. If you look for defensive options within an offensive shot, you can go for the tough ball without *selling out* (giving your opponent a wide open table).

The layout in Figure 19-9 is a perfect opportunity to play a two-way shot. Unless you're a fairly advanced player, the angle on the 1 ball makes for a pretty tough cut. You've got to sneak the 1 ball past the 7 and into the side pocket, while the cue ball goes off the long rail for position on the 2 ball.

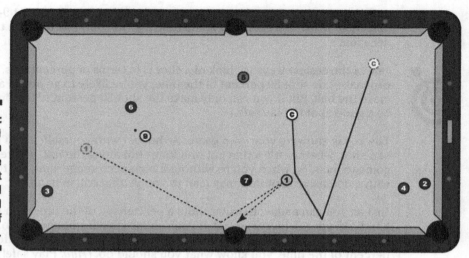

Figure 19-9:
Play the 1
ball with
a bit more
than pocket
speed, and
you should
be okay if
you miss.

But a natural safety is tied in with this shot, should the unfortunate happen
and you miss. When you approach this shot, think to yourself, "If I'm going to
miss, I will miss on a certain side of the pocket." You still want to try to make
the shot, but, in Figure 19-9, err on the side of aiming the 1 ball on the left
side of the pocket. This way, should you miss, the 1 ball will hit off the long
rail and might hide behind the 7, 6, or 9 ball. All the while, the cue ball will
head to the other side of the table in position for the 2 ball.

If you make this shot, great. You've got position on the 2 to continue your
run. If you miss, you may be in good shape should you play the shot
accordingly — meaning you hit the 1 ball with near pocket speed and miss
on the right side of the pocket.

The battle between being a confident player and being a realistic player
doesn't have to cause problems. For example, planning on what happens
if you miss is being a realist. While the ultra-confident player may think
he'll never miss, it's going to happen. Be a realist when planning your shot.
Then you can be confident in your ability to execute the shot you choose —
whether it be offensive, defensive, or a bit of both.

Handicapping 9-Ball

While 9-ball is a game that's tailor-made for TV — it's fast, the basics are easy
to learn, and it often forces players to try spectacular shots. But the reason

9-ball is so popular among amateur players (and among those players who like to place a friendly wager on a match) is because it's so easy to handicap.

By *handicap,* I mean it's easy to modify or level the playing field between players of different skill levels. Unlike 8-ball, which is limited when it comes to modifying rules or establishing tactical advantages, 9-ball is pretty straightforward.

Here are a few of the ways players play the game of 9-ball to make things easier on a player with less skill:

- **Giving games on the wire:** You can change the number of games each players has to win. A common handicap in 8-ball, giving up games (called *giving games on the wire*) is an easy way to negotiate a fair match.

- **Giving up the breaks:** Breaking in 9-ball is always an advantage. The breaker will have control of the table should something be pocketed. So, if a strong player gives up the breaks to a weaker player, the weaker player has the advantage.

- **Giving balls:** You may overhear a player say, "She's giving me the 7." This phrase means that one player is giving another a second ball that could win the game. Should the first player make either the 7 or the 9 ball, he would win the game.

  As you can imagine, you can play with this handicap in a number of ways. Some players give away the 7 with the stipulation that you can't make it with a combo and it has to be called. Or you could give up the 7 and 4 so that the other player has to make either the 4, 7, or 9 to win the game.

When you're just starting to learn 9-ball, ask for a lower numbered ball as an out. Having the 4, for example, against a stronger player will force you to approach that ball as if it were an end-game scenario. You may not be able to run an entire rack of 9-ball. But just maybe, you can clear three balls so that you can treat the 4 ball like it was the game-winner.

Handicapping is a creative endeavor. Don't be afraid to throw out other stipulations that you think can even the playing field, whether specifying that the stronger player has to bank the 6 or the stronger player has to pocket the 8 with her opposite hand. While this section describes the most common handicaps, you can experiment to keep your practice matches lively.

Chapter 20

Pool's Many Other Games

. . . .

In This Chapter

▶ Becoming familiar with one-pocket and straight pool

▶ Accommodating more than a pair of players

▶ Getting to know snooker

▶ Introducing the basics of three-cushion

. . . .

*I*f you think 8-ball and 9-ball are the be-all and end-all of your options at a pool table, you're sorely mistaken. Certainly the most popular disciplines, these games are just two of the ever-growing number of ways to compete with a cue, a table, and few balls.

Some games emphasize position play, shot-making, and supreme execution, while others place a premium on strategy, matching players' wits against one another. And while 8-ball and 9-ball are often a starting point for many players in pool, you have many other games to choose from. Some games even take place on completely different tables! Others place limitations on which pockets you can use on a standard pool table. So regardless of your style and preferences, you can find a game for you.

In this chapter, I cover two games favored by many professional players — straight pool and one-pocket. While the best shooters may prefer these games, a non-pro is still capable of having a little fun. I also cover multiplayer games, which can open up some interesting possibilities and can lead to some interesting situations. Finally, I cover snooker and three-cushion billiards, two games that take place on entirely different equipment.

Running into Straight Pool

Many professional players favor straight pool, which requires a high level of skill and a bunch of experience and creativity. These games can be great ways for players of all levels to pick up and redefine different parts of their game.

Aptly named, *straight pool* is pretty straightforward: Make a ball, get a point. Make another ball, get another point. If you're the first to a certain number of points, you win.

In straight pool, you can shoot any ball (no matter the number or whether it's striped or solid) in any pocket in any order. Sounds pretty simple, but you'll quickly see it isn't so. Also, you've got to plan ahead. After you make all but one ball, the 14 pocketed balls are reracked (see Figure 20-1), so you have to make the free-floating ball in a manner that allows you to send the cue ball into the stack, breaking them open so that you can keep pocketing balls.

You can see that the 14 balls are reracked just like they would be in a normal 15-ball pyramid with the top ball removed. The goal with the last remaining ball from the last rack (the 5 ball in Figure 20-1) is to pocket it while sending the cue ball into the *stack* — pool terminology for any cluster of balls around the footspot. If the cue ball can run into the stack, you should send a ball into position for your next shot.

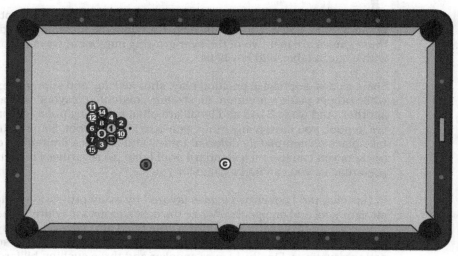

Figure 20-1:
In straight pool, 14 balls are racked when one is left on the table.

Another name for the game is *14.1 continuous*, which is a reference to the fact that you can keep going and going and going because you have one ball to lead you into the next rack of 14. You continue shooting until you fail to make a ball legally, at which point it's your opponent's turn.

Straight-pool games are played to a predetermined number of points (30 can be a good starting point), so you continue pocketing balls — each worth one point — until you reach the set number.

Just as in 8-ball and 9-ball, you can foul if you fail to drive a ball to a rail after cue-ball contact. But in straight pool, a foul doesn't result in your opponent receiving ball in hand. Instead, the player who fouls loses a point, and play continues. A player who fouls in three consecutive strokes is penalized 15 points.

Breaking

Straight pool is a *call-shot game*, meaning that you have to announce which ball you're going to make and where it's going. Calling the shot is pretty tricky to do on the break. Plus, if you fail to make anything, your opponent has a wide open table to start picking her way through balls. So, the best plan is to use a safety break (see Chapter 11).

Obviously, if you have the choice, you don't want to break. But if you must, try to disrupt the rack as little as possible. You must hit two balls to the rail to avoid fouling, so you want to send two balls to rails while leaving the cue ball all the way on the other side of the table. Figure 20-2 shows a standard break in straight pool.

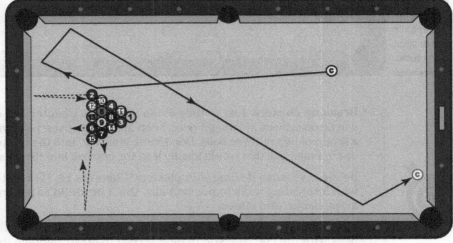

Figure 20-2: Hit the cue ball off the rack's corner and back up-table.

Clearing balls

With 15 balls, six pockets, and nothing prohibiting certain balls from going into certain pockets, you've got options. But sometimes all the possibilities can be paralyzing. When it comes to clearing a rack of balls, these guidelines can keep you on the straight and narrow:

✔ **Think three balls ahead.** You want to keep planning for future shots, so have a plan on how you're going to pocket the next three balls. Don't worry about position for every single ball; you'll feel overwhelmed in a hurry.

✔ **Work outside in.** Some strategists recommend picking off the outlying balls first. In Figure 20-3, this strategy means you'll try to pocket the 2, 4, and 6 balls first. Not only are the balls sitting near pockets, but you'll clear paths for other balls to go in those same pockets.

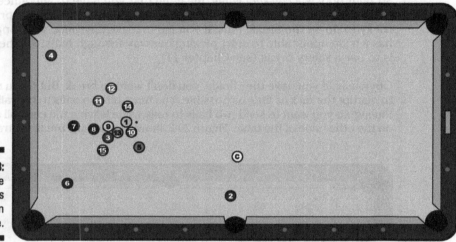

Figure 20-3:
Clear off the outer balls first to open the table.

✔ **Break up clusters.** Just as they are in 8-ball (see Chapter 18), clusters can be disastrous in straight pool. Keep in mind that you need to break up a group of two or three balls. Don't force your way into the cluster. Instead opt to find a ball that would ideally lead the cue ball into the cluster.

Be creative when dealing with clusters. Chapters 14, 15, and 16 deal with interesting ways to pocket balls. Don't be afraid to get creative with kicks, banks, and kisses.

✔ **Avoid unnecessary contact.** When you can avoid bumping other object balls with the cue ball, you're best served to do so. Sending the cue ball into other object balls can lead to unpredictable results. And control is everything in straight pool. Keep the cue ball from hitting other object balls, and you'll be in better shape.

✔ **Identify the break ball.** Because you need to have a ball on the table to break open the next rack, you'll have to do some planning once you get toward the end of a rack. The break ball should be located near the top of where the balls will be racked, but it can be anywhere around the stack that allows you to pocket it while sending the cue ball into the racked balls.

✔ **Identify the key ball.** After you know which ball you'd like to use to break open the next rack, you need to identify a *key ball*. The key ball is the ball you pocket before the break ball. Ideally, you'd like to find a key ball (second-to-last ball) that would allow you to leave the cue ball in perfect shape for the break ball (last ball). Figure 20-4 is one example of a solid key ball.

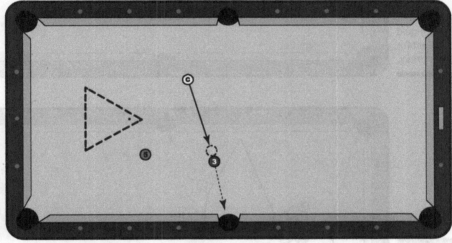

Figure 20-4:
A stop shot on the 3 gives you a good angle on the break ball.

Making the break shot

The opening break is a safety against your opponent. The break shot occurs after you've made all but one ball in a rack. This shot, as you may guess, is very different than the opening break. This break is an offensive opportunity.

Ideally, you'd like to be somewhere in the shaded region in Figure 20-5. In this position, you've got a natural angle at the stack, and the shot on the 11 ball isn't that difficult.

But if you don't land in perfect shape for the break, don't worry. You've got plenty of options. Figure 20-6 shows three less-than-ideal situations that can still lead to a successful break shot — it just may be a bit more difficult.

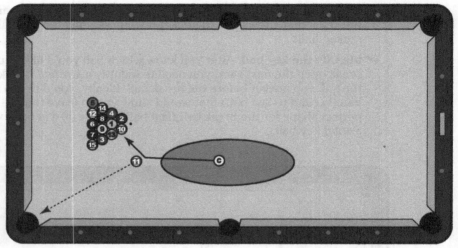

Figure 20-5:
Land in the shaded region, and you should be set for your break.

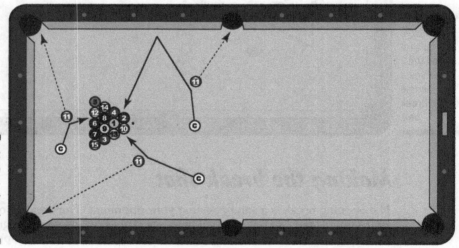

Figure 20-6:
Here are three possibilities for your break shot.

Unlike a break shot in 8-ball or 9-ball, your break in straight pool doesn't have to be earth-shattering. You don't need to spill balls all over the table. Instead, you just want to push a few balls into the open so that you have some options. As a rule, plan to hit the stack firmly, but don't go out on a limb to really crack the rack.

Playing safe

With so many balls on the table, you can still find yourself without a clear offensive path. When you're out of offensive options, you can play defense by leaving the cue ball in a position where your opponent will be in a tough spot.

Figure 20-7 shows a situation where you don't really have a viable option to pocket a ball. Even if you can bank a ball or come up with a creative shot, you may be better off hiding the cue ball in the stack.

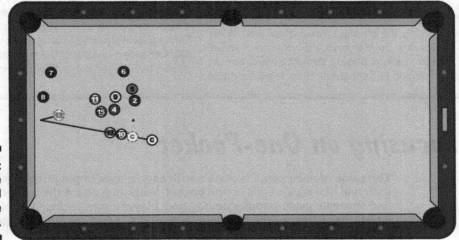

Figure 20-7:
Try to freeze
the cue ball
against the
10 ball.

If you can lightly roll the cue ball into the 10, pushing the 13 to the short rail, you'll tie up your opponent in a pretty tricky spot. The cue ball will be frozen to the 10, so your opponent won't have an easy escape from this position.

Experimenting with straight pool

Straight pool is considered a game that tests a player's all-around skill. You need to have control of the cue ball, you need to be able to make difficult shots at times, and you need to be able to think ahead.

These reasons are exactly why developing players can learn so much by playing straight pool. So what if it takes you a million hours to get more than 14 balls? You'll be making the most of your practice time because you're working on a whole bunch of important skills all at the same time.

If you're practicing by yourself, spread all 15 balls on the table as they might be during a game of straight pool. Have a cluster of seven or eight balls around the footspot, with another six balls on the same half of the table near the rails and corner pockets. Leave one or two balls on the other half of the table (or at least between the two side pockets). This setup will help you re-create game-like conditions when you're hoping to up your straight-pool skills.

Willie Mosconi's 526

Every sport has iconic numbers. Wilt Chamberlain's 100-point game in basketball, the 2,000-yard rushing mark in football, and Joe DiMaggio's 56-game hitting streak in baseball are just a few examples. Pool's number is 526. That number refers to an incredible run by possibly the greatest player of all time, Willie Mosconi. On March 19, 1954, Mosconi ran 526 balls in a row playing straight pool during an exhibition in Springfield, Ohio. If you're doing the math, Mosconi ran an unbelievable 35 consecutive racks!

Almost every straight-pool player can tell you what her high run is. And chances are, that number is nowhere near Mosconi's famous feat. It may take a player a lifetime to reach 100 balls. Only pro-level players can brag about runs over 200. And only a handful of the top professional players have ascended north of that figure.

Focusing on One-Pocket

The game of one-pocket is played with each player hoping to pocket more than half of a rack's balls in one pocket. Without a doubt the most cerebral and strategic game popular among pool players, one-pocket is a collection of intricate safeties, subtle position plays, and — when the time is right — an explosion of offense.

In one-pocket, you first have to determine which player is shooting at which pocket. The player who is going to break chooses which corner pocket he'd like to shoot at, leaving the other corner pocket for the opposing player.

You want to call the pocket that's opposite of the side you're going to hit the rack. So if you're hitting the back-right corner of the rack, you want to call the back-left corner pocket. Like straight pool, one-pocket is a game best started with a defensive break. Because you can't be sure to pocket a ball in your pocket, you want to keep the balls grouped around the footspot, with maybe two or three balls heading toward your pocket.

Here are a few tips to help you execute a successful break in one-pocket (see Figure 20-8):

✔ Aim to contact the head ball just before the ball in the second row. Hitting the second ball will send the head ball toward your pocket, while the cue ball will head to the short rail.

✔ Use a bit of inside English (left English in Figure 20-8) to help kill the ball on the long rail. (See Chapter 10 for more on English.)

✔ Speed control is critical because you need to keep the object balls near your pocket. Also, you want the cue ball to come to a rest on the rail next to your opponent's pocket.

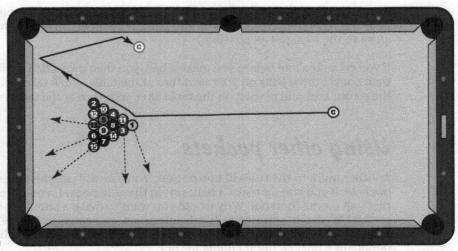

Figure 20-8:
Send a few balls toward your pocket and leave your opponent without a shot.

Winning the game

One-pocket is a game of great strategy. Often, one game (that's one rack, not even a best-of-five match) can last well over an hour as players trade safeties in the hope of gaining a tactical advantage. The goal is to make eight balls in your pocket. But if you make six balls and miss, you could leave your opponent in perfect shape to get eight of his own.

Often, a player will play to position balls by his pocket, without actually pocketing them until he knows he can do so and still have control of the table. But in general, you want to keep your opponent from having clear looks at balls in his pocket, while improving your own standing.

Your opponent can shoot any ball into his pocket. Oftentimes, you want to leave the cue ball either by your opponent's pocket or frozen (or close to frozen) to the head rail. Putting the cue ball in these spots will limit your opponent's options.

One-pocket is a thinking person's game 98 percent of the time. Most of the shots are very precise safeties, meant to adjust the layout of balls slightly in the shooter's favor. But after a player has put himself into position to win, he often has to do so with some high-powered shot-making. It's a strange thing to see: Players lightly tapping balls around for 45 minutes, only to see one of them start firing at his hole like it was ablaze!

Fouling

There is a unique way of counting fouls in one-pocket that's a bit like straight pool. Should you not send a ball to a rail after cue-ball contact, you lose one point. And because points are balls made, you also have to take one of your balls out from the collection area and place it back on the table (on or as close to the footspot as possible).

If you commit a foul before you make a ball, you then owe a ball. So if you foul, then pocket three balls on your next turn at the table, you'll take a ball out of the return area and place it on the table after your turn at the table is over.

Using other pockets

Another quirk to the rules of one-pocket: You can still use the other four pockets. If you should make a ball, say, in the side pocket, you simply respot that ball on the footspot. Why would you want to make a shot in the wrong pocket? Well, if it's strategically advantageous, you can move a ball from near a pocket to the center of the table. Similarly, you can make a ball in your opponent's pocket, but it counts for her.

One-pocket is such a complex game, you're best off learning it from someone with a little experience. Many of the same types of shots arise multiple times, so experience — *knowing the shots* — pays off.

Handicapping one-pocket

The rules of one-pocket allow for a fairly easy handicapping system. The most common way to even the playing field between players of different skill levels is to change the number of balls each player has to make to win. In an even game, each player tries to make eight balls. But you can switch that so the more skilled player has to make nine balls to his opponent's seven balls. Or, an even larger handicap is one player on ten balls and the other on six.

Also, because the person who breaks is at an immediate advantage, you can have the weaker player break to give him an advantage. And, as in most disciplines, you can always give up games on the wire, so two games on the wire means one player has to win two games while the other has to win four.

Popular Variations: 10-Ball and Rotation

Many players still play the following two games, which are pretty similar to 9-ball — similar enough that I only lightly touch on the differences in rules, setup, and so on:

✔ **10-ball:** What's the difference between 10-ball and 9-ball? If you said, "one ball," you're not a smarty pants. You're right. 10-ball and 9-ball have two other differences, though:

- 9-ball is primarily a game where anything goes. If you miss a shot on the 3 ball but you knock in the 9, you win. Well, 10-ball is a call-shot game, meaning you have to call the ball you intend to make and the pocket where you're going to make it.

- The second major difference is the rack. Ten balls are arranged in a triangle with four rows. This slight change from the diamond shape in 9-ball makes a *tremendous* difference. You can manipulate the 9-ball break so that it becomes predictable. Pro players can find ways to consistently pocket balls on the break (including the soft break; see Chapter 19). Well, with 10-ball, the best thing to do is let 'er rip. The power break is still best to scatter the balls, while you still maintain control of the cue ball, of course. And with one more ball on the table, it's that much harder to *run out* (clear all the balls) from the break.

All in all, for the average amateur player, 10-ball isn't all that different from 9-ball. But for many spectators and players, 10-ball is the preferable game for the professionals.

✔ **Rotation:** Some of the best players in the world come from the Philippines, where the most popular game is *rotation*. Rotation is a game much like 9-ball, only with a full rack of 15 balls. Like 9-ball, you must hit the lowest numbered ball on the table first. But unlike 9-ball, you get points corresponding to the number on the ball you pocket — so if you hit a 1–12 combination, you get 12 points.

Games are played to 61 points, which is 1 more point than half the total available in one rack of balls. Also, because you must hit the lowest numbered ball in rotation, you may want to keep an eye out for combinations. Making a 1–10 combination gets you the same amount of points as making the 1, 2, 3, and 4 balls.

Having to hit the lowest numbered ball on a table covered with as many as 15 balls can be tricky. Think about a game of 8-ball after the break, only now you can only aim at one ball! So, while rotation takes a considerable amount of skill to navigate packed tables, it also forces you to kick, bank, and kiss balls.

If you find 15-ball rotation too difficult, try to modify the game a bit by using just 9 balls. Play to 23 points (because 45 points are available in every rack). You'll have an easier time hitting the lowest ball, and the games will go quicker with fewer points needed to win.

Multiplayer Games

If you and two friends are at a table, you may want to all play a game at once. Luckily, pool players' ingenuity isn't restricted to one-on-one games. Outside of team versions of 8-ball and 9-ball, multiplayer games are considered more lighthearted endeavors — ways to incorporate more players into the action and not true tests of pool skill.

Cutthroat

Cutthroat is probably the most widely known multiplayer game. Ideally, three people play it, but you can also play with five. If you're playing cutthroat with three players, each person gets five balls (1–5, 6–10, or 11–15). And unlike most pool games, you actually want to keep your balls on the table in cut-throat. When only one player has balls on the table, he wins.

Allowing a player to choose his group after pocketing a ball is one way to determine who is shooting at what. In this scenario, say Player 1 breaks and pockets the 4. He'll want to shoot a ball in the 4 ball's group (the 1, 2, 3, or 5) and declare himself either the middle group or the high group. Player 2 may want to pocket a ball from that same low group (leaving Player 3 two balls down) or a ball from one of the other two groups on her turn. She then can choose the third group and have a ball advantage on both players.

In 8-ball (see Chapter 18), you want to pick the group without many balls tied up in clusters because they'll be difficult to pocket. Well, because you want to keep your balls on the table in cutthroat, the group with balls tied up in clusters is desirable. These balls will be difficult for your opponents to pocket, so they'll have a tough time knocking you out of the game.

Cutthroat is a fun game to get multiple players involved. The strategy isn't too heavy, and players of different skill levels should be able to at least compete with one another.

Kelly pool

If you've ever been in a pool hall and heard a certain rattling sound like someone on the table next to you was playing a game of Parcheesi, you have at least been *near* a game of Kelly pool. A game any number of people can play, Kelly pool involves a pill bottle filled with 15 beads, each numbered to correspond with a ball in the rack.

The game is played just like rotation (see the "Other Games: Rotation and 10-Ball" section), with a 15-ball rack and players needing to contact the lowest numbered ball first. The beads, though, add an interesting twist to the game. Each player shakes the bottle and takes a bead, which is kept secret from everyone else. Whatever number you draw is the ball that you need to make to win the game.

If someone else makes your game-winning ball, though, you're eliminated. Play continues until someone makes the numbered ball corresponding to the pill they drew.

8-ball and 9-ball for teams

8-ball and 9-ball work best as two-player games, but you can still incorporate more players. You can play both games as team events. If two players are on each team, you can trade off from shot to shot or switch every inning.

If an 8-ball team has one strong player and one beginner, it can be beneficial for the newbie to play so that the players switch off after every shot. The expert player is able to leave makable shots for her teammate, so the beginner has a chance to pocket some balls. Also, the skilled player is capable of getting out of tricky spots should her beginner teammate lose control of the cue ball while pocketing a ball.

Playing team 8-ball or 9-ball is also helpful for beginners because of the interaction with another player. So many times, one player who is struggling with a particular concept may be afraid to ask for help or may not know who to ask. But in team games, it's in the best interest of the team to share knowledge and communicate.

Three-Cushion Billiards

Often, pool is referred to as *pocket billiards*. Well, the cynic might ask, what is billiards without the pockets? The answer to that question is the carom games. Using tables that have no pockets (see Figure 20-9), caroms involve sending the cue ball off of one ball and into another. The most popular carom game is *three-cushion,* which involves sending your cue ball off of one ball and three rails and into another ball.

The rules of three-cushion are surprisingly simple:

✔ You use three balls (usually one red, one yellow, and one white).

✔ Each player has his own cue ball (one has the white, the other has the yellow).

✔ You're required to send the cue ball into one ball and off three cushions before it hits the second ball.

Other than that list, there really aren't many rules!

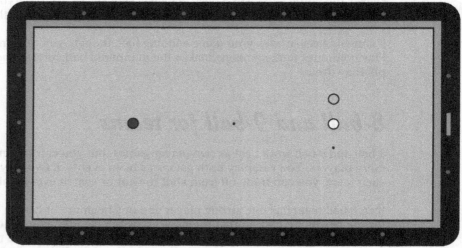

Figure 20-9:
A billiard
table has
no pockets,
but the lack
of pockets
doesn't
make things
any easier.

To make a successful shot (which is worth one point) in three-cushion, you can mix things up when it comes to the first ball and three rails. You can hit a rail, the first ball, and then two more rails before hitting the second ball. Or you can hit three rails and then the two balls. Or you can hit four rails, the first ball, and then four more rails before hitting the second ball. You see, you can score points in many different ways (though that last example isn't necessarily the smartest idea).

Three-cushion can be very difficult for players who are unfamiliar with the cue ball's angles after hitting a ball and after hitting a rail. But if you'd like to simplify things, throw out the provision that you need to hit three cushions. Just work on hitting the two other balls with your cue ball, without worrying about hitting the rails. (This version is actually known as *straight-rail* — a game that was popular decades before three-cushion.)

Maybe the most important thing for a rookie in caroms (either straight-rail or three-cushion) is seeing the big ball. When you send your cue ball off another ball and around the table, you want to give yourself a little room for error. The big-ball concept is one way to make a shot easier on yourself. Balls that are near a rail or corner are effectively harder to miss because you can either hit the ball directly or hit the rail before the ball. Can you see how the red ball in Figure 20-10 is big?

Whether you're playing three-cushion or straight-rail, practicing a carom game every now and then can help you play better pocket billiards. Caroms require great knowledge of the cue ball's path after contact with a ball. And increasing your understanding of and control with the cue ball is never a bad thing.

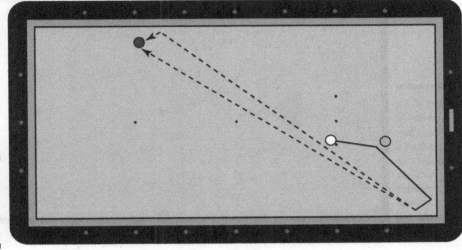

Figure 20-10:
The red
ball is "big"
because it's
by a rail.

Snooker

If you get to the point where a pool table is too small and the pockets look too big, snooker is your game. Popular in the United Kingdom and Asia, *snooker* is a cue sport much like pool, with some differences in equipment and scoring.

Snooker is played on a table that measures 12 feet by 6 feet (3 feet longer than a professional-sized pool table) with pockets that are approximately 3.5 inches wide.

As you can see in Figure 20-11, snooker is played with more balls than any pool game. You use 15 red balls and 7 colored balls. Snooker is played by accumulating points, with each colored ball having its own point value — reds are worth 1, yellow 2, green 3, brown 4, blue 5, pink 6, and black 7.

But you can't just clear all the balls in any order. You must first make (or *pot*, as it's called in snooker-speak) a red ball. Only then can you take aim at a colored ball. If you then make a colored ball, you get the corresponding points, and the ball is then replaced in its original spot. You can continue alternating between red balls and colored balls until you've cleared all the reds. At that point, you're to pot all the colored balls in order from least valuable to most valuable (from yellow to green to brown to blue to pink and finally to black).

The colored balls are re-spotted after you make them, so you can pot the same colored ball after every red ball. Because the black ball is worth seven points, it's usually best to aim at sandwiching as many black balls between reds to maximize the number of points you accumulate during each turn.

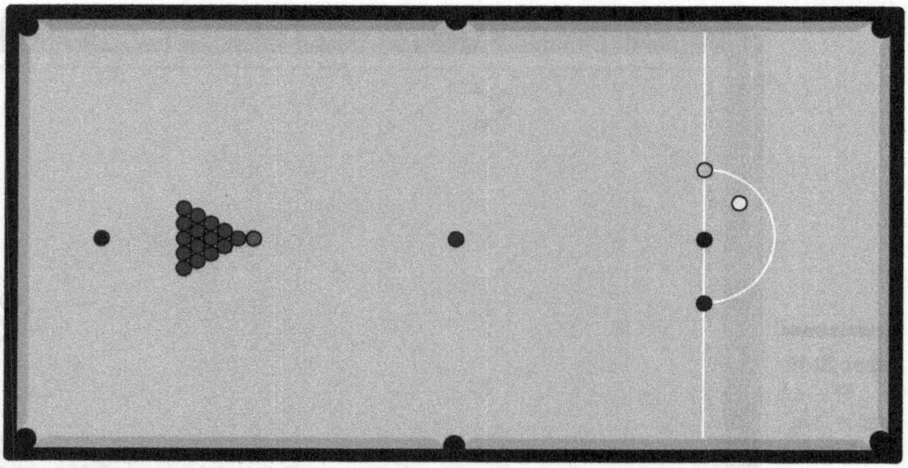

Figure 20-11:
A snooker table is bigger than a pool table and has smaller pockets.

The player with the most points when all the balls are cleared wins that game — known as a *frame*. You can play matches to any predetermined amount of games, whether it be a best-of-5 match or best-of-35, like the world championship match.

Breaking and playing

Surprisingly, the break in snooker is quite similar to that of straight pool. Because you can't be sure to make a ball and have a shot on a colored ball, you want to use a safety break.

As in straight pool, the goal is to clip the side of the stack (the red balls, in this case) and have the ball come all the way back up the table (see Figure 20-12). Ideally, the red balls would still be grouped close together, while the cue ball is stuck near the top rail. Your opponent would be hard-pressed to have a shot in this situation, so you're at an advantage.

Like straight pool, a game of snooker usually starts with both players gently massaging the main stack until one player has an offensive option. At this point, she can go ahead and try to pot a red ball to start the scoring.

But safety play is still an important aspect of snooker. As a general rule when you're playing safe, you want to keep the cue ball near the corner pockets farthest from the stack of red balls. This strategy forces your opponent to play a very long shot on what should be a difficult cut into the opposite corner pockets.

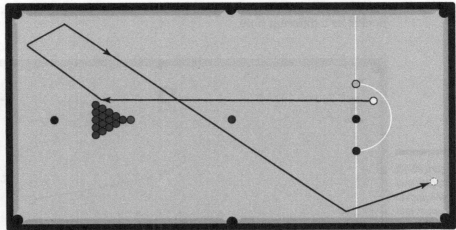

Figure 20-12:
You want
to clip the
back corner
ball and
keep the
ball up near
the top rail.

Another option for a safety is what's called a *snooker*. A snooker simply means leaving the cue ball hidden behind a colored ball so that the incoming player is unable to make a straight hit on a red ball. These types of safeties are similar to what you can do in 8-ball (see Chapter 18) and 9-ball (see Chapter 19).

Snooker's variations

You can play snooker in several different forms. Here are a few of the most popular takes on the standard version:

- ✔ **Short rack:** This version is an express way to play the game. You use only 10 red balls instead of the standard 15, so frames progress quicker because you need to pot fewer balls.

- ✔ **Snooker pool:** You can play snooker on a pool table, though you'll need a set of snooker balls sized for a pool table. (Pool balls are 2¼ inches in diameter; snooker balls are 2¹⁄₁₆.)

- ✔ **Golf:** One common variant combines the game play of golf with snooker. In golf, each player has his own cue ball and object ball. Each player begins with the object ball placed in the direct middle of the table and the cue ball in the *D* (the semicircle area near the top of the table). First, you want to pocket the object ball in the top-right pocket. When you make the ball in that pocket, the object ball is respotted in the middle of the table, and the cue ball remains where it stopped. You next have to pocket the ball in the upper side pocket, working clockwise around the table.

Figure 20-13 shows the numbered pockets, similar to a golf course, with each pocket as a different hole.

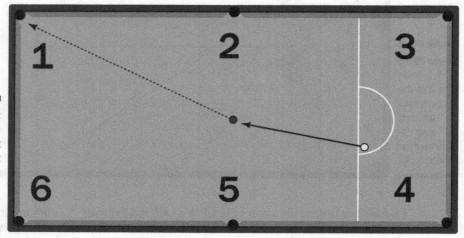

Figure 20-13:
In golf, you will pocket an object ball in the pockets going clockwise.

Part V
Gearing Up

The 5th Wave   By Rich Tennant

In this part . . .

In this part, I run through some of the peripheral subjects involved with the sport. While picking up a cue
and playing seems easy, you need to know how to be a
discerning customer when you're looking to choose a cue
off the wall of your favorite pool hall (or if you want to
bring home a pool table for your own living quarters).
I also cover the mental side of the game, which some
players say is 90 percent of the challenge. Finally, I offer
several drills to help you work on just about any area of
your game.

Chapter 21

Equipment Check: Looking for Quality Tools

In This Chapter

▶ Spotting a quality cue

▶ Prolonging your cue' life

▶ Buying other tools

▶ Purchasing a table

---

1 think the saying goes something like, "A good carpenter never blames his tools." But you and I aren't carpenters; we're pool players. And the excuse of faulty equipment has been a trusty defense for errant shots for as long as the game has been in existence.

But you shouldn't settle for second-rate gear just to have a convenient alibi for a missed shot. In fact, because pool is a sport that requires an incredible amount of precision, top-quality equipment is an absolute must.

You need to know what to look for when you're browsing for a cue or accessories. Also, if you're in the market for a pool table, I share with you some nuggets of info to digest before you make what can be a major purchase.

In this chapter, you discover the keys to becoming a well-informed shopper. So, even though you'll always have the possibility of blaming substandard equipment for your failures, if you read this chapter, you shouldn't have to.

Finding a House Cue

When you walk into a poolroom, you'll be quick to notice the number of cues available for you to choose from. These *house cues* — named because they largely stay in house — are often run-of-the-mill cues made from one piece of wood and are available for general public use. And while house cues are often well worn and even slightly abused, you can take steps to make sure that you choose the best cue available.

House cues are rarely in pristine condition, though you should be able to find one in serviceable shape. A house cue with a relatively smooth, clean shaft will be easier to handle than one covered in grime, simply because you'll notice it less while running it through your grip hand. The cleaner the shaft, the less friction exists between the wood and your hand.

Wanting a tip?

The most important part of any cue is the tip. Ironically, the tip is also the part most commonly overlooked by most beginner players searching for a house cue. But because this little piece of leather will be the only part of your cue making contact with the cue ball, it better be in good shape.

First, you need to differentiate between types of tips. To be frank, I don't think many room owners maintain their house cues, simply because they don't have to. These sticks are heavily used and sometimes abused, so upkeep isn't a high priority.

With that in mind, some house cues have inexpensive removable tips that can easily be replaced when broken or worn out. These so called *slip-on tips* are commonly found on house cues in bars. When available, though, you'll want to nab a cue with the type of tip shown in Figure 21-1. This cue has a one-piece tip that is attached directly to the cue's *ferrule* — the piece between the wood shaft and the leather tip. These cues usually provide a better hit because the tip is fastened directly to the stick via the ferrule, instead of the bulky slip-on tip that is placed over the end of the cue.

Figure 21-1:
This cue has a proper ferrule and tip.

The next thing you want to look for is the shape of the tip. Shopping for a house cue, you want to look for a cue tip that's rounded in a nice, even manner. A properly shaped tip is crucial if you want to hit the cue ball anywhere other than the exact center.

You'll know a tip is properly shaped if it's curved somewhere between the roundness of a nickel and dime. While you may not be pulling your change out in the middle of a poolroom, you can make a good estimation on a tip somewhere between completely flat and one that's pointed like an arrow.

One thing to avoid is a *mushroomed* tip, where the top has been smooshed down so that the leather looks like the top of a mushroom. Basically, this kind of tip has crossed the line from well-worn to time-to-replace.

Shooting for straight

You also need to check the straightness of the cue. While the tip is the most vital piece (see preceding section), the most immaculate tip in the world can't help you if your cue is the shape of half of a hula hoop.

You can check the straightness of your potential stick in two ways:

✔ **The most popular method is simply rolling the cue back and forth on the bed of the table.** If you see any wobble, you'll know the cue has a kink in it.

You're not being judged on the speed at which you roll the cue. Do it nice and slow so that you can really study the cue's shape and observe whether the tip jumps up and down.

✔ **The second way to check for any warping is to hold the butt of the cue right up to your eye and sight down the shaft.** Rotate the cue and see whether you notice anything that seems off. This method is effective, but it's easier to miss little imperfections than when you just roll it on the table and go.

Lifting weights

The average cue weighs 19 ounces, but house cues are usually readily available in anywhere from 18 to 21 ounces. When it comes to choosing which weight is best for you, it's all a matter of personal preference.

For example, consider the weight of a cue on the break shot. Some players prefer a heavier cue, thinking the big lumber will crush the cue ball into powder. Other players prefer a lighter cue, thinking the increased hand speed during the stroke leads to a more powerful break.

In the end, experiment and choose the one to your liking.

Buying Your First Cue

After you've invested a little time into your game, you may want to make a financial investment. Buying a cue is by no means a necessity for a developing player, but playing with one cue should lead to a certain level of comfort when you play. After all, an increased level of comfort and performance is the primary reason you're looking for a cue. Regardless of how much fun you have picking out a house cue or using your friend's stick, you want something that is, well, *yours*.

Money isn't everything

Luckily for you, the billiards industry has got you covered when it comes to sticks aimed at the first-time buyer. These models, ranging in price from $40 to a few hundred bucks, are geared to be durable, steady cues that offer players a way to own a quality cue without making a massive investment.

If you've got a briefcase full of $100 bills, great. If not, don't worry. The truth is that money doesn't buy playability. After you get above $500 or so, you're paying only for the decorative aspects of the cue — the fancy inlays, the ornate designs, the frills.

There's something to be said about form, but if you're looking for function, you can find it for a fair price.

Checking the specs

After you have an idea what you want to spend, you can work out the details of your cue. You have plenty to consider because you can customize almost every part of the cue to your liking.

Figure 21-2 shows a standard cue with all the parts labeled. When you're in the market for your own stick, here are a few things to consider:

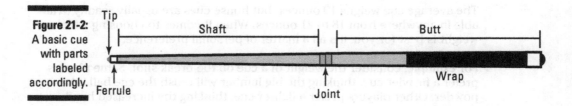

Figure 21-2: A basic cue with parts labeled accordingly.

Tip

Shaft

Butt

Ferrule

Joint

Wrap

✔ **Cue length:** From house cue to collector's item, most modern cues are 58 inches. While you may consider going up or down a few inches, this length should suit the large majority of body types.

✔ **Shaft material:** The *shaft* of the cue — the part from the joint to the ferrule — can be made of fiberglass, graphite, or a wide array of woods. If you can get a quality maple shaft for a price that works, it's hard to beat Mother Nature.

✔ **Wrap:** Most cues have a wrap near the *butt* (back end) to prevent your grip hand from slipping. You have a number of options to choose from, all based totally on personal preference. Linen is the most common, though you can get anything from leather to rubber to nothing.

✔ **Shaft taper:** House cues are evenly tapered from the tip on down, but you can buy a *pro-tapered shaft* — meaning the diameter remains the same from the tip back to a certain point on the shaft. For your first cue, try to find a shaft with a shorter pro-taper so that you'll have an easier transition from the shape of house cues to your own cue.

✔ **Joint:** You screw a two-piece cue together at the joint, which can be made of metal, wood, or plastic. Players will always disagree about what type of joint is best; just know that each material changes the weight distribution of the cue as well as the feel at impact. (Regardless, metal is the most common joint on affordable two-piece cues and should be fine for beginner and intermediate players.)

✔ **Tip:** The tip is the most important part of a cue. Tips vary from soft to hard, though inexperienced players are best served with a medium to medium-soft tip. (See the earlier section, "Wanting a tip?")

Cue cases

After you buy a cue, you may need to get a case to hold it. Starting out, you'll be fine with an 11, meaning the case can hold one butt and one shaft, as opposed to a 24, which holds two butts and four shafts. (The first number indicates how many butts the case holds, while the second indicates the number of shafts.)

The most modest cases available are flexible and padded, protecting your stick from dents and dings. But for a few more bucks, you can get a hard case that will protect your cue from any damage — save for the extreme.

Know that if you want to express yourself, the case is one way of doing it. You can find no shortage of ways to decorate a cue case, from patches to stitching to autographs of pro players to anything else you can think of. Naturally, a subdued empty canvas can say as much about you as anything else. . . .

Feel it out

I want to stress the importance of feel — how the cue feels in your hands and how it feels when you're hitting balls. If a $1,000 cue feels like a warped toothpick, and a $40 starter feels like silk, go with the one that you think feels best.

Excuse my turn as an amateur psychologist, but having confidence in your cue is an absolute must. You have to believe that you're a better player thanks to your cue. If not, why would you want to lug it around?

To that end, don't be afraid to shop around. Ideally, you're going to be using this little bundle of wood for some time, so you want to find the one that's right for you.

Maintaining Your Cue

Cues can last for decades — whether or not yours will depends on the level of TLC you provide over the life span of your cue. Keeping your cue in top-playing condition is surprisingly easy if you incorporate a few procedures into your routine.

Your tip's top shape

Keeping your tip in perfect condition requires a two-pronged approach that gives attention to both its shape and its scuff:

- **Shape:** After a few hundreds hits, your tip is going to flatten out. An overly flat tip gives you less control of the cue ball on off-center hits, even to the point of miscues — where the tip skims off the ball instead of properly striking it.

  So, take care of your tip, and it'll take care of you. Carry a tip *shaper* in your cue case. A shaper is a small concave piece of metal with a gritty surface. You grind the cue tip against the shaper so that the outer rim of leather is removed, returning your tip to the proper shape.

- **Scuff:** Another problem your tip will face over time is the smoothing of its surface. As the leather gets tamped down, you'll have a harder time applying chalk evenly, which can lead to miscues.

  Again, a little tool will go a long way to solving this problem. A tip *tapper* has an abrasive edge, similar to the *scuffer,* that you gently tap over the leather. It will scuff up the surface, leaving it more adept at accepting and holding chalk. Most stores or Web sites that carry billiard accessories offer a two-in-one tool that's both a shaper and a scuffer.

The shaft: Keep it clean

Grime, grit, chalk, talc . . . plenty of foreign substances are going to make their way onto your cue's shaft. Even after a few hours at the table, you'll notice how the shaft might feel a little stickier as it runs through your bridge.

The secret to keeping a nice, smooth shaft isn't that difficult: Just clean it after every use. It may not sound like a lot, but just rubbing the shaft with a damp washcloth, followed by a massage with a dry towel, should do wonders.

If you need to step it up a notch, rub the shaft with a touch of rubbing alcohol on the washcloth. Again, use a dry towel to make sure that you remove as much moisture as possible.

If you're dealing with an extreme case of gunk and grime, trust a professional. Most pool halls either have a repair shop in-house or know of an industrious cue doctor. For a couple of bucks, you can get your shaft newly sanded and sealed so that it'll be as good as new.

You can clean the ferrule with a wet washcloth, but take care if you're really scrubbing. If water and pressure can't get it clean, try a tiny dab of toothpaste. The grit should help restore the whiteness, without damaging the surface.

Joints, butts, and wraps

Maintaining the integrity of the rest of the cue is fairly simple. Keep your cue out of harm's way, whether that be in your house, in your car, or at the pool hall. One of the most common reasons for warping is extreme temperatures, so avoid dropping the stick in the trunk of your car for the winter if you're in Minnesota or for the summer if you're in Phoenix (to be safe, make that year-round, Arizonians).

Keep your cue in its case in a safe place, and you should be ready to draw that weapon whenever you want for years to come.

Accessorize Your Game

What's a sport without the accompanying gadgetry? Golf's got an entire industry of toys (of varying usefulness) that can keep your gear in playing shape. Well, pool's got some tools of the trade as well:

> ✔ **Chalk:** When it comes to chalk, be a high-roller. All chalk is relatively cheap — usually less than a buck for a cube — but the better quality stuff is necessary to get a nice, even application on your tip. A good

cube of chalk won't appear flaky or coarse when applied. Price often dictates quality, so don't settle for the lower-end options.

When it comes to choosing a chalk color, you don't want to clash with whatever color cloth you play on. If you're buying chalk to keep in your cue case, go with blue because most public tables will have blue or green cloth. If you're buying chalk for your home table that's another color, buying a similar shade to that of your table will keep you from seeing unsightly chalk marks all over the table.

✔ **Scuffer and shaper:** You'll need a scuffer and shaper to maintain your cue. You can find plenty of little trinkets that accomplish both of these tasks, all for around $10.

Along with the scuffer, keep a plain, old washcloth with your cue or around your home table. A washcloth is essential if you want to keep a clean cue.

✔ **Balls:** If you think about the amount of punishment doled out to pool balls, you may want to invest a little bit more money into your set. While the cheapest sets of 16 balls (15 colored balls and a cue ball) are available for $50 or so, buy a quality set of durable resin balls.

As for the cue ball, you should get one with a normal set of balls. But some players prefer to spend a little extra on the cue ball because it's constantly in play and always the ball being hit by the cue. It's not necessary, but if you want to upgrade, you have plenty of different types to choose from. Many bar tables have a cue ball that is a different weight than the other balls (to allow the table to tell which ball should go to the cue-ball return hole), which can really change game play. A quality cue ball with a standard weight should only cost $20 or so.

Like your cue, balls collect grime and gunk over time. With all the chalk dust flying around the pool table and whatever gets caught in the pockets, balls will pick up dirt quicker than you may think. Don't be afraid to give them a good wash with warm water and just a dab of dish soap.

As a rule, look for your accessories at a pool-centric retail outlet — or at an online store that specializes in pool equipment. Avoid the sporting-good store aisles at the big department stores because they usually carry the cheapest and less effective versions of the tools you'll need.

Choosing a Table

So you're in the market for a table. Whether you plan on using it daily or weekly or yearly, you'll have plenty of options to get the exact product you want. Because table manufacturers compete with so many other in-home entertainment options for your dollar, they have all different models for all different homes. Run through the following sections, and you'll be an informed consumer when you walk in the showroom.

Know what you get at each price point

I'll cut to the chase. Before I get into the ins and outs of size and such, I want to detail what you'll get for the amount you've got budgeted for your table.

Within the billiards industry, it's no secret that most Americans assume that they can get a high-end pool table for $1,500 to $1,700. While someone can get a serviceable, quality table for that amount, it's probably the *least* you'll want to spend if you plan on the table being a fixture in your game room for years to come.

You can certainly buy a $400 table, but it will be about as discount as you'll find. You may be able to play on a less expensive table for awhile, but you might experience very different conditions from a pool hall. Plus, lower-end tables are sure to show signs of wear very quickly. But pool players say it's better to play on anything than not play at all, so a $400 table is better than twiddling your thumbs!

With more of an upfront investment, in that $1,500 range, you can get a table that plays about as well as any of the high-end tables, though it may have a rather simple design.

When you get up into the $3,000-and-up price range, you're paying more for the aesthetically pleasing parts of the table — the ornate woodworking and inlays.

So before you go shopping for a table, know what you're looking for and what you're willing to spend. From there, the rest of your decisions will fall into place.

Figure out what size fits best

The table in the corner of your favorite watering hole is probably a 7-footer, while professional tournaments are held on 9-foot tables. The *barbox* — the 7-foot tables commonly found in bars — is the smallest available table. Which one is right for you depends on the amount of space available in your home.

Table 21-1 outlines the necessary space for each model of table. Notice how the different cue lengths affect the overall space needed. The common cue is 58 inches, so if possible, plan on having that much room open for your table.

Table 21-1	Minimum Room Sizes for Different Tables		
Table Size (Feet)	48-Inch Cue	52-Inch Cue	58-Inch Cue
7	11'3" x 14'6"	11'11" x 15'2"	12'9" x 16'
8	11'8 x 15'4"	12'4" x 16'	13'2" x 16'10"
8 (oversized)	11'10" x 15'8"	12'6" x 16'4"	13'4" x 17'20"
9	12'2" x 14'4"	12'10" x 17'	13'8" x 17'10"

An all-too-common mistake is to underestimate the amount of space needed to play an unimpeded game of pool. If you're unsure what size table you can accommodate, err on the side of a smaller model. You'll be thankful when you have to hit a cue ball up against a rail — it'll be much easier when the back end of your cue isn't butting up against the wall.

Play on the bed you made

First and foremost, make sure that the bed of your table is made of slate. Often, inexpensive tables are constructed with cheap composite wood. If you want to get your money's worth, get a table with a slate bed. Anything else is just a temporary toy.

Most tables have a slate bed between ¾ and 1½ inches. While a bed of ¾-inch slate should be fine for recreational play, thicker cuts offer more stability (with an increase in weight).

Some pool tables can weigh a ton — literally. This weight is primarily due to the heft of the slate bed, which is absolutely necessary to ensure that you have an even playing surface. If you settle for a table with an inferior bed, it may not play as true as slate, which can discourage people from using the table.

Call the pocket

When it comes to choosing what kind of pockets you want on your table, denim or corduroy won't be options. Instead, you'll have to decide whether you want drop pockets or a ball-return system.

Drop pockets hold the balls directly in the pocket. This design is the most common because it's less expensive and quieter.

Ball-return systems, though, are a viable option for your home table. These tables have rails or channels that go from each pocket to a return tray by the foot of the table. Think of a coin-operated bar table — the balls drop down and head to a little storage area until you put in a few coins to release them. An at-home table with a ball-return system has the same setup.

Dress your table cloth

Thanks to modern scanning and printing techniques, you can put just about anything on the cloth of your table, whether that be a vacation photo or the logo of your favorite team. Feel free to express yourself with the color and style of cloth, but know that green and blue are the two colors favored by professionals because they offer the best contrast to the balls.

Also, many offbeat colors will show stains and chalk more than the standard colors. But if you absolutely must have the table cloth match the electric purple drapes, you can make that happen.

You've probably heard someone refer to the table's cloth as felt. Well, it's not. Cloth is most often wool-based, with some including synthetic fibers. Among pool players, I'd recommend simply referring to the cloth as just that and avoiding any felt references.

Look for a worsted wool cloth for your table. While you can certainly get a professional-grade cloth with a little investment, a middle-of-the-road worsted wool option should be durable and playable.

Consider style and substance

You'll see a wide variety of styles of tables — from sleek black modern tables to the classic oak tables. For tables in the $1,000 to $2,000 range, the design is often straightforward and simple because most of your money is going toward the playability of the table. Still, you should have the option to make sure that the table seamlessly fits into your home.

Cruising through a few retailers' Web sites, such as brunswickbilliards. com and imperialusa.com), you should be able to get an idea of what design you'd like. After you have what you want in mind, you'll have a working vocabulary when you walk into a showroom (that is, assuming that you don't just construct your dream table online, which is certainly a possibility).

Think about table accessories

In just about any retail outlet in the country, you're sure to see model rooms set up within the showroom. A pool table isn't just sold as a pool table. Rather, a table is sold as the centerpiece to a full recreation room, with a whole host of various accessories.

Because the table is the centerpiece, and the most expensive part, of the game room, you can get accessory packages at a discounted rate if you buy them with the table. Look for deals on bar stools and chairs to accompany your table.

Along with the table, consider adding a few of the following items to complete your home game room:

- ✔ **Table light:** While you certainly don't need a table light to play, lights are relatively inexpensive and can greatly improve playing conditions, especially if the table is going in a basement or under-lit room.

   Look for a light with at least three fixtures so that you'll decrease the shadows cast over balls. Also, make sure that the light is spread evenly over the entire playing surface. If you see dark spots at the edges, you know those pesky shadows will cause some problems.

- ✔ **Cue racks:** Keep the cues organized with a rack. Either wall-mounted or free standing, cue racks can extend the lives of house cues by keeping the sticks out of harm's way in between playing sessions. Again, racks are available for about $30 up to a few hundred bucks, so they shouldn't be too hard to squeeze into your budget.

- ✔ **Ball racks:** You've probably heard the ball rack referred to as *the triangle*. It is imperative to have a good rack. Look for a wooden or hard molded plastic model, which will allow you to push the balls together.

   Many "accessory" sets offer flimsy plastic racks. Try to get an upgrade so that you'll have a quality rack that will last for more than awhile.

- ✔ **Bridges to somewhere:** Getting a *mechanical bridge* — that cue with the funny-looking contraption on the end — is fairly simple. Most retail outlets sell plastic bridges that can slide over regular house cues. With the $4 fitting and a $10 one-piece house cue, you'll be all set when it comes to bridges.

Chapter 22

Pool Is Mental: Winning the Head Games

In This Chapter

▶ Maintaining a positive attitude

▶ Keeping your head in check

▶ Trusting yourself

▶ Maximizing your knowledge of the game

*O*ne of the most fascinating — and maddening — aspects of pool is the very large divide between what you can *see* and what you can *do*. Believe me, you aren't the only one to plan how you're going to pocket three or four balls, only to miss the first shot that looked super easy.

Unlike a sport like baseball, where you can rely a little on reaction and instinct, pool is a game where everything is stationary until you create motion. If you want to be successful, you need to be in the right state of mind to do so.

As you begin to develop an understanding of your own capabilities and overall skill level, you'll also notice that some days you'll play better than others. And part of making sure that you're always ready to play your best is developing a proper mental approach to the game. Whether that means practicing with the radio on full blast to help you deal with distractions or just working on your in-game focus, you shouldn't ignore the mental side of pool.

In this chapter, I discuss the game inside your head. In addition, I cover how reaching a certain level of self-awareness is a vital stage in your development as a pool player. You need to be honest with yourself, while still being encouraging.

Staying Positive

By no means am I breaking new ground in the field of sports psychology when I tell you staying positive is important. But in a game like pool, a positive mental attitude is exceptionally important. When you're confident and optimistic, you're trusting your body to do what it's learned during your time playing pool.

Projecting confidence

It's by no means easy to walk around a pool table like you're the king of the world when you just missed a straight-in shot on the 8 ball. And I'm not saying you should be strutting around all the time. You do, however, need to project some level of self confidence for two reasons:

- ✔ **To improve your own performance:** Tell yourself you're going to make a shot before you attempt it. Tell yourself that you're a good player. Even if you have to fake it, having the *appearance* of a confident player will improve your performance.

- ✔ **To show your opponent no fear:** In tennis, you're never supposed to drop your shoulders and pout after a point. Why? Because it allows your opponent to see that he's winning, that he has an edge. So when you're playing pool, you can't allow your opponent to see you in a moment of weakness. Showing frustration only saps your confidence and fuels your opponent.

Projecting confidence doesn't mean slipping into a delusional state where you think you can do no wrong. You must be honest with yourself, but you still need to approach every situation as if you are in complete control — because you are!

Practicing confidence

Building confidence in yourself and in your game is a process. Just as you want to constantly improve as a player, you also want to become a more confident, self-assured player. To this end, you can do a few things to allow yourself to succeed.

Give yourself a chance to succeed

When you find yourself stymied by a shot, don't make it harder on yourself than it has to be. To improve, you need to work on certain skills over a period of time. You're not going to be a great player overnight, but you can gradually improve in certain areas.

As an example, I want to point out a common problem among beginners. Look at the shot in Figure 22-1. With the cue ball across the table and a thin cut needed to pocket the 1 ball, it's certainly no gimme.

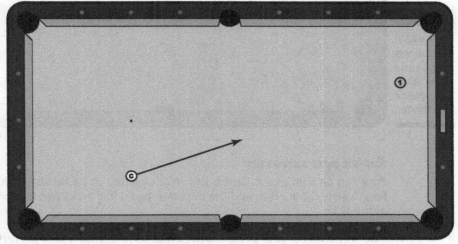

Figure 22-1: This shot isn't exactly easy, so boil it down to the basics.

So how do you work on the skills necessary to make this shot? Easy.

First, you want to develop confidence in making a shot at this angle. Instead of leaving the cue ball five diamonds away, shorten up the shot. Set up the shot in Figure 22-2.

By working on the shortened version of your original problem, you allow yourself to start with a situation where you can succeed.

When you can pocket the shot with the cue ball at Position A five times in a row, move the cue ball back one diamond to Position B. You're still shooting from the same angle, but now you have to be more precise with the cue ball. You can continue pushing the cue ball back to Positions C and D until you're at the point five diamonds away.

REMEMBER

You can use this method of practice, where you start out with an easier shot and incrementally increase the difficulty, with just about any area of your game. Just remember to take it easy on yourself. Gradually work up from basic to advanced.

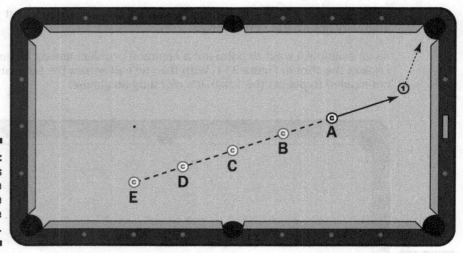

Revisit past successes

Pool can be a bit of a rollercoaster ride. One day you'll be able to hit a table-length straight-in shot, and the next day you'll feel lucky not to hurt yourself at the table.

One way to keep your progress in perspective is with a *pool player's journal.* No, I don't mean you'll be writing "Dear Diary" entries. But you will be keeping track of things you do well (while also noting things that cause you to struggle). Because dwelling on the not-so-good days is easy, a pool journal can help remind you what you did right when you played well — whether that means getting a full night's rest or wearing your lucky underpants.

Your journal is your business, and you can include pretty much any info you'd like, but try to explain why you played well (or what else you could have done if you played poorly). A written record can include both mental and physical practices because the ultimate goal is giving yourself hints on what you can do to play better.

Thinking Straight: Keeping Your Head in Line

You want to keep things consistent. So just as you should take the same number of practice strokes on each shot, you should try to establish a pattern of thoughts leading up to any and every shot.

In the most basic sense, every shot you'll face on a pool table has two stages — choosing a shot and then executing it. The problem is that these practices are very different. The first involves evaluating countless situations and consequences to find the best option for you. The second requires you to quiet your mind in an almost Zen-like sense to let your body do what it's supposed to do.

If this concept sounds a little hard to grasp, it should. The mental aspect of pool is different for everyone because it takes place completely in your own head.

Choosing a shot

When you approach the table, the first thing you must do is choose a plan of action. This first step is your planning stage. Whether you're going to play safe or try to win the game, you should be completely focused on considering your options.

When you think about what you're going to attempt to do with your next shot, you want to be very specific in your goals. If you're going to try to make a specific ball, you want to think about exactly where you want to leave the cue ball after the shot. You want to think about *how* you're going to get the cue ball to that destination.

As an example, here's a list of a few points you'll need to settle before you try an offensive shot. While certainly not an exhaustive list, you must have these things covered before you're done planning your shot:

- ✔ Have you pinpointed an exact contact point on the object ball that will send it to the intended pocket?
- ✔ Where exactly do you want the cue ball to come to a stop after pocketing the object ball?
- ✔ Where must you hit the cue ball to leave the cue ball in the chosen position?
- ✔ What speed is needed to pocket the ball and leave the cue ball in perfect position?
- ✔ Is the path you've chosen the easiest way to get position on the next shot?

After you're sure you've found a plan that will lead to a successful shot, you're ready to get down on a shot. But only then, when you have considered every aspect of a shot, are you ready to approach the next step in the mental process of making a shot.

Thinking about execution

When you're ready to get down on a shot, you're totally and completely certain that you can successfully execute the plan you've made.

During your preshot routine (see Chapter 2), one of the last steps is lowering yourself into the shot, which means assuming a proper stance and taking your practice strokes. After you're in the proper position, you should only be concerned with doing exactly what you planned. Down on a shot is no time to think about playing safe or going three rails for position instead of two.

If you question your original plan at any time while you're down on a shot, step away from the table and start over. Just as I talk about being confident in yourself, you must have faith that your plan is going to work. If you don't, you're doomed to miss the shot, unless you get back up and take time to reformulate your plan.

As far as your frame of mind during a shot, you should be completely focused on sending the cue ball in the correct direction with the proper speed for the intended shot. What complicates this situation is the relationship between your mind and body. While philosophers have discussed this topic for a few millennia, pool players have a different term for the perfect cooperation between your head and your hands: in stroke.

What is called *the zone* in sports is known as being *in stroke* in pool — a weirdly surreal state of mind where your mind and body are working together in perfect unison. You're not overthinking; you're not brain-dead. You're playing your absolute best by executing at the highest level you possibly can.

While this state is pretty elusive and just as ambiguous to describe, you can take steps to make sure that your head is in the right place during your game. Think of the steps from planning to execution, all without having anything get in your way.

Dealing with distractions

Distractions are plentiful in pool (and poolrooms!), and learning to deal with them is an essential skill if you want to play consistent — and consistently good — pool. Learning how to deal with these situations, whether it's the annoying song on the jukebox or your friends giving you a hard time, is a skill that takes practice.

As you spend more and more time around a pool table, you'll be able to deal with minor distractions. With some experience, you'll learn to remain focused on what you want to accomplish, instead of allowing a small distraction to cause you to miss.

Because pool is such a mental game, you'll need to develop this impenetrable focus. Focus will help you deal with the infinite variety of distractions, whether you're at a pool hall or in a friend's basement.

Some not-so-sportsmanlike players will intentionally try to distract you during your shot. I cover this practice, known as *sharking,* in Chapter 6, but it's worth repeating: An opponent can't get to you if you don't let him.

But what do you do when you're down on a shot, ready to pull the trigger on a shot, when something or someone acts as a distraction? Well, in the simplest terms, there are two things you *can* do. Either step back from the shot and start over or continue with your routine and shoot as if nothing happened.

You can make arguments for both sides. Some say stepping back only acknowledges that the distraction has affected you. Others say going on with the shot is foolish because you're no longer completely focused. It's by no means an exact science, but if you're still 100 percent sure that you can make the shot, go ahead and shoot it. If not, step back and start over.

If you aren't 100 percent sure, step back. Returning to the start of your pre-shot routine (see Chapter 2) will allow you to get back into your comfort zone.

As you gain experience with all the different kinds of distractions that will pop up, you should increase your level of focus while also gaining an understanding of when you should back off and when you should continue shooting.

Turning up the pressure

I'm guessing if you play a few buddies in your basement, the pressure situations won't be too suffocating. But if you start playing in leagues and tournaments, you may have to deal with the prospect of nerves.

So until you find yourself in the final of the World 8-Ball Championship, how can you practice playing under pressure? Well, simulating that kind of pressure is probably impossible, but you can get familiar with pressure situations by incorporating games into your practice routine.

For example, if you're working on hitting *spot shots* (where the cue ball is in the center of the table and the object ball is on the footspot), see how many times out of ten you can make a ball on the footspot with the cue ball anywhere on the dotted line (see Figure 22-3).

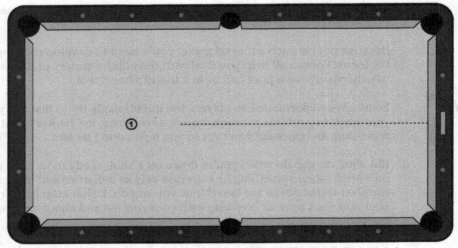

Figure 22-3:
How many
times can
you make
this shot
out of ten?

However many times you make it in your first ten tries, try to beat that number the next time. This exercise is a simple way of tricking your brain to focus, but at least it gets your competitive juices flowing — even if you're only playing yourself.

Finding ways to incorporate some sort of competitive edge into your practice time will also help you stay interested. How fun is it to do the same drill over and over for two hours? Not very.

Know Too Much: Being Honest with Yourself

I said before that pool is a game where you might know how to accomplish something, but consistently fail to do it. The disconnect between what you know and what you can do is often a complicated mental struggle.

No matter your skill level, you have to have a firm grasp on what you can and can't do if you want to be successful. If you've only been playing for a few months, you're not going to try to draw the cue ball back off of three rails for perfect position on the next ball. Conversely, if you're comfortable with an otherwise difficult shot, you should make the most of this skill.

All in all, it's vitally important that you play within yourself. In Chapter 13, I talk about playing position three-balls ahead. If you're still a pool newbie, thinking three balls ahead only complicates things for you.

To this end, it's not totally foreign for players who start taking the game a little more seriously to actually get *worse* in the first few weeks. Imagine if you started reading everything about pool you could get your hands on. You'd know everything there is to know about a complex concept such as English (see Chapter 11), but you wouldn't have the practical experience to execute difficult shots.

When you're new to the game, try not to overcomplicate things. You may be intrigued by all your learning, but try to simplify your approach to the game.

Nothing is more important than a solid foundation of the fundamental skills of pool. As you continue learning more and more about the game, don't forget to revisit and practice the fundamental aspects of your game, such as your stance, bridge, and stroke.

Chapter 23

Drilling It Home: Practice Techniques

. . . .

In This Chapter

▶ Maximizing your practice time

▶ Using drills to isolate certain skills

▶ Keeping practice lively with a few games

. . . .

So some hotshot kid walks into a pool hall, thinking he's destined to be the next great hustler. He starts tooling around on a table, making a few shots but missing plenty more. After an hour or so, he walks up to the counter, where an old-timer is jockeying the cash register with his face buried in yesterday's sports page.

"Hey, mister," the kid says. "You know I'm going to be the best pool player ever?"

"Oh, yeah?" the old man replies. "Well, I hope you're ready to give up your little girlfriends. And I hope you're ready to quit playing baseball. I hope you're willing to sleep on pool tables for the next 10 years, playing 18 hours a day, stopping only to shovel food in your face or lay your head down for an hour or two — because that, and a truckload of natural talent, is what it'll take to be the best."

The kid's a little put off by the crotchety old man. "Oh, well," he says. "I'm just going to go home and play some video games."

While (mostly) a joke, this story shows how becoming the best isn't easy, but you can shorten the learning curve if you practice effectively and efficiently. In this chapter, I tell you how to practice and what to practice so that you can get better without limping around with a stiff back from sleeping on pool tables.

Making the Most of Practice

Before getting to *what* you should be practicing, I want to cover *how* you should be practicing. No matter if you play for three hours a day or a few hours a month, you should be interested in getting the most out of what time you do spend at the table. Otherwise, you're just wasting time, right?

Check out these tips for maximizing your practice time:

✔ **Stay fresh.** If you're going to practice for more than an hour, take a 5 or 10 minute break every 45 minutes. You don't want to be a zombie with a cue stick, so give your mind time to freshen up.

✔ **Focus.** Whether you're at your house or at a pool hall, you'll certainly be faced with distractions — TV, beverages, friends. And while these things are certainly part of a leisurely game of pool, you want to limit them while you're practicing. If limiting them means bearing down for 30 minutes so that you can socialize and kick back for an hour, then it's a better solution than lazily shooting for an hour and a half.

✔ **Get warm.** Take some time to loosen up. Start by just casually pocketing some balls, concentrating more on feeling comfortable and less on results. Also, start with fairly simple shots — get accustomed to hearing the ball hit the back of the pocket.

✔ **Stay objective.** You want to be honest with yourself while you're practicing so that you can work on things that need a little improvement. Try not to get too confident or too frustrated when you practice. If you start putting yourself down, you'll just be practicing how to be negative.

✔ **Improvise.** Drills help, and exercises are good for you, but don't be afraid to keep things lively. If you want to create different ways to work on specific things, go for it.

✔ **End on a positive.** Don't throw your hands in the air after a miss and give up for good. Make your last shot or last few shots. It sounds simple, but ending on a high note will leave a good last impression.

The rest of this chapter focuses on specific drills in a number of different skills.

Working on the Fundamentals

Wanting to work on the basics? Then start with these fairly straightforward drills, which are a few quick ways to check that everything is in line with your stroke. The drills aren't that sexy, but you won't be spending much time on them — a few minutes at the start of each practice session should be enough. These exercises are just to check that your stroke is operating as it should.

Tip to tip

It can't get much easier than this drill, can it? In Figure 23-1, the cue ball is on the footspot. All you want to do in this drill is hit the cue ball down off the middle of the short rail so that it comes directly back to the tip of your cue.

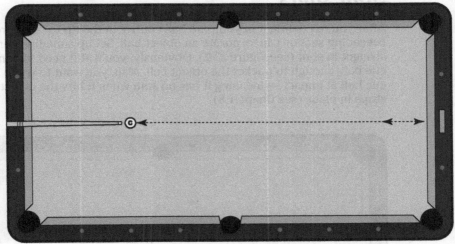

Figure 23-1:
Try to hit the cue ball straight down the table so that it comes directly back to you.

You can easily overlook this little drill, but it may just be the best way to diagnose any problems with your stroke. It will benefit every player, no matter the skill level, to try it from time to time.

Here are a few things you can look for:

✔ If you're not hitting the cue ball off the exact center of the short rail, your cue may be offline at impact, causing the cue ball to deflect to the right or left.

✔ Should the cue ball head straight down the table but then veer offline on the way back, you may be putting English (sidespin) on the cue ball by mistake. This error is common among developing players. Concentrate on hitting the cue ball at center-ball (right in the middle) so that you avoid imparting unintentional English on the cue ball.

✔ Check that your cue follows the cue ball after impact, right along the line of the shot (down the middle of the table). If the cue is turning to the right or to the left, you may be clenching your back hand.

✔ Because you want to see whether the cue ball comes back to the tip of your cue, you must stay down in your stance as the cue ball travels down and back.

✔ For more precision, use a striped ball instead of the cue ball. With the stripe lined up to your target at the center of the far rail, hit it like you normally would. The stripe shouldn't waver as the ball rolls down and back.

Stop shots

After you're confident in your cue-ball control in the tip-to-tip exercise (see preceding section), incorporate an object ball. Set up a medium-length, straight-in shot (see Figure 23-2). Obviously, you'll still need to control the cue ball, enough to pocket the object ball. Also, you want to try to kill the cue ball at impact — meaning it has no spin when it hits the object ball, so it stops in place (see Chapter 8).

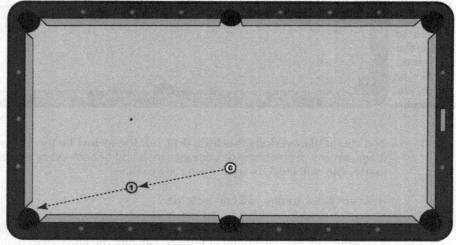

Figure 23-2: A stop shot requires a straight stroke and a little cue-ball control.

When you're making the shot in Figure 23-2 without difficulty, increase the distances between the pocket and the 1 ball and between the 1 ball and the cue ball. This distance increases the difficulty, so you'll be fine tuning a nice, straight stroke.

Some players have a bit of a phobia when it comes to long, straight shots. It may be because players become accustomed to shooting at an angle. But more likely, straight-in shots can cause problems because they expose flaws in a player's stroke.

You really don't aim on a straight shot, so any error must be attributed to execution. If a player misses straight-in shots over a matter of time, it may be due to faulty fundamentals — a scary thought for any player.

The reality is that straight shots can tell you a lot about your stroke. So, if you're confident in pocketing a lengthy dead-on shot, you'll be on your way to a fundamentally sound stroke.

Fine-Tuning Your Shot-Making Skills

You can never be *too* good at making shots, so stay sharp with these exercises.

More than any one drill, the single best way for you to improve as a shot-maker is to face your fears. If you have trouble with a particular shot, don't avoid it, because it's going to pop up in a game.

Work on your problem area, whether it be rail shots or backward cuts or whatever. Keep things simple by starting with an easy version of the shot. For example, if you want to work on shots along the rail, begin with the object ball one diamond from the pocket, then go to two, and then three.

After you face your fears, you're ready for a drill that's simple and to the point: Line up 15 balls across the table and start firing them into the corner pockets (see Figure 23-3). When you begin a line of 15 balls, you can be fairly flexible with your shot selection because you have so many options. But when things wind down, you'll be best served thinking a few balls ahead so that you can stay in shape.

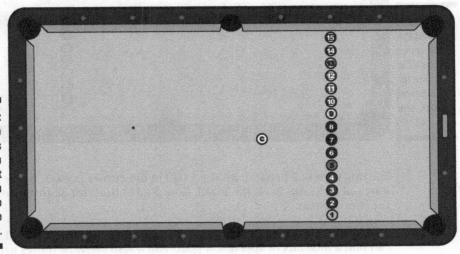

Figure 23-3: Move the line of balls farther from the pocket when you want to up the difficulty.

The first time you try this drill, line up the balls along the headstring (meaning they're two diamonds away from the pockets). As you improve, you can move the line of balls back so that each shot is a bit more difficult.

Controlling Your Cue Ball

If you want to work on controlling the cue ball, you're in luck. You can find no shortage of drills focusing on fine-tuning your cue ball's behavior.

The L drill

A famous exercise, the *L drill* is an effective way to practice because of its simplicity in design and complexity in execution. As no surprise, the balls are lined up in an L shape around a corner pocket (see Figure 23-4).

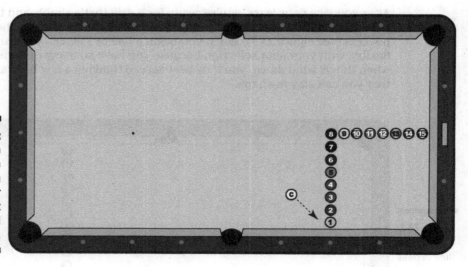

Figure 23-4: Pocket the ball, leave yourself in position for the next ball, and repeat.

Starting with ball in hand, hit the 1 ball in the corner pocket, bouncing off the long rail for position on the 2 ball. Now pocket the 2 for position, move on to the 3, and so on.

Sounds easy, but you'll discover you can quickly get out of line unless you can find a nice mix of speed and spin. You'll also see how things get a little more interesting as you get to the 5, 6, and 7 balls out in the middle of the table. You're sure to see plenty of different angles after a few minutes with this drill.

Circle drill

This toughie includes cue-ball control and pattern play, but you're going to face some tricky shots if you want to clear the table. As the name suggests, in the circle drill, you arrange balls in a circle in the middle of the table, as shown in Figure 23-5. Start with six or seven balls, working your way up to all 15 as you go.

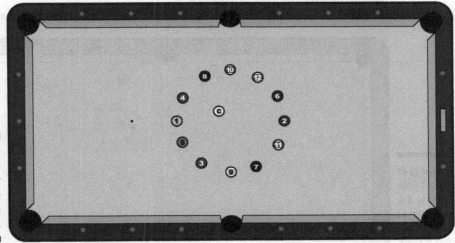

Figure 23-5: Staying in the center of the table is a little tricky.

Take ball in hand to start and shoot at any ball toward any pocket. Here's the rub: You can't allow the cue ball to leave the circle or come into contact with any of the object balls.

You'll be forced to think ahead, keeping the cue ball in the middle of the table while you fire balls in all directions.

The center of position play

You'll often be faced to choose between a few different routes to get position on your next ball. So, with that in mind, have some fun with your cue ball. The basic goal with this drill is to leave your cue ball in the middle of the table, regardless of how it got there.

Set up any kind of shot you'd like (though I'd recommend one on the easier side because you want to focus on position and not pocketing the ball). With a piece of paper as a landing strip or a piece of chalk as a target, try to plan at least two different routes to the center of the table.

In Figure 23-6, you can see that you have a few ways of getting from the 9 ball to the center of the table. You can try to draw the cue ball straight back, use follow to the short rail, or go two rails. As you work with different options on different shots, you should notice that less cue-ball movement is often easier, though you'll see some exceptions.

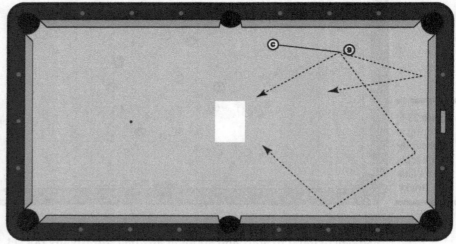

Figure 23-6:
Find your way to the center of the table after making the 9 ball.

Breaking

In Chapter 4, I talk about the keys to a good break. One of the most important factors is controlling the cue ball after it explodes the rack. This drill requires a little more work than the other drills involving controlling the cue ball because you'll be racking a bunch. But remember, if you have a good break, you'll win more games. Win more games, and you'll be racking less in the long run.

You can play this "game" with either an 8-ball or 9-ball rack, so go with whichever you prefer. Break the balls just as you would in a normal game. If the cue ball stops in the gray area of the table shown in Figure 23-7, you get a point. If it doesn't, your imaginary opponent (the ghost) gets a point.

To up the difficulty, you can make the rails out of bounds, meaning the ghost gets a point if you hit one.

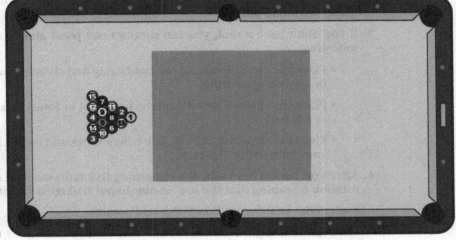

Figure 23-7:
Keep the
cue ball
centered
after the
break.

Making a Game of It

One way to keep practice lively is to challenge yourself, so instead of just going through a pattern of mindless activities, you'll add a competitive element to your routine. The following sections describe a few of the many games that you can play.

Allen Hopkins Q Skills

One of the greatest players of the last few decades, Allen Hopkins came up with the *Q Skills Test* as a way of rating players according to skill level. The idea is that, with all the pool players running around, there has to be a way of categorizing everybody according to skill level.

Here's a rundown on the basics behind this neat little test:

1. **Rack all 15 balls in any order, break from the headspot, and tally your score.**

   Determine your points as follows:

   - If you scratch, subtract one point (so you would begin at negative 1).

   - If the cue ball jumps off the table, subtract two.

   - Balls made on a scratch break stay down and do not count as points.

   - If you don't scratch, all balls pocketed count as one point.

2. **After the break, if you have a shot, begin shooting balls, which are each worth one point.**

3. **If you don't have a shot, you can subtract one point and do any of the following:**

   • Place the cue ball behind the headstring and shoot at any ball below the headstring.

   • Place the cue ball directly on the headspot or footspot and shoot at any ball.

   • Place the rack over the cue ball where it lies and move the cue ball anywhere within the rack.

4. **After you pocket ten balls, the remaining five balls must be shot in rotation (meaning that the lowest-numbered ball must be hit first).**

   Each of the final five balls is worth two points.

5. **When you miss, your turn is over.**

Try this game ten times, counting your score from each *inning,* or turn at the table. The theory behind this drill is that over an extended period of time, players will gravitate toward their skill levels. A novice might score a few high innings, but everything will shake out with enough of a sample.

Table 23-1 shows how scores equate to skill levels. While it may be cool to see how you fit into this grid, where you fall isn't really important in the long run. What *is* important, however, is that your scores keep going up over an extended period of time.

Table 23-1	**Q-Skills Test Scores**		
Rank	*# Per Inning*	*# in 10 Innings*	*# in 50 Innings*
Recreational	0–3	0–30	0–150
Intermediate	3.1–6	31–60	151–300
Advanced	6.1–9	61–90	301–450
Developing Pro	9.1–12	91–120	451–600
Semi-Pro	12.1–16	121–160	601–800
Professional	16.1–18	161–180	801–900
Touring Pro	18.1–20	181–200	901–1,000

If you want to try this test, spend 15 minutes to get your initial score. From that point, you can try it again every week or month and chart your progress.

This test is a great way to assess your skills, but it shouldn't be the main source of your practice. You want to build skills by targeting specific areas of your game. Do that, and your performance in the Q Skills Test will only improve.

Playing the ghost

Sit around in a pool hall long enough, and you'll hear someone talk about *playing the ghost*. Not nearly as spooky as it sounds, this drill refers to someone playing a solitaire version of a game.

No matter the discipline, though it's most commonly associated with 9-ball, the *ghost* is an imaginary player that never misses a shot. So if you're playing the ghost in 9-ball, you'll break and begin shooting (regardless whether you made anything). If you make the 9 ball, you win. If you miss anywhere along the way, the ghost wins.

Being able to run out more often than not in 9-ball is something only the best players can do, so you may want to start small. Start playing with just three balls. Break the little triangle open and start shooting. If you make all three balls, you win. If not, the ghost got you.

As a way of ending your practice session, play the ghost in a race to seven games, using however many balls you think is appropriate. If you win seven games before he does, add another ball. If you lose by a considerable margin, take a ball off the table.

Part VI
The Part of Tens

The 5th Wave   By Rich Tennant

"Must be the darn cue stick's not straight but I can usually perform these trick shots much better than this."

In this part . . .

In his part, I give you practical advice on a range of topics. I offer a list of ten of the most popular trick shots. Do one of these shots for your friends, and you'll discover the nifty feeling of pulling off something that looks impossible. In addition, I give you practical advice when it comes to ten frequently experienced problems. From losing control of the cue ball to getting bored with practice, pool is loaded with concepts that can trip up the average player.

Chapter 24

Mastering Ten Trick Shots

1t's often said that the best players in the world make everything look easy. When it comes to trick shots, though, the goal is to pull off what looks impossible (or at least very, very difficult).

The greatest trick shot artists in the world know the simple truth — that these artistic and often mesmerizing shots aren't about winning a game or tournament. Instead, they're about entertainment. They're about setting up the audience to expect one thing, but delivering another. With these ten shots, some of which are more about the setup than a super-complex execution, you can be on your way to getting a gasp from your audience.

The Butterfly

The butterfly is perhaps the most well-known trick shot of all time. The aim is to pocket all six balls in six different pockets. What makes this dazzling shot so appealing is that, even without a world-class stroke, you can make it! The truth is this shot is mostly in the setup, with a little bit left over for the execution.

In Figure 24-1, the six balls are arranged in groups of three, which kind of looks like a butterfly. To set up like Figure 24-1, place the 1 and 2 balls just less than one ball's width apart in the middle of the table lengthwise. Now you can place the 3 and 4 balls.

Some important points for this arrangement:

✔ The centers of the 1 and 3 balls should line up with the near point in the upper-right corner pocket (shown by the dotted line). The same is true with the 2 and 4 pointing at the inside point in the lower-right corner pocket.

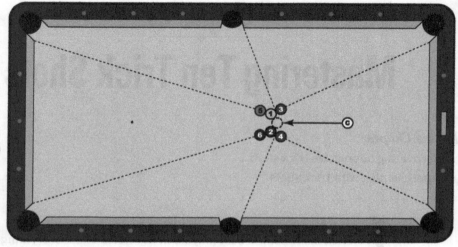

Figure 24-1:
Six balls,
six pockets.
Impossible,
right?

- If you draw a line perpendicular from the line connecting the centers of the 1 and 3 balls, it should point directly to the near edge of that pocket. Again, it should be the same with the 2 and 4 and the lower side pocket.

- When the 2 and 4 balls are in place, they should be in line with the diamond to the right of the side pocket.

- The 1 and 5 balls should be lined up with the inside point on the upper-left corner pocket (shown by the dotted line). The 2 and 6 should be in line with the lower-left corner pocket.

With the balls arranged properly, strike the cue ball with an even, controlled stroke so that it hits the 1 and 2 at the same time. Each ball should go into a corner, as shown in Figure 24-1.

The Hustler Bank

I'd be willing to bet you're never going to see the hustler bank arise naturally in a game of 8-ball. But that didn't stop Hollywood from using its simplicity and apparent impossibility in the greatest pool movie of all time, *The Hustler*.

As shown in Figure 24-2, freeze the 8 ball to the long rail, just an inch or two away from the point of the pocket. Now, freeze the cue ball to the 8. This shot appears impossible because the 8 ball has no place to go should you cue into it. However, the cushion is flexible, so if you hit as high on the cue ball as possible, you can push the 8 ball into the rail, as the cue jumps up and out of the way of the 8 as it heads toward the corner pocket.

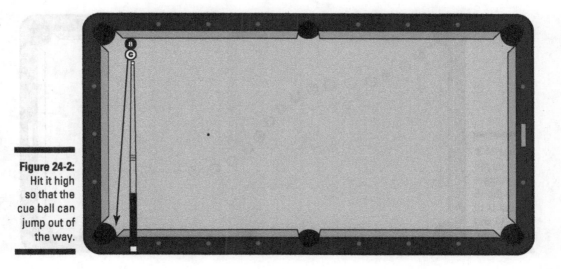

To start, you want to line up directly in line with the two balls. If you hit this shot with a bit of right English, the spin will cause the cue ball to throw the 8 ball back toward the corner pocket. It's important that you use an open bridge so that the cue can deflect up off the cue ball and out of the way.

The Snake Shot

The snake shot is another shot that places more emphasis on setup and less on a masterful stroke. This shot is a fancy-looking 15-ball combination that is almost as much of a domino experiment as it is a pool shot.

Put the 15 a few inches from the corner pocket, as shown in Figure 24-3. Place the 14 ball just a ball's width (2¼ inches) from the 15 so that the line of centers is close to being in line with the 15 and the corner pocket.

Repeat this step for all 15 balls. You can snake the balls in one direction or the other, but you want to make sure that the angle from one ball to the next is not too extreme. If you have trouble connecting the cue ball with the 15 ball, move the balls a bit closer together.

When you're ready to go, hit the cue ball with an even, smooth stroke. Any speed should be fine, but start with a slower hit on the cue ball to increase accuracy.

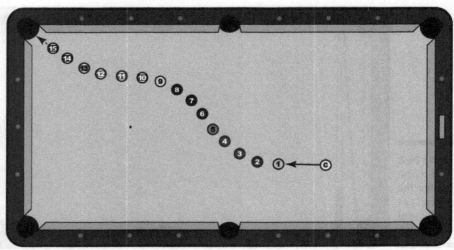

Figure 24-3:
Line up the
centers
from the 15
to the 14 to
the 13 and
so on.

Mizerak's Just Showin' Off

The just-showin'-off shot hit the big time thanks to Hall of Famer Steve Mizerak's series of Miller Lite beer commercials. One of three shots that The Miz hit in a single 30-second ad, this special shot was the stunner.

With the cue ball even with the 1 ball and one diamond away, load up on high left English, as shown in Figure 24-4. You want to hit the 1 ball on its right side, sending the cue ball toward the upper-left corner.

Some important points to note:

- ✔ The 3 and 5 have to be slightly closer to the center of the table than the 1 and 2 so that the 1 will hit the 5 and then drop in the bottom side pocket.

- ✔ A line drawn between the centers of the 4 and 5 should be aimed directly at the right point of the corner pocket. (The 4 and 5 should point to the edge of the pocket because the 5 will throw the 4 to the left . . . right into the pocket.)

- ✔ The 1 and 2 should be lined up straight across the table and not directly into the side pocket on the top of Figure 24-4.

You want to hit the cue ball firmly because it will have to travel around the entire table and hit the 6 in the top-left corner. Also, you should use a bit of left English (one tip or a bit more) to help the cue ball find its way to the 6.

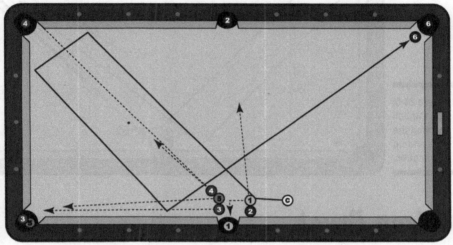

Figure 24-4:
Don't beat yourself up if you can't pocket all six.

Life on the Railroad

Speed's the key with this railroad shot. Well, first you need to have three extra cues to use as props, but the next crucial element is great speed control. Set the shot up with all three cues in the top-right corner pocket, as shown in Figure 24-5. First, place two cues directly on the table so that they line up perfectly with the 3 ball. The cues will be the tracks for the cue ball to roll right into the 3.

Next, the third cue will be somewhat open to the table. Place the butt of the cue on top of the other two cues. This cue will be a guide for the cue ball to roll up and the over to the other two.

Like in the previous shot, you want to use high left English, hitting the cue ball at about 10:30 if you look at the ball's face like a clock. You'll need to strike this shot firmly so that the cue ball has enough speed to travel around the table, hitting three rails on its way up the two cue sticks. If you hit it at just the right speed, the cue ball will climb up the cues and then roll back down to pocket the 3 into the side pocket.

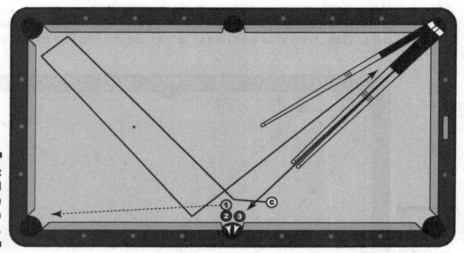

Figure 24-5:
Run the ball
around the
table and up
the cues.

Prison Break

This prison-break shot is another situation that may not happen organically, but that shouldn't hurt the presentation. Pretend the layout in Figure 24-6 is the scenario in a game of 8-ball. You're up, and you're stripes.

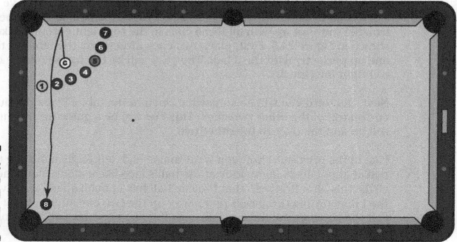

Figure 24-6:
Go off the
rail and
over the
blockers.

As you can see, you need to hop the cue ball over the blocking balls by way of the long rail. To hit this shot, elevate the butt of your cue 30 degrees. This downward angle on the cue ball will cause it to hop off the table a bit. If you strike the cue ball with the necessary force, it will hit the rail. The compressed cushion will push the cue ball into the air and over the other object balls.

You really have to stroke this shot. Focus on popping the cue ball off the table with your cue. Hit the cue ball with a short punch of a stroke, similar to the technique of a jump shot, described in Chapter 16.

First on the Three

When you're with friends, this 3-ball first is a great way to get a laugh (or, if you're looking for a beverage or cab fare, you can always propose a friendly wager). With the 1, 2, and 3 balls on the end rail (as shown in Figure 24-7), you're going to proclaim for all to hear that you intend for the cue ball to hit the 3 ball first.

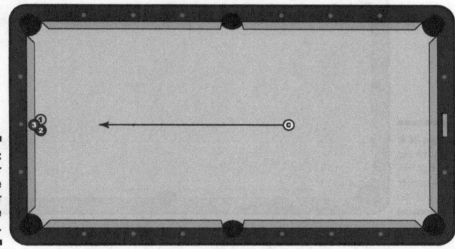

Figure 24-7: Throw your hip into the table after hitting the cue ball.

Tell your audience that your cue will only touch the cue ball as it would in a normal stroke and the cue ball will never leave the table. Still, it will hit the 3 before the 1 and 2 balls. Looks impossible, right?

First, I deal with the setup. Freeze the 1 and 2 balls against the short rail. Gently place the 3 ball on the edge of the cushion, so that it is resting on the 1 and 2 ball. Getting all three balls to stay on the end rail may take a little work, but it's absolutely vital that the 3 ball is teetering on the edge of the cushion and the two balls.

Line the cue ball up so that it's a straight shot for the point right between the 1 and 2. Now comes the hook: Gently roll the cue ball toward the three balls. When it's close, throw your hip against the side of the table. The force should rattle the three object balls so that the 1 and 2 slide to the side while the 3 drops down in perfect position for the cue ball to make contact.

Frozen Treat

Here's one that is simple, but will still baffle the average pool novice. In the frozen-treat shot, the cue ball and 8 ball are frozen together in a perfect line on the first diamond on the short rail (see Figure 24-8). It's not a stretch to think it would be impossible to send the 8 ball anywhere but straight ahead, right?

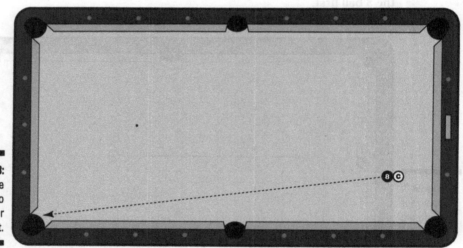

Figure 24-8: Throw the 8 ball into the corner pocket.

Well, this shot is in the trick shots chapter, so wrong. You can make this shot using something called throw. *Throw* is the friction between two balls at the moment of impact, which can cause the struck ball to deviate from the line of centers.

So, in the example in Figure 24-8, load up on high right English and hit the cue ball at about 3:00. You must hit the 8 ball with a smooth stroke so that the cue ball can throw the 8 on its course to the pocket.

Clearing the Way

This shot is known as the *football shot* because it resembles a quarterback running through a hole left by a bunch of blockers who cleared the way. Much like the snake shot, the football shot (in Figure 24-9) is a chain reaction that is heavily dependent on the setup.

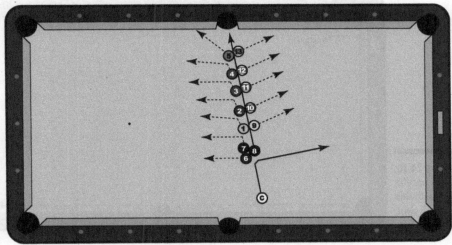

Figure 24-9:
The key is sending the cue ball off the 6 and into the 8.

The most important part of this shot is that the cue ball should carom off the 6 ball before hitting the 8. Hitting the 6 first will send the 7 ball into the 1, which will start the chain reaction that splits up the 10 blocking balls. As those spread from the center of the table, the 8 ball will gently roll toward the side pocket, provided that the cue ball caromed into the 8 at the correct angle.

This shot is by no means easy, but if you tinker with the setup a bit, you should be able to get it.

If you're having trouble getting a good hit on the 8, clear off all the balls except the 6, 7, and 8. Try sending the cue ball off the 6 and into the 8. If you can make the 8 with just three balls, you should be able to do it with 13.

Don't Try This at Home

Want something a little more . . . um, extreme? Try the out-of-midair shot, which has been a staple of trick shot at exhibitions for years. The legendary player and showman Jimmy Caras was the first to popularize pool's version of the William Tell shot.

With a little help from some cubes of chalk, you can shoot a ball out of a trusting friend's mouth.

1. **Ask your willing assistant to lay across the table so that the center of his mouth is around one diamond off the short rail (shown by the dotted line in Figure 24-10).**

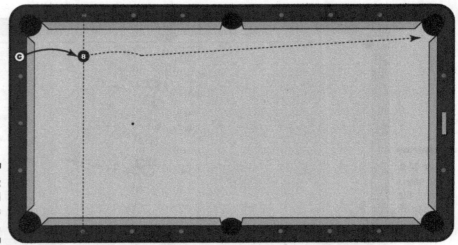

Figure 24-10:
Be careful
with this
8-ball shot.

2. **Ask your assistant to hold a piece of chalk in between his teeth.**

3. **Place the 8 ball in the divot on the exposed side of chalk, and you've got your target.**

4. **When the human ball holder is in place, stack two pieces of chalk on the short rail so that they're in line with the 8 ball and the far corner pocket.**

5. **Place the cue ball on this stack, and you're ready to take aim at the 8 ball.**

   Ideally, the cue ball will hit the 8 ball near its vertical axis, sending the 8 straight into the far corner pocket. If the cue ball hits above or below the center of the 8 ball, it may miss your assistant.

It's hard to hurt somebody while playing pool, but not impossible. This shot is about as full-contact as pool can get, and even then, you shouldn't be running the risk of any major injuries. But if you're going to try this shot, make sure that you're confident in your abilities to jump the ball to the proper height. Oh, and if you're the trusty assistant, don't be afraid to cover your face with your hands!

Chapter 25

Overcoming Ten or So Common Problems

• •

In This Chapter

▶ Troubleshooting your game for a few common mistakes

▶ Recognizing what you're having problems with and finding a solution

• •

*N*ot all pool players are alike, but many make similar mistakes. And because thousands of pool players have gone before you, enduring all the growing pains of learning the game on their own, you can benefit from those experiences. In this chapter, I cover ten or so common problems that all burgeoning pool players have had to overcome.

From tips on making your solo practice sessions interesting to keeping your cue ball under control, this chapter is designed to troubleshoot your game so that you can avoid common pitfalls.

Following the Cue Ball

When an object ball is hanging in a pocket, just an inch from the edge, the shot looks so darn easy. All you have to do is tap the ball in. You can hit the ball just about anywhere and it'll fall, so what's the problem? To start, some players have a tendency to hit this shot by putting follow (topspin) on the cue ball, which can lead to the cue ball following the object ball into the pocket for a scratch.

This problem has two solutions:

▸ **Hitting lower on the cue ball:** If the cue ball is in close proximity to the object ball, you should be able to avoid the scratch by hitting the cue ball just below center on the vertical axis. A low hit will keep the cue ball from gathering topspin on its way to the object ball so that it stops in place after knocking the object ball into the pocket. The farther the cue ball is from the object ball, the lower you have to hit in order to keep the cue ball from rolling. So if you're more than half a table away from the object ball, you should be hitting as low on the cue ball as possible (about halfway between the center and the lower edge).

✔ **Hitting the object ball slightly off center:** You can also avoid a scratch by hitting the object ball off center. In this situation, the cue ball can follow the cue ball into the pocket only if it hits the object ball near fully and has topspin. So if you can't (or don't want to) keep the cue ball from gaining follow, you can change the angle of impact on the object ball so that it can't follow forward into the pocket.

Because you can pocket the object ball by hitting it just about anywhere, create an angle if you're shooting directly at the ball and pocket. Aim to hit the object ball to one side of the pocket so that the cue ball will deflect in the opposite direction. This technique, which you can use in certain situations where you're trying to play position, is known as *cheating the pocket.*

As you can see in Figure 25-1, you have a relatively straight-in shot on the 1 ball. Instead of aiming to hit the 1 in the middle of the pocket, hit it to the left side of the pocket so that the cue ball will head toward the short rail — and out of danger for a scratch.

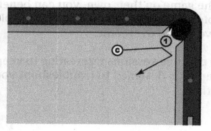

Figure 25-1:
Cheating
the pocket
will keep
you from
scratching.

Miscuing No More

Avoiding a *miscue* — where the cue tip slips off the cue ball instead of making proper contact — is more about developing correct habits than some super-technical bit of info. A player miscues for several reasons:

✔ **Forgetting to chalk the cue tip:** Get in the habit of chalking your cue before every single shot. You may get away with forgetting now and then, but I promise that forgetting to chalk the cue tip will catch up with you. Getting a fresh, even layer of chalk on your cue tip before every shot will guarantee that you won't miscue (at least not because of a lack of chalk). Chalking the cue tip may sound pretty labor-intensive, but it really isn't. Try to incorporate the five-second process of chalking your cue into your preshot routine. Make it a habit, and you'll hardly notice that you're doing it all the time.

✔ **Hitting too far from the center of the cue ball:** The second way of avoiding miscues is paying close attention to the *miscue limit,* which is the farthest distance from the center of the cue ball you can hit without the tip sliding off the cue ball's surface. A conservative estimate of the miscue limit puts it at about halfway between the center of the cue ball and its edge (see Figure 25-2). You may be able to stray a bit farther from center, at times, but this distance keeps you making solid contact with the cue ball.

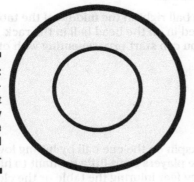

Figure 25-2: The miscue limit is halfway between the center and the edge.

If you're going to stray far from the center of the cue ball, try to keep your cue as level as possible; changing the angle of the cue at impact only increases the chances of a miscue.

✔ **Using a cue with a misshapen tip:** A deformed cue tip can also lead to miscues. With a $5 tool, you can keep your cue's tip nice and rounded (about the curvature of a nickel or dime). Be sure to scuff up your cue's tip once in awhile (see Chapter 21).

Losing Control of the Break

With all the power that goes into a break shot, you can easily lose a bit of control. You might include some body movements into your break stroke that aren't a part of your normal routine, and you're definitely looking to maximize power.

But anything done to up your power shouldn't be at the expense of control. A powerful break is worthless without the ability to control it. So if you're losing control of the cue ball on your break — scratching, mishitting the head ball, jumping the ball off the table — you need to dial it down a bit.

Here's a checklist that will help you control your break:

- ✔ **Limit any and all body movement.** If you've incorporated any weight transfer, cut it out. Until you can consistently hit the head ball full (so that the cue ball sits in the middle of the table), use just your back arm to power the break.

- ✔ **Firm up your bridge.** Double check that your bridge hand is clasped tightly around the cue stick. A strong bridge keeps the cue from sliding away from the center of the cue ball.

- ✔ **Return to center.** Put the cue ball right in the middle of the table. A centered cue ball keeps you locked in on the head ball in the rack. When you can control this break, you can start experimenting with other spots on the head string.

Failing to Draw

The *draw shot,* where you put backspin on the cue ball by hitting low, can be a tough nut to crack. For one, some players are a little hesitant to hit the cue ball below its equator. Perhaps they fear injuring the table or the cloth, or they fear hitting *too* low and popping the cue ball up in the air. Whatever the reason, the draw shot may not come naturally.

Oftentimes, a player will line up a draw shot by placing her cue nice and low on the cue ball, only to hit the center of the cue ball on her final stroke. The cue ball won't draw back after hitting the object ball, so the player is left to ask, "How did I not put backspin on that ball?"

The key is contacting the cue ball where you originally aimed. Forget about the chances of miscuing, and you shouldn't be thinking about what the table's owner is going to do if you put a three-foot rip in the cloth. Focus on a smooth stroke, with a cue that's as level as possible.

And possibly the most important component of the draw stroke: Don't forget to follow through! You may be tempted to jab at the ball with a short, punchy follow-through, but an abbreviated follow-through isn't going to help you out. You need to teach yourself to follow through as you would normally. Focusing on following through helps you maintain a smooth stroke, accelerating the tip of the cue before it strikes the cue ball.

Keeping Focused: Pocket versus Position

In the course of one shot, you've got a lot to think about. But one mistake that can leave you scratching your head is using too much mental energy on pocketing the ball at the expense of playing position for your next shot, and vice versa.

You can achieve a happy balance to accomplishing both goals of a shot. Unfortunately, this balance isn't always as easy as having a 50 percent chance of making the ball and a 50 percent chance of playing position for your next shot. The ratio changes with each shot. For example, a ball that's hanging in the pocket is a cinch to make, so playing position will occupy most of your focus. Conversely, a full-table bank shot will require you to almost exclusively focus on executing the shot, while only giving a few seconds to thinking about position.

Whatever the shot may be, make a conscious effort to address it appropriately. You can only have so many thoughts running around your head at once, so make sure that you're addressing the shot properly.

Scratching Too Often

Scratching is never fun, but it can become a real pain when you're totally surprised by it. Planning your cue ball's path to the next position only to see it fall into a pocket can cause you to question yourself, which can lead to confidence issues.

So here's a quick checklist to keep you from putting the white ball down a hole:

- ✔ **Remember the 90-degree rule.** If the cue ball hits an object ball with stun (no spin), it'll deflect at a 90-degree angle from the object ball's direction. Looking for situations where the cue ball could go into a pocket if it deflects at a 90-degree angle can help you avoid scratches. If such a shot would send the cue ball toward a pocket, put follow or draw on the cue ball. If a 90-degree angle is safe, you know a stun shot won't lead to a scratch.

- ✔ **Send the cue ball to the middle of the table.** A ball that hits a rail and crosses the exact center point on the table can't scratch (unless it goes off numerous rails). So, if you're sending the cue ball to a rail, plan for it to cross the middle of the table.

- ✔ **Simplify!** If you can play position for your next shot without hitting a rail, that's good. If you can get in position by going off one rail instead of two, do it. Keep things simple, and you'll keep better control of the cue ball.

Getting Bored with Practice

It's easy not to like doing drills. Lining up ball after ball and hitting the same shot 50 times isn't exactly the most exciting activity you can pursue. But, while you can improve by just shooting balls aimlessly, you need to have some structure to your practice time to get the most out of it.

When you get bored with whatever you're doing, get creative. Think of games to play against yourself. Increase the pressure of the situation by placing a bet with yourself. (For example, if you succeed, you can skip doing the dishes for the night, but if you fail, it's time to get scrubbing.)

Also, keep things fresh by ending your time at the table by doing something fun. Check out the games in Chapter 23 for a few ideas.

Rechecking Your Fundamentals

You're going to have good days, and you're going to have bad days. But when you find yourself in a slump that lasts more than a few days, you need to go back and check your fundamentals. Run down this checklist to see whether something's outta whack:

- **Staying down?** Don't come up from your stance until the cue ball stops (or you need to get out of a ball's path).

- **Staying straight?** Put the cue ball on the foot spot and hit it down to the far short rail and back. If everything is in line, the cue ball should come right back to your cue tip. Keep upping the power on the shot to see whether you stay straight for firm strokes.

- **Bridging loose?** If your bridge hand isn't completely still before, during, and after every shot, it can be a big problem. Make sure that your bridge hand is planted firmly on the table and that your fingers aren't moving.

- **Following through?** If you've got the space, you should finish a stroke with the cue tip at least 6 inches past the point of contact. An abbreviated follow-through can lead to an inconsistent, jerky stroke.

- **Feeling comfortable?** If you're in your stance, and you feel uncomfortable or strained, something's wrong. You want to be balanced and relaxed.

Attempting the Cue-All Solution

If you hit any shot a million times, you'll probably have a pretty good grasp on it. When you're struggling with any shot or situation or technique, the best cure is practice.

But not just any type of practice. Try to isolate one specific thing you want to work on and then get after it. While you may not hit a million balls in your lifetime, a few dozen can do wonders for your game and for your confidence!

Index